A CONCISE DICTIONARY OF
ENGLISH IDIOMS

A Concise

DICTIONARY

of

ENGLISH IDIOMS

By

WILLIAM FREEMAN

PUBLISHERS   *The Writer, Inc.*   BOSTON

First Edition	1951
Second Impression	1951
Second Edition	1952
Fourth Impression	1963
Fifth Impression	1965
Sixth Impression	1967
Seventh Impression	1969

Library of Congress Catalog Card Number: 74–92873

Printed in Great Britain

INTRODUCTION

In compiling this book, I have done my best to keep two objects in view.

The first of these has been to furnish anyone, native or foreigner, who is interested in the less formal aspects of the English language, with a simple and practical Guide to the idioms—or, at any rate, some of those which contrive with such extraordinary frequency to entangle themselves in our speech and writing.

Idioms, simply because they *are* idioms, have a habit of evading or ignoring the accepted rules of grammar, few though such rules are in English. These friendly, colloquial little phrases that everyone uses and believes he understands are in many cases beyond logical analysis, and convey implications totally unconnected with the normal meanings of the words themselves.

" I've just been telling off that black sheep of the family, Jane," says a gossip, " for leading her mother a proper dance. I suppose she thought she'd make a splash in that new rig-out of hers when she went to look up the Browns. The airs she gave herself, trying to put Mrs. Jones out of countenance, cutting old Miss Robinson, and giving young Simpkins the glad eye ! "

If any fellow-countryman of mine is inclined to be pityingly and patronizingly amused at the difficulties of a foreigner in grasping these perfectly respectable sentences, will he set himself the task of converting them into straightforward, grammatical, non-idiomatic English ?

He will then, I fancy, continue to pity the foreigner, but no longer to patronize him.

My second object covers ground which, strictly speaking, has nothing to do with that branch of grammar which we call syntax, or sentence-construction, but concerns itself with the origin and history of many idiomatic phrases, that is to say with another branch—Etymology. In short, I want this book to be a good deal more than a dictionary : I envisage it as one to be dipped into, even—so fast and far does my ambition run !—as a solace and diversion during an insomnia-ridden night.

As to the general arrangement, that, of course, had to be alphabetical. It is indeed doubly alphabetical, the idioms being grouped under main headings, and subdivided further under individual headings.

This alphabetizing involved difficulties that were inescapable.

Idioms in general do not consist of simple words—how many times and with what fervour have I wished they did !—but of groups of words, among which in many cases there is more than one " key " word which might be used in the index. In " *Go to the wall* ", for example, the entry might be under " go " or with equal justification under " wall ". Again, should " *A bread-and-butter letter* " be indexed under " bread-and-butter " or " letter " ?

No definite and comprehensive rule can be laid down, but I have done my best to meet such cases by cross-references.

As for the examples given, let me say that they are *not* drawn from the works of eminent defunct—and incidentally hopelessly out-of-date—writers, but are, in the traditional words of the pavement artist, " all my own work ". Further, they are in the plainest, most ordinary language. Further still, if the idiom embodied in any example be replaced, word for word, by the definition, the reader will discover that (allowing for minor modifications of tense, numbers, et cetera) the sense is identical; in other words, that the precise implication of the idiom is conveyed.

There are certain deliberate omissions. These include :

(1) Single words, the idiomatic variations of which can be discovered in any ordinary dictionary.

(2) Provincial idioms, those in dialect, and others no longer in general use.

(3) Technical idioms, and those evolved during the late wars, many of which are of so fugitive a nature that they are already obsolescent.

(4) Slang phrases which might involve the speaker or listener—or both—in embarrassment.

(5) Latin and Greek tags.

(6) Foreign phrases and terms, and purely commercial terms.

(7) Idioms indicated by initials only.

The abbreviations are few and simple. They are :

Abbrev. = Abbreviated
Abbreviation
Lit. = Literal meaning
Met. = Metaphorical meaning
Old f. = Old fashioned
Or. = Origin
S. = Slang (but *not*, as already indicated, slang which
is objectionable : merely phrases which are
too colloquial for use in any form of writing
in which " good style " is desirable—an essay,
a thesis, a poem).

ACKNOWLEDGMENTS

IT is difficult, in a book of this type, to distribute one's thanks adequately. A considerable number of dictionaries, of which Webster's and the noble Oxford are the chief, have helped me. Other creditors are the erudite E. C. Brewer for his *Dictionary of Phrase and Fable*, Sir W. G. Benham for his Book of Quotations, James Main Dixon (*English Idioms*), a number of school books which formed a useful source of reminders, and Roget's *Thesaurus*, every word of every page of which I read.

I also desire to record my especial thanks to Messrs. J. M. Dent & Sons, Ltd., for allowing me to incorporate the small collection of idioms which appeared in *English for Foreigners*, an earlier book of my own published by them.

To the innumerable unofficial enthusiasts who, on being told what I was writing, instantly reacted with " Ah, but have you got this one ? " this book should, perhaps, be dedicated. But it isn't.

DICTIONARY OF IDIOMS

A B C : The first rudiments ; the beginning.
Henry doesn't know even the A B C of dancing.

Abeyance : IN ABEYANCE. In a state of waiting or suspense until some decision is made.
The question of Mary's marriage is in abeyance till her mother comes home.

Abide : ABIDE BY *or* WITH. Remain faithful to an agreement or decision ; remain with a person.

Above : ABOVE ALL. That which is of the greatest importance.
Above all, be truthful.

ABOVE-BOARD. Honest and unconcealed.
His conduct has been entirely above-board.

Abuse : TERMS OF ABUSE, *or* ABUSIVE TERMS. Bad and violent language.
He constantly addressed her in terms of abuse.

Accommodate : ACCOMMODATE ONESELF. Adjust oneself to the circumstances ; accept the conditions.
They will have to accommodate themselves to poverty and hard work.

ACCOMMODATE WITH. Supply with ; allow the use of.
We can accommodate you with a sitting-room and two bedrooms.

Accord : OF ONE'S OWN ACCORD. Voluntarily ; without being compelled.
He went to the police of his own accord.

WITH ONE ACCORD. Unanimously ; all together.
They cheered the King with one accord.

ACCORDING TO ; IN ACCORDANCE WITH. As agreed or arranged.
The goods will be sent in accordance with your instructions.

Account : AN ACCOUNT TO SETTLE. Lit., A debt to pay ; commonly used in referring to a grudge or a grievance.
I have an account to settle with Harry for the lies he told.

A GOOD ACCOUNT OF. A satisfactory story about.
I was glad to receive a good account of the boy's work.

ESTEEM OF NO ACCOUNT. A rather pedantic and old-fashioned equivalent to "consider valueless".

GONE TO HIS ACCOUNT. Died ; gone to another world in which the good and evil he did in this one will be judged.

KEEP AN ACCOUNT OF. Keep a record of.

ON ACCOUNT. As partial payment.
He owed £50, and sent me £10 on account.

ON ACCOUNT OF. Owing to ; because of.
She left her husband on account of his unsatisfactory habits.

ON NO ACCOUNT. In no circumstances ; a negative to which no exceptions may be made.
On no account walk home by the river.

ON THAT ACCOUNT. For that reason.

OPEN AN ACCOUNT. Deposit a sum of money in a bank for the first time.

SQUARE ACCOUNTS. Take some action which will cancel out a wrong, and make one equal with one's adversary.

TAKE INTO ACCOUNT. Make allowance for.
The judge, taking into account the prisoner's youth, set him free.

Accountable : BE ACCOUNTABLE FOR. Be responsible for.
You will be accountable for every penny I have lent you.

Ace : WITHIN AN ACE OF. Within a very little distance of ; very nearly indeed.
The boy was within an ace of being drowned.

Achilles : ACHILLES' HEEL. Or. Mythological. The weak or vulnerable spot in a man's character or circumstances. According to the legend, Achilles, with the exception of one heel, was protected against every weapon his enemies might use.

Acquit : ACQUIT ONESELF. Conduct or exhibit oneself ; behave.
The boy acquitted himself in battle like a brave and experienced soldier.

Act : ACT A PART. Conceal one's real emotions, etc., as an actor does.

She smiled cheerfully, but I knew she was only acting a part.

ACT UPON. Take definite action because of what one knows.

The police heard of the murder, and at once acted upon the information they received.

ACT UP TO. Behave in accordance with.

I hope you'll act up to the good advice I've given you.

IN THE ACT. Actually doing it.

The man stole my purse. I caught him in the act.

Adam : NOT KNOW FROM ADAM. Used of someone completely unknown and unfamiliar.

Mrs. Smith is a friend of mine, but I don't know her husband from Adam.

THE OLD ADAM. The natural primitive instincts, without morality ; original sin.

The old Adam made him knock his enemy down.

Addition : IN ADDITION TO. Furthermore ; as well as.

In addition to a fine, he was sent to prison.

Address : PAY ONE'S ADDRESSES TO. An old-fashioned, formal phrase ; court ; make love to with the object of marrying.

Many men had paid their addresses to the beautiful heiress.

Advantage : HAVE THE ADVANTAGE OF. Be in a superior position, physically or morally.

I had the advantage of a first-class education.

TAKE ADVANTAGE OF. 1. Gain through another person's ignorance or innocence.

The dealer took advantage of the poor woman's ignorance and bought the picture for five shillings.

2. Act at a propitious or fortunate moment.

I took advantage of the fine weather to-day to play tennis.

Affirmative : IN THE AFFIRMATIVE. Equivalent to " Yes ". See IN THE NEGATIVE.

After : BE AFTER. 1. Intend.

What are you after ? what do you intend ?

2. Pursue.

The thief knew the police would be after him.

Age : AT AN ADVANCED AGE. Very old.

My mother died at an advanced age.

FROM AGE TO AGE. From one long historical period to another.

GREEN OLD AGE. Very old, but with the implication of being healthy as well.

UNDER AGE. Less than twenty-one years old.

Agog : ALL AGOG. In a state of excitement.

Aid : IN AID OF. To help; with the object of assisting.

A concert will be given in aid of the Nurses' Fund.

Air : AIR A GRIEVANCE. Bring forward for discussion some hardship, grievance or other matter which should be made public.

These grievances were aired in Parliament last week.

IN THE AIR. In a state of uncertainty; unsettled.

We go to Paris on Monday, but after that all our plans are in the air.

See CASTLES IN THE AIR.

INTO THIN AIR. Into nothingness. To " vanish into thin air " is to disappear entirely.

Airs : GIVE ONESELF AIRS. Try to impress people with one's superiority. Similar to PUT ON AIRS, PUT ON SIDE, SHOW OFF.

Since she's moved into a house with a garage, Mrs. Sympkins has given herself insufferable airs.

Alarm : GIVE THE ALARM. Arouse one's household or neighbours when some disaster—a fire, burglars, etc.—is discovered.

FALSE ALARM. Untrue report of disaster.

We heard our house was burnt down, but it was only a false alarm.

Alert : ON THE ALERT. In a state of awareness; ready for anything that may happen.

All day the village was on the alert for the King's visit.

Alive : ALIVE AND KICKING (S.). Vigorous and active.

I'm glad to see that old Ben is still alive and kicking.

All : ALL ALONG. All the time; from the beginning.

He has known, all along, that I hate him.

ALL AT ONCE; ALL OF A SUDDEN. Suddenly; unexpectedly.

All at once there was a tremendous crash.

ALL FOR THE BEST. All for the ultimate good. (Commonly used to console someone for bad news.)

If her husband has left her, it's probably all for the best.

ALL THE BEST (S.). A common form of farewell, an abbreviation for " May all the best things happen to you".

ON ALL FOURS. **1.** Lit., On one's hands and knees, in the position of a four-legged animal. **2.** Met., Level with ; similar to.

This demand for money is on all fours with the one we received last week.

ALL IN ALL. Everything.

Mary was all in all to him.

ALL MY EYE AND BETTY MARTIN (S.). A term of contempt and disbelief said to be a corruption of " Ah, mihi, beate Martini " (= " Ah, (grant) me, Blessed Martin !). All complete nonsense.

ALL ONE. Of no importance ; immaterial.

It's all one to me whether you stay here or go home to your mother.

ALL OVER. **1.** Covering the entire surface.

The ground was all over snow.

2. Finished.

The man was dead, his troubles were all over.

3. (S.). Entirely in character ; characteristic.

Bill arrived late and very untidy—but that's Bill all over.

ALL OVER THE PLACE. **1.** Scattered untidily.

Collect your papers ; they are all over the place.

2. In many directions.

His work takes him all over the place.

ALL THE SAME. **1.** Alike, in a general sense.

Men are all the same.

It's all the same to me ; it will make no difference so far as I am concerned.

2. Nevertheless.

All the same, I'm not going.

ALL THERE (S.). Mentally alert and fit. (*Note.*—This idiom is generally used negatively.)

The poor old woman doesn't seem to be all there.

IT'S ALL UP (S.). Further effort is useless.

It's all up ; we are surrounded by the enemy.

See THE GAME'S UP.

FOR ALL THAT. Nevertheless ; in spite of.

He is blind, but for all that, he's the happiest man I know.

WHEN ALL'S SAID AND DONE. The conclusion, stated briefly. When all the facts are considered.

When all's said and done, Peter is less to blame than John.

Allot : ALLOTTED SPAN. The time allowed. Frequently used in reference to the seventy years which, according to the Bible, is the normal period of human life.

The old lady has passed the allotted span by nearly twenty years.

Allow : ALLOW FOR. Leave a margin of time or space.

We must allow for the train being late—it always is.

Allowance : MAKE ALLOWANCES. Excuse.

We make allowances for her rudeness—she has never been taught good manners.

Alternative : HAVING NO ALTERNATIVE. Having no choice or option ; being unable to do otherwise.

The judge has no alternative but to sentence the murderer to hang.

Ambition : THE HEIGHT OF AMBITION. Strongest, most powerful desire.

To be an engine-driver was the height of his ambition.

VAULTING AMBITION. Abbrev. quotation. " Vaulting ambition that o'erleaps itself ", from Shakespeare's *Macbeth.* Ambition which is too great to be fulfilled.

Ambush : LIE IN AMBUSH ; IN WAIT FOR. Conceal oneself for the purpose of attacking.

The natives lay in ambush in the jungle.

Amends : MAKE AMENDS. Compensate for some injustice or wrong.

This will make amends for John's unkindness.

Anchor : COME TO ANCHOR. Lit., When a ship lowers her anchor, and ceases to move. Met., Stop ; halt.

The old lady wandered round the room, and finally came to anchor opposite George.

RIDE AT ANCHOR. Or. nautical. A ship is said to " ride " at anchor when she swings backwards and forwards while anchored.

Answer : ANSWER BACK. Retort ; reply impudently.

If I scold the boy, he always answers back.

ANSWER ; BE ANSWERABLE FOR. Accept responsibility.

The captain has to answer for the discipline of his company.

KNOW ALL THE ANSWERS. Be alert and well-informed.

I've been talking to young Smith ; he's a smart lad, and seems to know all the answers.

Appear : APPEAR FOR. Represent legally or officially.

Sir John Smith, K.C., appeared for the plaintiff.

TO ALL APPEARANCES. To the eye ; outwardly.

He was to all appearances a gentleman.

Appetite : WHET THE APPETITE. Increase one's desire to eat.

The long walk had whetted the appetites of the guests.

Apple : APPLE OF ONE'S EYE. See under **Eye.**

APPLE-PIE ORDER. Perfectly tidy and neat.

Apron : TIED TO ONE'S MOTHER'S APRON-STRINGS. Met., In the position of a small child who is compelled to rely on its mother for everything ; humiliatingly dependent.

The poor fellow has been tied to his mother's apron-strings all his life.

Arm : AT ARM'S LENGTH. Lit., The length of one's extended arm.

He held the picture at arm's length.

Met., In a state of formality and unfriendliness.

Jones rarely speaks to his wife ; he keeps her at arm's length.

A BABY IN ARMS. A child too young to walk.

WITH OPEN ARMS. With warmth and pleasure.

The kind old woman received the stranger with open arms.

Armed : ARMED NEUTRALITY. Nominally at peace, but actually unfriendly and prepared for war.

Arms : BEAR ARMS. Lit., Carry weapons.

The Government has called on all men capable of bearing arms.

TAKE ARMS ; TAKE UP ARMS. Go to war.

UNDER ARMS. Equipped with uniform and weapons and ready to fight.

Within a month the entire German forces were under arms.

As : AS IT WERE. In other words ; speaking metaphorically.
He was, as it were, intoxicated by the soft air and sunshine of spring.

See SO TO SPEAK, and IN A MANNER OF SPEAKING.

Ascendancy : GET *or* OBTAIN THE ASCENDANCY. Become the stronger, physically or morally.
As time passed, the wife gradually gained ascendancy over her weak-willed husband.

STAR IN THE ASCENDANT. Rising in power or popularity, as a planet rises in the sky.
George's social star is in the ascendant ; he dined yesterday with a duke.

Ashes : REDUCE TO ASHES. Completely destroy by fire.
In less than an hour the cathedral was reduced to ashes.

Assign : ASSIGN A CAUSE. Give a reason.
The doctor was unable to assign a cause for her illness.

Assurance : MAKE ASSURANCE DOUBLY SURE. Quotation from Shakespeare's *Macbeth*. Make absolutely certain.

Astray : GO ASTRAY. Stray. Lit., Wander from the right path. Met., Depart from what is correct.
He has gone astray in his statement.

Attention : PAY ATTENTION TO. Attend to ; listen to.
Please pay attention to these instructions.

RIVET ONE'S ATTENTION. Concentrate ; fix one's mind upon.
In spite of the noise and confusion on board, my attention was riveted on a girl leaning over the rail.

Attitude : STRIKE AN ATTITUDE. Stand or sit in a dramatic, self-conscious position.
The actor, striking an attitude, quoted Shakespeare.

Avail : LITTLE, OR NO, AVAIL. Almost (or quite) without any result.
She often implored her husband not to go out, but her words were of little avail.

Avenue : LEAVE NO AVENUE UNEXPLORED, *or* EXPLORE EVERY AVENUE. Employ every possible source of information ; make every possible enquiry.
We'll explore every avenue to find a way out of your difficulties.

See LEAVE NO STONE UNTURNED (under **Stone**).

Away : AWAY WITH YOU ! An old-f. phrase, spoken either angrily or facetiously, meaning " Depart, go ! "

Axe : AXE TO GRIND. A private and personal object to achieve or favour to obtain.

I guessed when he asked for an interview that Smith had an axe to grind.

B

Back : BACK OUT OF. Withdraw from an agreement.

George promised to contribute £20, but backed out of it when the time came.

BACK STAIRS. Lit., The inferior staircase used by the servants, in a large house. Applied as an adjective (1) to servants' gossip and (2) to indirect and unofficial influence.

He obtained the post through back-stairs influence.

BEAT BACK. Compel to retreat.

The enemy attacked, but were beaten back.

BEHIND ONE'S BACK. When one is absent. (The phrase is always used in connection with slander and unpleasant gossip.)

The old woman told lies about the boy behind his back.

BREAK THE BACK OF. Complete the most difficult or the chief part of.

We shall break the back of the work by to-night.

GO BACK (*a*) ON A PERSON ; (*b*) ON ONE'S WORD. (*a*) Betray ; desert ; (*b*) contradict or withdraw (a statement, etc.).

(*a*) *He went back on me, and joined a rival firm.*

(*b*) *He went back on his promise and refused to lend me the money.*

HANG BACK. Linger ; fail to advance.

I asked for someone to help me carry the poor woman, but the crowd hung back.

PAY BACK. Repay money or benefits.

Here's five shillings ; pay me back next week.

PUT ONE'S BACK UP (S.). Annoy ; make hostile. (From the manner in which a cat arches its back when angered.)

John's rudeness always puts my back up.

See RUB UP THE WRONG WAY.

WHEN ONE'S BACK IS TURNED. When one is absent, or occupied over some other matter.

He laughed at his master when the old man's back was turned.

Background : KEEP *or* REMAIN, IN THE BACKGROUND. Remain inconspicuous and unnoticed.

I'm going to keep in the background during the discussion.

Backwards : BACKWARDS AND FORWARDS. Similar to TO AND FRO, which see.

Bacon : BRING HOME THE BACON (S.). Provide the necessary money for food, etc.

Tennyson didn't earn much by his plays ; it was his poetry that brought home the bacon.

SAVE ONE'S BACON (S.). Enable one to escape or succeed.

He would have failed at the examination, but his history paper saved his bacon.

Bad : A BAD EGG ; A BAD HAT ; A BAD LOT (S.). A person with a thoroughly bad character.

BAD DEBTS. Debts which are " written off " as complete losses. See WRITE OFF.

BAD FORM. Not accepted as socially correct ; ill-mannered.

It is bad form not to speak to one's hostess at a dance.

GO BAD. Become stale or rotten.

GO TO THE BAD. Surrender to evil influences ; abandon all social or moral conventions.

Thompson has gone to the bad completely since his wife died.

Bag : BAG AND BAGGAGE. Luggage ; all one's portable possessions.

He was turned out of the hotel, bag and baggage.

Balance : STRIKE A BALANCE. Balance or weigh certain objects or facts against one another, in order to discover their comparative value or importance. (Used especially in connection with financial accounts.)

Striking a balance, I should be happier with Mother than with Father.

ON BALANCE. The result of such examination, and similarly used.

On balance, we're £50 richer.

Bald : BALD AS A COOT. Absolutely hairless. (A coot is a water-bird, one species of which has a flat covering on its forehead, which gives it an appearance of baldness.)

Bale : BALE OUT. 1. Remove water or other fluid from a vessel by means of a ladle, pail, etc.

A big wave swamped the boat, but the crew succeeded in baling out the water.

2. Escape from an aeroplane by parachute.

We baled out behind the enemy's lines.

Ball : THE BALL AT ONE'S FEET. Or. Football. Every quality and opportunity of being successful.

George will become famous ; he has the ball at his feet.

KEEP THE BALL ROLLING. Continue the conversation or proceedings successfully.

My host had very little to talk about, and it was difficult to keep the ball rolling.

OPEN THE BALL. Or. Dancing. Make a formal and definite beginning.

The magistrate opened the ball by asking the policeman to give his evidence.

Bank : BANK HOLIDAYS. General holidays on which all banks as well as shops are closed ; consequently an official holiday.

Bargain : BARGAIN FOR. Anticipate ; plan.

We didn't bargain for so many people coming to tea.

DRIVE A HARD BARGAIN. Conclude a bargain the terms of which are harsh.

Old Jones agreed to finance the business, but he drove a hard bargain.

INTO THE BARGAIN. In addition ; extra.

He bought the house, and the furniture into the bargain.

STRIKE A BARGAIN. Reach a final compromise.

We argued for a long time over what I should pay, but finally struck a bargain.

Bark : BARK UP THE WRONG TREE (S.). Make a mistake ; a false assumption.

If you think George was responsible for the rumour, you're barking up the wrong tree.

HIS BARK IS WORSE THAN HIS BITE. What he threatens to do is worse than what he actually does.

John says that he'll half kill the boy when he catches

him, but his bark is worse than his bite, and I don't suppose he'll do more than send him to bed without any supper.

Battle : BATTLE ROYAL. A general fight. See PITCHED BATTLE.

ENGAGE IN BATTLE. Attack ; fight.

GIVE BATTLE. Fight with ; attack.

The English gave battle to the enemy soon after sunrise.

IN BATTLE ARRAY. In battle order ; ready to attack.

Marlborough's troops were drawn up in battle array.

PITCHED BATTLE. One in which both sides are fully engaged.

Bay : AT BAY. In a situation so desperate that one is compelled to turn and face one's enemies. See FIGHT WITH ONE'S BACK TO THE WALL.

BAY THE MOON. Howl, as certain animals do, at the full moon. (To " bay " is to utter a deep bark or cry.)

Be : BE IT SO. An old-f. version of " Let it be so ". A general acceptance of a statement, etc.

I shall leave early to-morrow morning.

Be it so. I will have breakfast ready.

BE NO MORE. Cease to exist ; die.

Our poor old dog is no more.

See BREATHE ONE'S LAST ; PASS AWAY *or* OVER ; PEG OUT ; GATHERED TO ONE'S FATHERS.

BE OFF WITH YOU ! A peremptory order to depart.

I don't give money to beggars—be off with you !

Beam : ON ONE'S BEAM-ENDS. Or. Nautical. In a desperate and almost hopeless condition. (Lit., The term is applied to a ship when it is tilted so far over one side that it is resting on the ends of its crossbeams, or supports, and is consequently in great danger of sinking.)

Tom has lost his entire fortune, and is on his beam-ends.

See ON ONE'S UPPERS.

Bear : BEAR A CHARMED LIFE. Be almost incredibly fortunate in escaping disasters and accidents.

The bullet missed my uncle by less than an inch—he bears a charmed life.

BEAR DOWN. Press down ; overcome.

BEAR DOWN UPON. Or. Nautical. Lit., To approach a vessel from the weather side. To approach with determination or with an obvious purpose.

The Professor bore down on the undergraduate.

BEAR ENQUIRY, INVESTIGATION, *etc.* Produce a satisfactory answer to enquiries. (Frequently used in the negative.)

The business he has been connected with since he left prison won't bear enquiry.

BEAR FALSE WITNESS. Swear to things which one knows to be untrue ; tell lies about.

I will not bear false witness against my friend.

BEAR MALICE, *or* A GRUDGE. Retain bitter or angry feelings, usually as the result of a dispute or quarrel.

I hope you won't bear malice after what has happened.

BEAR A MEANING. Convey a meaning.

That sentence doesn't bear the meaning you seem to think it does.

BEAR IN MIND. Retain in one's memory.

Bear in mind that the train leaves at midnight.

BEAR THE NAME. Possess the name.

Their son bore the name of his grandfather, and was christened Joseph.

BEAR OUT. 1. Lit., Carry away.

They bore out the body.

2. Confirm ; support.

His statement bears out what the police told me.

BEAR THE PALM. Be the best ; the winner ; worthy of the palm, an honour which was in Roman days given to the victor.

They are all clever girls, but Ruth bears the palm for beauty.

BEAR UP. Sustain one's strength and spirits.

Her father's death was a terrible shock, but the poor girl is bearing up well.

BEAR WITH. Endure.

The invalid is very irritable, but we try to bear with him.

NO BEARING ON. No connection with ; irrelevant.

You deliberately struck the man ; the fact that it was a wet day has no bearing on the matter.

See BESIDE THE MARK, and BEGGING THE QUESTION.

BEARS DATE, SIGNATURE, *etc.* Has written upon it.
His latest letter bears date April 1st.

Bear-garden : Used in reference to a place—generally a room—in a condition of extreme tumult and confusion.
The children left the nursery looking like a bear-garden.

Beard : BEARD THE LION IN HIS DEN. Confront boldly one's opponent or superior in his own home or office, and discuss the matter in dispute.
I'm going to beard the lion in his den to-morrow, and ask him plainly why he hasn't increased my salary.

Beat : BEAT ABOUT THE BUSH. Avoid or delay a straight-forward discussion ; approach a subject in a roundabout way. Or. Hunters beating bushes and similar hiding-places to discover if game is hiding there.
I wanted to talk about our marriage, but Joan would beat about the bush.

BEAT DOWN. 1. Crush opposition.
The rebellion was beaten down.

2. Compel a person to reduce his price.
He wanted five shillings, but I beat him down.

BEAT HOLLOW (S.). Be entirely superior to.
We thought Tennyson a great poet, but Shelley beats him hollow.

BEAT IT (S.). Depart at once.
Don't stay here—beat it.

BEAT OFF. Repel.
The garrison beat off all the enemy attacks.

DEAD BEAT. Utterly exhausted.
After walking all day in the rain, we were dead beat.

Bed : BED OF ROSES. A state of ease and luxury. (Frequently used with a negative.)
Life to-day is far from being a bed of roses.

Bee : BEE IN ONE'S BONNET (S.). Obsession ; some particular idea or conviction, usually slightly crazy.
He has a bee in his bonnet—he insists the earth is not round but flat.

MAKE, *or* FOLLOW, A BEE LINE. Proceed in a straight line, as a bee does on its way home.

Beggar : BEGGAR DESCRIPTION. Be so extraordinary that one cannot find words in which to describe it.

The splendour of the Coronation beggars description.

Begging : BEGGING THE QUESTION. See under **Question**.

Behalf : ON BEHALF OF. As a substitute for, or representative of, someone.

The chairman signed the document on behalf of the company.

Behaviour : BE ON ONE'S GOOD, *or* BEST, BEHAVIOUR. Conduct oneself as correctly and properly as possible.

Charles was on his best behaviour throughout the interview.

Behind : BEHIND THE SCENES. Or. Theatrical. Secretly and unofficially.

Plans for the next election are going on behind the scenes.

BEHIND THE TIMES. Late ; unfashionable.

You are behind the times with your information.

Her dress was extremely behind the times.

See OUT OF DATE.

Belief : BEYOND BELIEF. Unbelievable ; astounding.

EASY OF BELIEF. Easily believable.

It is easy of belief that his people were gentlefolk.

STAGGER BELIEF. So strange or unexpected that one can hardly believe it.

Below : HIT BELOW THE BELT. Attack unfairly. Or. Boxing. In prize-fighting a boxer may not strike his opponent below the belt worn round the waist.

It was hitting below the belt for his father to threaten to write to Mary about the other girl.

Bend : BEND ONE'S STEPS. Walk in a specified direction.

After lunch I shall bend my steps homeward.

See BETAKE ONESELF.

Benefit : GIVE THE BENEFIT OF THE DOUBT. Assume that a person is innocent when it is not certain that he is guilty.

The milk jug was empty, and the cat sitting near, but we gave him the benefit of the doubt.

CONFER A BENEFIT. Act beneficially ; be advantageous.

This new discovery will confer a benefit on all invalids.

Bent : BENT UPON. Determined to take a certain action.
> *John was bent upon walking the entire distance that same night.*

TOP OF ONE'S BENT. As much as possible ; very thoroughly.
> *George was enjoying himself to the top of his bent.*

Berth : GIVE A WIDE BERTH TO. Or. Nautical. Avoid ; keep as far from as possible. A berth is any place in which a ship can anchor.

Beside : BESIDE THE MARK *or* POINT. Irrelevant ; unconnected with the matter being discussed.
> *Your statements are beside the mark.*

See NO BEARING ON and BEGGING THE QUESTION.

BESIDE ONESELF. In such a state of emotion that one is incapable of knowing what one is doing.
> *George was beside himself when he heard that Mary was in the wrecked ship.*

Best : AT BEST. Even in the best possible circumstances.
> *A fox is, at best, an unsatisfactory pet.*

BEST MAN. The bridegroom's chief friend and assistant at a wedding.

FOR THE BEST ; ALL FOR THE BEST. For the best that can happen ; for the ultimate good.
> *She has gone back to her husband, and it is probably for the best.*

Betake : BETAKE ONESELF. Old f. Go ; proceed to.
> *It is late ; I shall betake myself to bed.*

See BEND ONE'S STEPS.

Better : BETTER HALF. Wife (a gently-ironic complimentary phrase).

BETTER ONESELF. Improve one's worldly position.
> *Young William has left the village to better himself.*

GET THE BETTER OF. Triumph over ; prove stronger than.
> *Her kindness of heart got the better of her anger, and she forgave him.*

THINK BETTER OF. Reconsider, and decide to alter one's plan (usually from prudence or fear).
> *He was going to protest, but thought better of it.*

Between : BETWEEN OURSELVES, *or* BETWEEN YOU AND ME. Speaking privately and confidentially.
> *Between ourselves, I don't think he will live much longer.*

Beyond : BEYOND EXPECTATION. Beyond anything expected.

> *The beauties of Florence in spring were far beyond his expectation.*

BEYOND THE PALE. Beyond the limits of decent society, good manners and moral limitations. In Ireland, the property of the English kings used to be separated from that owned by the inhabitants, which was known as being beyond " the pale".

> *The man's cruelty puts him beyond the pale.*

Bid : BID FAIR TO. Appear likely to.

> *The daughter bids fair to be even more beautiful than her mother.*

BID WELCOME, FAREWELL, *etc.* Lit., Tell a visitor to consider himself welcome. To express a welcome, or a farewell greeting.

> *My hostess came to the door to bid me farewell.*

Bill : BILL AND COO (S.). Speak lovingly and intimately. An allusion to the sound—billing and cooing— made by doves and pigeons.

> *We'll leave the two young people to bill and coo together.*

Billingsgate : Bad language ; abuse. Billingsgate, the London market in which fish is bought and sold, is supposed—traditionally and unjustly—to be the place where the worst language is used.

Bird : AN EARLY BIRD. Or. The proverb, " The early bird catches the first worm." An early arrival.

> *The entertainment did not begin till eight, but we were early birds, and got to the hall at seven-thirty.*

BIRDS OF A FEATHER. Or. The proverb, " Birds of a feather flock together." People of the same type, or with the same views.

> *She murmured bitterly, " Birds of a feather", went to look for Peter in the public-house and found him there.*

A BIRD IN THE HAND. Or. The proverb, " A bird in the hand is worth two in the bush." Immediate possession or payment is worth twice as much as a mere promise to pay at some later date.

> *He offered me a shilling ; it was not much, but it was a bird in the hand, and I accepted the money.*

BIRD OF ILL OMEN. Lit., A bird—e.g. the raven, the owl or the crow—whose appearance is supposed to indicate the coming of bad luck. Applied to any person who has a reputation for bringing bad news.

The postman has proved a bird of ill omen three times this week.

BIRD OF PASSAGE. Lit., A bird like the swallow, starling, etc., which migrates from one country to another according to the season. A person who is constantly travelling from place to place and has no permanent home.

Perkins left for Rome again yesterday—he's a regular bird of passage.

KILL TWO BIRDS WITH ONE STONE. Produce two results with a single action.

When in town I'll kill two birds with one stone and visit Mrs. Smith and my sister.

Birthday : BIRTHDAY CLOTHES, *or* SUIT. No clothes at all ; naked, as one is born.

The small boy dashed out of the bath in his birthday clothes.

Bit : NOT A BIT (OF IT). Not at all.

Are you afraid ? Not a bit of it.

Bite : BITE, *or* LICK, THE DUST. Be killed in battle.

May all our enemies bite the dust.

BITE ONE'S HEAD OFF. Speak angrily and sharply to a person.

Because I ask for some money, you need not bite my head off.

TWO BITES AT A CHERRY. Two separate attempts to achieve a result.

There's no need to make two bites at a cherry ; we can finish all our packing this afternoon.

Black : BLACK ART. Art or craft derived from the Devil ; vile and supernatural practices.

IN ONE'S BLACK BOOKS. In disfavour ; with a bad reputation.

George has been in his uncle's black books ever since he forgot the old man's birthday.

See BOOKS, GOOD and BAD.

BLACK LOOKS. Evil, angry looks. See BLACK AS THUNDER.

BLACK AS THUNDER. Darkly; furiously. (An imaginative exaggeration, as thunder itself has no colour; the word used should be " thundercloud ".)

He gave me a glare as black as thunder, and asked me what I wanted.

IN BLACK AND WHITE. In writing or print.

Here is his story, set down with complete frankness in black and white.

Blackmail : LEVY BLACKMAIL. Obtain money or some other advantage by threatening to reveal some past disgrace or scandal.

The villain levied blackmail for ten years before his victim went to the police.

Blanket : WET BLANKET. A person who by his manner or conversation extinguishes the cheerfulness and enthusiasm of others (as, literally, a wet blanket extinguishes fire).

She talked of nothing but her husband's death, and was a complete wet blanket.

Blind : BLIND IMPULSE. An illogical impulse.

Some blind impulse made me tell her my secret—I have been glad ever since that I did.

NONE SO BLIND. Abbrev. for proverb, " There's none so blind as those who won't see." No one is so difficult to persuade as a man who is determined not to listen to arguments or persuasion.

I've told her a dozen times that she is being cheated, but there's none so blind.

BLIND SIDE. The aspect of a man's character in which he is tender-hearted or weak.

Mary can always get on the blind side of her grandfather and persuade him to take her to the cinema.

BLIND STAGGERS (S.). An unsteady, staggering walk, due to illness or drunkenness.

There's old Peter, going home with the blind staggers as usual.

Block : A CHIP OF THE OLD BLOCK. One exhibiting the characteristics of his parents or ancestors.

Young Bill is going to be a clever actor—he's a regular chip of the old block.

Blood : BAD BLOOD. Ill-feeling ; antagonism.

> *There's been bad blood between the brothers ever since Jack came home.*

ONE'S BLOOD BEING UP. Being excited and angry.

> *His blood was up, and with a shout he dashed into the fight.*

See HOT BLOOD ; MAKE ONE'S BLOOD BOIL.

BLOOD IS THICKER THAN WATER. Relations are more closely connected than mere friends or acquaintances, and should receive better treatment.

> *He was my nephew, and remembering that blood is thicker than water I helped him.*

BLOOD SPORTS. Sports that involve the shedding of blood—fox-hunting, deer-hunting, etc.

BLOOD-SUCKER. Lit., An animal, such as a leech, a vampire-bat, or a mosquito, which lives on the blood of living persons. Met., One who lives by blackmail, lending money at high interest, or otherwise taking a cruel advantage of other people's fortune.

BLOOD-AND-THUNDER. Highly sensational ; melodramatic.

> *I rather like blood-and-thunder stories.*

See PENNY DREADFUL.

BLUE-BLOODED. Aristocratic, of gentle birth (from the fantastic idea that the blood of aristocrats was bluer than that of " common " people).

> *Though one of the most blue-blooded families in the land, they are desperately poor.*

IN COLD BLOOD. Deliberately ; coolly.

> *The murderer shot his victim in cold blood.*

IN HOT BLOOD. In anger.

> *I struck him in hot blood, and now I'm sorry.*

See BLOOD BEING UP ; MAKE ONE'S BLOOD BOIL.

IN THE BLOOD. Part of one's nature—born with one.

> *I hate cats, and so did my father—it's in the blood.*

MAKE ONE'S BLOOD BOIL. Make one furiously angry.

See IN HOT BLOOD ; ONE'S BLOOD BEING UP.

A PRINCE OR PRINCESS OF THE BLOOD. A member of the Royal Family.

Blot : BLOT ON ONE'S SCUTCHEON. Or. Heraldry. A disgrace ; an injury to one's good reputation. The 'scutcheon (or escutcheon) is the shield on which the coat-of-arms is depicted.

His brutal treatment of his daughter will always be a blot on his scutcheon.

BLOT OUT. Efface ; obliterate ; forget.

Let us blot out the memory of past misery, and look forward to a happy future.

Blow : BLOW HOT AND COLD. Be inconsistent and unreliable. From Æsop's fable of the countryman who blew on his fingers to warm them, and then on his porridge to cool it.

I don't want an acquaintance who will blow hot and cold, and whom I can't trust.

BLOW OUT. 1. Verb. Extinguish.

Blow out the candle.

2. Noun (S.). A large and luxurious meal.

We had a tremendous blow-out at the hotel.

BLOW OVER. Subside. Lit. applied to a storm of wind, etc.

The storm will soon blow over.

Met., Applied to quarrels, disagreements, etc.

Mary and I have frequent quarrels, but they soon blow over.

BLOW UP. 1. Explode.

The mine blew up soon after we passed.

2. (S.). Blame severely.

I'm going to blow up the builder for his bad work.

BLOWN UPON (S.). Spoilt ; defiled. (Meat is said to be " fly-blown " when a fly has deposited its eggs on it.)

He had a good character ten years ago, but it has been considerably blown upon since.

Blue : BLUE FUNK (S.). Extreme fear.

Arthur was in a blue funk when you sent for him.

BLUE RIBAND *or* RIBBON. Highest attainable honour or prize. Or. The blue ribbon worn with the Order of the Garter.

That horse won the Derby — the blue riband of racing.

BLUE RUIN (S.). Complete and absolute ruin.

Unless we appoint a new manager, the firm will end in blue ruin.

DARK BLUES AND LIGHT BLUES.   The Oxford and Cambridge teams or crews, the terms being derived from the respective colours worn, especially in connection with the annual boat-race.

HAVE THE BLUES (S.).   Be deeply depressed.
The entire staff seems to have the blues this morning.

Bluff : CALL A MAN'S BLUFF.   Or. The card game of poker. Challenge a statement or action which one believes has nothing to support it.
I called his bluff : if he could produce his authority as a police officer, I would allow him to search the house.   He muttered that he had left it at home, and went away.

Blush : AT THE FIRST BLUSH.   When glanced at casually, or for the first time.
At the first blush the Government proposals seem generous.

PUT TO THE BLUSH.   Compelled to blush for shame.
The lies he told would have put Ananias to the blush.

BLUSHING HONOURS.   Or. Shakespeare's *Henry VIII* : " And bear his blushing honours thick upon him ".   Publicly awarded honours, titles, etc.

Board : BOARD WAGES.   Wages paid by an absent owner to servants who " board " in their own houses while he is away.

Boat : IN THE SAME BOAT (S.).   Similarly situated.
It's no use grumbling—we're all in the same boat.

Bob : BOB UP.   1. Lit., Rise suddenly.
There was a splash in the pond, and a duck bobbed up.
2. (S.).   Met., Arrive suddenly.
We were having dinner when the Browns bobbed up.
(*Note.*—This idiom, followed by " again ", is frequently used to indicate more than one sudden appearance.)

Body : IN A BODY.   Collectively ;   all together.
The deputies arrived in a body.

Boil : BOIL OVER.   1. Lit., Boil so that the fluid rises above the edge of the saucepan or kettle.   2. Met., Become so angry that self-control is lost.
Stories of cruelty to children always make me boil over.
See MAKE ONE'S BLOOD BOIL.

Bold : MAKE BOLD TO ;   MAKE SO BOLD AS TO.   Old f., Dare to.
May I make bold to ask your name, sir ?

Bolster : BOLSTER UP. Add facts to a statement in order to support it.

The sailor bolstered up his story of the shipwreck by describing the ships which passed him.

Bolt : BOLT UPRIGHT. Absolutely straight and perpendicular. (*Bolt* here refers to an arrow with a knob on the end, used for shooting rooks.)

A BOLT FROM THE BLUE. A sudden and entirely unexpected disaster. The " bolt " is a thunderbolt, and the " blue " is a cloudless sky from which no storm is to be expected.

There came a bolt from the blue—our rich bachelor uncle got married.

Bone : BONE OF CONTENTION. The subject of argument or dispute.

The property left by their father was a bone of contention between the brothers.

A BONE TO PICK. A matter for reproof or blame.

I have a bone to pick with you in connection with your unpunctuality.

See A CROW TO PLUCK.

Book : BOOK MAKER. *Not* a manufacturer of ordinary books, but a professional racing man, colloquially known as a " bookie ", who makes a living by accepting bets from the public (punters). The bets recorded form collectively a " book ".

BRING TO BOOK. Bring to justice ; punish.

He has been robbing the public for thirty years, but the law will bring him to book in the end.

IN ONE'S GOOD BOOKS (*or* BAD). Liked and appreciated, or the reverse. (Also BLACK BOOKS.)

That young man is in everyone's good books.

SPEAK BY THE BOOK. Quote exactly and literally from some authority. (This phrase is more frequently used in the negative.)

Without speaking by the book, I am sure there is a law against cycling on that path.

SUIT ONE'S BOOK. Agree with one's plans.

That arrangement will suit my book very well indeed.

TAKE A LEAF OUT OF A PERSON'S BOOK. Follow his example.

I think I'll take a leaf out of Father's book and go to bed early.

Boot : TO BOOT. Old f., In addition to ; also.

I paid him what he asked, and five shillings to boot.

Border : BORDERING ON. Near to ; almost.

The servant's manner was abrupt, bordering on insolence.

Born : BORN BEFORE ONE'S TIME. Possessing ideas and theories that belong to a later period in history.

King Alfred, who was born before his time, thought that every English child should be taught to read and write.

Borne : BORNE IN UPON ONE. Impressed upon one's mind.

It was borne in upon her that they would never meet again.

Borrow : BORROWED PLUMES. Anything worn or assumed to which one is not entitled. Or. Æsop's fable of the jay who made herself ridiculous by adding peacock's feathers (or plumes) to her own.

Mary looked charming in her borrowed plumes ; she had taken, without asking, her aunt's fan and jewellery.

Bottle : BOTTLE-NECK. A passage which becomes suddenly narrow, like the neck of a bottle, through which objects are compelled to move slowly ; hence (Met.), anything which causes a delay.

The bottle-neck in the Brentford Road is an intolerable nuisance to traffic going to and from London.

BOTTLE UP. Suppress.

He bottled up his anger and said nothing.

Bottom : AT THE BOTTOM OF. Really responsible for.

The complaint is signed by the director, but old Parkins is at the bottom of the whole business.

BOTTOMLESS PIT. Hell.

TOUCH BOTTOM. Lit., Reach the bottom of the sea.

The boat's keel touched bottom.

Met., Reach the lowest depths of misery, poverty or disgrace.

At last he touched bottom, and was reduced to begging in the streets.

See ROCK-BOTTOM.

Bound : I'LL BE BOUND. I am certain.

You will arrive late again to-morrow, I'll be bound.

OUT OF BOUNDS. Beyond the official boundary or limit.

All the hotels in the town have been placed out of bounds for the troops.

WITHIN BOUNDS. 1. Within the official boundary or limit. 2. Within reasonable limitations and restraint.

She could never keep her temper within bounds.

WITHIN THE BOUNDS OF POSSIBILITY. Just possible.

It is, of course, within the bounds of possibility that the shipwrecked crew may have reached some desert island.

Bow : DRAW THE LONG BOW. Exaggerate.

When he was describing his escapes in the war, Bill was certainly drawing the long bow.

TWO STRINGS, *or* ANOTHER STRING, TO ONE'S BOW. An alternative, a second plan in case the first should fail.

If I can't borrow the money from Uncle John, I've another string to my bow—Uncle Peter.

Bowl : BOWLED OVER. 1. Lit., Overturned ; knocked down.

The poor old man was bowled over in the rush to the train.

2. Met. (S.). Overcome.

When I heard the news I was completely bowled over.

Box : IN THE SAME BOX. In a similar condition.

The Smiths are trying to find a hotel for the night, and we're in the same box.

See IN THE SAME BOAT.

Brain : BRAINS TRUST. A group of intelligentsia, meeting to discuss and answer questions and problems, usually sent them by correspondents.

CUDGEL ONE'S BRAINS. See **Cudgel.**

RACK ONE'S BRAINS. See **Rack.**

MAKE ONE'S BRAIN REEL. Stagger one mentally. Applied to an almost incredible statement or fact.

The number of stars now visible to astronomers makes one's brain reel.

PICK A PERSON'S BRAINS. Question him informally and more or less tactfully in order to obtain special information.

Bran : BRAN, *or* BRAND, NEW. Absolutely new. From the Anglo-Saxon *brand*, a torch. Or. Fire-new— applied to metal goods taken straight from the fire in which they were made.

What do you think of my brand-new bicycle ?

Brazen : BRAZEN OUT. Defiantly defend, or deny.

He brazened out his determination to spend the money as he chose.

Breach : BREACH OF THE PEACE (*strictly speaking,* THE QUEEN'S PEACE). Any action which breaches or breaks the law and may lead to violence and disturbance. See BREAK THE PEACE.

BREACH OF PROMISE (*to marry*). Legal phrase for the breaking of a formal promise, usually but not always on the man's part, to marry.

Margaret is going to sue Edward for breach of promise.

HEAL THE BREACH. Bring a serious or prolonged quarrel to an end.

George and Jane will not speak to one another ; her mother is trying to heal the breach.

Bread : BREAD-WINNER. The person whose earnings support the family.

John's father was an invalid, and his mother became the bread-winner.

Break : BREAK AWAY. Free, or detach oneself, by a definite effort.

I broke away from the association ten years ago.

BREAK THE BANK. " Bank " in this case refers to a private or public gambling organization (Monte Carlo, etc.), in which a gambler has a run of luck lasting long enough to cause the " bank " to run out of funds, and to be compelled temporarily to stop the play.

BREAK DOWN. I. Smash by force.

We shall have to break down the door to get in.

2. Cause to diminish and finally disappear.

The Queen's charm broke down her visitor's nervousness.

3. Collapse under great pain or emotion.

When at last she heard he was dead, she broke down completely.

See BREAK UP.

BREAK FORTH. Escape from.

Cheers broke forth from the crowd when the hero appeared.

See BREAK OUT and BURST FORTH.

BREAK NEW GROUND. Begin something new or different.

We shall break new ground in the spring by opening a shop at Liverpool.

BREAK THE ICE. Break an uncomfortable silence ; put an end to formality or stiffness.

The President broke the ice by asking me how I liked New York.

BREAK IN. 1. Enter a building by force.

The burglar was arrested outside the bank as he was breaking in.

2. Interrupt.

I could tell this story better if so many people didn't break in.

3. Train someone, usually an animal, in obedience.

I've spent nearly six months breaking in my pony.

BREAK A JOURNEY. Interrupt it by stopping at some point on the way, and resuming the journey later.

We are breaking our journey at Chester for one night.

BREAK A LANCE. Argue with ; attack verbally. Or. The Tournaments of the Middle Ages, in which competing knights, armed with lances, challenged one another to combat.

The landlord liked argument, and was always willing to break a lance with visitors on the subject of socialism.

BREAK LOOSE. Escape.

The dog broke loose from its chain.

See BREAK AWAY.

BREAK THE NEWS. Convey startling and usually bad news as tactfully and gently as possible.

John's father has died ; you'll have to break the news to the boy.

BREAK OFF. End suddenly.

We were discussing our plans, but had to break off when Emily came in.

BREAK OUT. 1. Lit., Force one's way out.

He broke out of prison, but was caught again later.

2. Met., Begin violently and generally unexpectedly.
A roar of cheering broke out.

See BREAK FORTH and BURST FORTH.

BREAK THE PEACE. Break the law by doing something
that may cause others to break it too, e.g. to try
to persuade a man to fight. See BREACH OF THE
PEACE.

BREAK THE RECORD. Surpass all previous performances.
*Old James broke the record in our village by living
to 105.*

BREAK STEP. Or. Military. Soldiers normally march
" in step " unless crossing bridges, when they
" break step " or march irregularly to reduce the
vibration.

BREAK THE THREAD. Interrupt a story, etc.
*I was telling the children my wonderful dream, when
you came in and broke the thread.*

See BREAK IN (2).

BREAK THROUGH. Penetrate the surroundings or im-
pediment.
The sun broke through the clouds.
The crowd broke through the lines of police.

BREAK UP. Lit., Break into small pieces. Met., End;
destroy.
*They were happy together, until the War came and
broke up their home.*

BREAK WITH. Have no further connection with.
I have entirely broken with the Company.

BREAK ONE'S WORD, *or* PROMISE. Fail to do what one
has undertaken to do.
*Michael has broken his word so many times that I
cannot trust him any more.*

Breast : MAKE A CLEAN BREAST. Confess all.
The murderer made a clean breast of his crimes.

Breath : ALL IN A BREATH. Breathlessly ; without pausing
to breathe.
*She explained, all in a breath, that she had missed
her train, had her purse stolen, and was lost in
London.*

THE BREATH OF ONE'S NOSTRILS. Vital ; absolutely
necessary.

The Englishman demands freedom ; it is the breath of his nostrils.

IN THE SAME BREATH. At the same time ; simultaneously. (Usually in connection with two contradictory statements.)

He told me he was a Communist, and in the same breath cheered the Queen.

TAKE AWAY ONE'S BREATH. Leave one breathless through intense astonishment, delight, etc.

Your offer is so generous that it takes my breath away.

UNDER ONE'S BREATH. Very softly ; almost in a whisper.

" I love him," she said under her breath.

WITH ONE'S LAST BREATH. To the end of one's life ; to the last. (Used metaphorically to add emphasis to a statement.)

I would maintain with my last breath that he is innocent.

Breathe : BREATHE ONE'S LAST. Die.

The old man breathed his last just before dawn.

BREATHE REVENGE, CURSES, BLESSINGS, *etc.* Murmur ; utter in low intense tones.

The aged traveller breathed a blessing on those who had given him shelter for the night.

NOT TO BREATHE A SYLLABLE. Remain absolutely silent ; keep secret.

I promised not to breathe a syllable about what he told me.

Bred : BRED IN THE BONE. Part of one's nature ; an inherent quality which cannot be changed.

His idleness, like his good looks, was bred in the bone.

Brick : A BRICK, *or* A REGULAR BRICK (S.). A thoroughly good fellow. Probably originating in the squareness, solidarity and general reliability of a brick.

BRICK UP. Fill up an opening in a building, cave, etc., with bricks.

There was once a window there, but it has been bricked up for centuries.

COME DOWN LIKE A TON, *or* A HUNDRED, OF BRICKS (S.). Blame severely and violently.

The manager came down on me like a ton of bricks for leaving the door of the safe open.

MAKE BRICKS WITHOUT STRAW. Or. Biblical. (The

Israelites were commanded to make bricks without straw.) Manufacture or produce something without the necessary material.

He wanted an iced birthday cake, but I've no sugar, and one can't make bricks without straw.

Brim : TO THE BRIM. Lit., to the edge of any vessel made to contain fluid. Met., To indicate absolute completion.

She was filled to the brim with happiness.

Bring : BRING ABOUT ; BRING TO PASS. Cause to happen.

It was gambling that brought about his ruin.

BRING TO BEAR. Concentrate one's efforts with some special object.

She brought to bear all her charm.

BRING TO BOOK. Detect someone in a mistake ; bring a wrongdoer to punishment.

The swindler was caught and brought to book.

BRING, *or* CALL, INTO BEING. Cause to exist.

His cruelty will bring into being bitterness and hatred in his home.

See BRING FORTH.

BRING TO A CLOSE. End ; conclude.

We are bringing our entertainment to a close with a firework display.

BRING FORTH. Produce ; display. (Lit. and Met.)

Whoever can bring forth a plan to prevent future wars deserves the world's greatest honours.

See BRING INTO BEING and CALL FORTH.

BRING FORWARD. Introduce ; initiate.

The Chancellor of the Exchequer brought forward a new scheme of taxation.

BRING HOME TO. Cause one to realize, to feel, to understand.

The sound of church bells brought home to him the happiness he had lost.

BRING ON. Start ; cause to begin.

His troubles may bring on a serious illness.

BRING UP THE REAR. Or. Military. Follow at the end.

Policemen on horseback brought up the rear.

BRING ROUND. 1. Bring from a short distance.

Mrs. Jones, who lives at No. 6, will bring round some apples.

2. Restore a person who has fainted.

We threw water over the woman to bring her round.

See COME TO.

BRING UP. **1.** Refer to some matter requiring discussion (also BRING FORWARD).

Please bring up the matter at our next meeting.

2. Care for and educate.

Young Peter was brought up by his uncle.

He was very well brought up.

BRING WORD. Convey information.

My servant will bring word when I am ready.

Bristle : BRISTLES WITH. Is made crowded and unpleasant with.

The journey bristles with dangers.

Broad : AS BROAD AS IT'S LONG. Either alternative will lead to the same result.

We could go there through London or through Kingston. As both routes will cost five shillings and take an hour, it's as broad as it's long.

BROADLY SPEAKING. Speaking generally; stated in simple terms.

Broadly speaking, the English are simple and friendly.

Broken : BROKEN ACCENTS. Imperfect or hesitating speech.

The boy, who seemed half frozen, begged in broken accents for a meal.

See BROKEN ENGLISH.

BROKEN COLOUR. A colour diluted or rendered impure with some other colour.

BROKEN ENGLISH. Inaccurate and imperfect English.

The Indian asked, in broken English, the way to London.

See BROKEN ACCENTS.

BROKEN REED. An ally or support who has proved useless or unworthy. (A reed is a tall kind of grass which, although stiff, snaps very easily.)

I asked him to give evidence in our favour, but he proved a broken reed.

Brow : LOW-BROW. One whose tastes are normally those of the less-educated types of people ; one who enjoys " popular " forms of art, literature and music as opposed to the classical.

HIGH-BROW. The opposite type ; a person whose

tastes are for the "superior", less subtle forms of art.

Brown : IN A BROWN STUDY. Apparently thinking deeply, actually hardly thinking at all ; in a mental vacuum. (The phrase is due to a faulty translation of the French *sombre pensée*. *Sombre* means not only brown, but gloomy, melancholy.)

Brush : A BRUSH. A light, casual encounter.
> *Our advanced troops had a brush with the enemy this morning.*

Brute : BRUTE FORCE. Physical force or strength, as opposed to moral force.
> *The police had to use brute force to take her to the station.*

Buck : BUCK UP (S.). Similar to **Buckle to.**

Buckle : BUCKLE TO (S.). Make an extra effort.
> *We shall have to buckle to if we are to catch that train.*

BUCKLE UP. Bend and collapse.
> *The iron supports of the bridge have buckled up.*

Buff : IN THE BUFF (S.). Unclothed ; nude.
> *The doctor examined the recruits in the buff.*

Build : BUILD UPON. Met., Rely upon.
> *He makes many promises, but it isn't safe to build upon them.*

Buoy : BUOY UP. Or. Nautical. Support ; encourage.
> *He was buoyed up by the knowledge that his wife still trusted him.*

Burn : BURN ONE'S BRIDGES *or* BOATS. Make a change of plan impossible ; make certain that the decision is final. If a general or sea captain wished to make his own retreat impossible, he burned the bridges he had crossed or the ships he had sailed in before the battle began.
> *Peter has burned his bridges, and written resigning his job.*

BURNT-OFFERING. Or. Biblical. Lit., The Jewish sacrifice to God of laying the body of an animal upon an altar, and burning it. Met., A humble offering or sacrifice of any description.
> *I made a burnt-offering of my scruples, and said I would do as she wished.*

Burst : BURST, BURST FORTH. Break out ; escape violently and excitedly.

A cry of horror burst forth from the crowd.

See BREAK OUT and BREAK FORTH.

Bury : BURY THE HATCHET. Forget past quarrels, and become friends. Or. The custom of the American Indians of ceremoniously burying their war-hatchets after making peace with an enemy.

See PIPE OF PEACE and LET BYGONES BE BYGONES.

BURY ONE'S HEAD IN THE SAND. Obstinately refuse to accept or face facts. Or. The legendary (and false) idea that ostriches bury their heads in the sand when in danger, believing that since they are unable to see their enemies, their enemies cannot see them.

For years his business has not been paying, but he buries his head in the sand and refuses to alter.

Business : THE BUSINESS END (S.). The effective end.

The robber attacked me, but I knocked him down with the business end of a broom.

GO OUT OF BUSINESS. Cease to trade or (less literally) continue one's usual work.

My father had a tailor's shop, but he went out of business after the war.

HAVE NO BUSINESS. Have no right.

You've no business to go into that room.

MEAN BUSINESS. Intend to take definite, and usually unpleasant, action.

There's a bull in the field, and I'm afraid he means business.

Butt : BUTT IN (S.). See STRIKE IN.

Buttonhole : Intercept and speak privately to.

I tried to buttonhole the President as he was leaving.

Buy : BUY IN. Purchase at an auction-sale on behalf of the seller.

There were no bargains at the sale ; all the best lots were bought in.

BUY OUT. Purchase the whole rights or interest in a business.

Old Smith has bought out all Brown's shares in Smith, Brown & Co.

   BUY UP. Purchase a complete consignment or collection.

By : BY AND BY. Soon ; in the near future.

   We'll meet again by and by.

   BY AND LARGE. In general terms ; comparing the advantages and disadvantages.

   By and large, how is your new business progressing ?

   BY HIM-(HER-)SELF. 1. Unaided.

   The baby can now walk by himself.

   2. Alone.

   I spent all the afternoon by myself.

   BY THE WAY. See under Way.

Bygones : LET BYGONES BE BYGONES. Let past quarrels or disagreements be ignored or forgotten. See BURY THE HATCHET and PIPE OF PEACE.

Byword : BECOME A BYWORD. Become notorious.

   The Duke's bad manners have become a byword.

C

Cake : HAVE ONE'S CAKE AND EAT IT TOO. Obtain two contradictory advantages from the same thing.

   You say you want to save your money for a holiday and go to the cinema every week, but you can't have your cake and eat it too.

   TAKE THE CAKE, BUN *or* BISCUIT (S.). Win the prize. Always used ironically in connection with some preposterous action or statement.

   Peter's idea that we might buy a plane and fly to America takes the cake.

Calculate : CALCULATED TO. Likely to ; tending to.

   His conduct is calculated to end in imprisonment.

   CALCULATE UPON. Expect ; estimate.

   We calculate upon a hundred people attending the meeting.

Call : CALL TO THE BAR. Or. Legal. Admit as a barrister. Qualified law students are " called " from the body of the hall to take part in legal proceedings. To be called *within* the Bar is to be made a Queen's (or King's) Counsel.

CALL FOR. 1. Demand.

The Army and Navy call for more men.

2. Arrive to take away or accompany.

We will call for you on our way to the concert.

CALL FORTH. Bring out, develop good or bad qualities.

The child's helplessness called forth all the best in him.

See BRING FORTH.

CALL IN. Recall something that has been issued, e.g. coins or stamps.

CALL TO MIND. Recall; remember (usually used in the negative).

I can't call to mind where I met you.

CALL NAMES. Abuse.

She called him every name she could think of.

CALL OFF. 1. Order to cease (occupation, etc.).

When the murderer was discovered dead, the police hunting him were called off.

2. Change one's mind, and abandon plans previously made; cancel.

We were going to give a dance, but decided to call it off.

CALL ON. 1. Visit, usually briefly and formally.

We must remember to call on Lady Putney.

2. Request.

The Chairman now called on Mr. Jones to address the meeting.

CALL OUT. 1. Raise one's voice; shout.

Call out the name of the winner.

2. Summon to keep public law and order.

Rioting began, and the Mayor had to call out the troops.

CALL OVER. Read through a list of names aloud, in order to ascertain who are present.

CALL IN QUESTION; QUESTION. Express doubt about.

I call in question the accuracy of those figures.

CALL THE ROLL. Similar to CALL OVER. See ROLL CALL.

CALL TO ARMS. Summon to battle.

England called her troops to arms, and prepared for war.

See JOIN THE COLOURS (under Colour).

Candle : BURN THE CANDLE AT BOTH ENDS. Exhaust one's energies over business or pleasure, or both ; go to bed very late and get up very early.

George looks half dead ; he's been burning the candle at both ends.

NOT FIT TO HOLD A CANDLE TO. Not fit even to assist ; not good enough even to be compared with.

John isn't stupid, but he isn't fit to hold a candle to his brother.

Cap : PUT ON ONE'S THINKING- *or* CONJURING-CAP. Or. A legendary magic cap worn by Eric XIV of Sweden which gave him special powers. Give a problem deep and serious thought.

I must put on my thinking-cap before I answer that question.

ASSUME THE BLACK CAP. Sentence to death. An English judge places a flat square of black silk— it is part of his full dress—upon his wig before formally sentencing a criminal to be hanged. (Covering the head is one of the traditional forms of mourning.)

A FEATHER IN ONE'S CAP. See under **Feather.**

CAP AND BELLS. Part of the equipment of a professional jester or fool of the Middle Ages.

That silly young idiot Smith evidently thinks he's entitled to wear the cap and bells.

CAP IN HAND. Humbly ; like a beggar.

I'm not going to Sir William, cap in hand, to ask for work.

IF THE CAP FITS. If the statement made is appropriate or true.

He called me a liar.

Well, you should know if the cap fits.

SET ONE'S CAP AT. Old f. Applied to a woman who is making a determined effort to persuade a man to marry her. The idiom originated in the idea that she put on her most attractive cap to catch him.

Miss Johnson is setting her cap at the rich widower, but I don't think she'll succeed.

Cards : ON THE CARDS (S.). Possible ; likely to happen.

It's on the cards that I may go to Australia.

PUT ONE'S CARDS ON THE TABLE. Be absolutely candid, and conceal nothing.

I told him I was putting my cards on the table, and hoped he would put his.

Care : HAVE A CARE ! Old f. Be careful ; take care.

Have a care that you don't drive too fast.

CARE NOTHING FOR. Take no interest in.

We never go to concerts ; John cares nothing for music.

Career : CHEQUERED CAREER. One including many changes ; successes and failures. A " chequered " pattern is one resembling a chessboard, with alternate squares of light and dark colours.

Carpet : ON THE CARPET(S). Called in by one's official superior for reprimand (the " carpet " being the one in his office).

Young Mason was on the carpet this morning for constantly arriving late.

See HAUL OVER THE COALS.

Carry : CARRY ALL BEFORE ONE. Be overwhelmingly successful.

At college and in society he carried all before him.

CARRY THE DAY. Reach final success ; win.

The bravery of our soldiers eventually carried the day.

CARRY OFF. 1. Take away by force.

The invading army carried off all the provisions in the town.

2. Conduct oneself successfully in a difficult situation.

He met the King, and carried off the interview well.

CARRY ON. 1. Or. Naval. Continue one's work or recreation.

Don't waste time, carry on with your sweeping.

2. Grieve.

She carried on terribly when her husband died.

3. Behave irregularly and badly.

I hear that young Smith has been carrying on with the Jones' daughter.

CARRY ONE'S POINT. Or. Archery. Succeed in convincing one's opponent.

George wanted Mary to marry him, and carried his point.

CARRY OUT ; CARRY THROUGH. Complete.

He carried through the work in a month.

Cart : IN THE CART (S.). In acute danger or difficulty. Or. In olden times a criminal was driven in a cart to the place of execution. Also IN THE SOUP.

PUT THE CART BEFORE THE HORSE. Make two statements in reverse order of their importance ; put the second and less-important thing first ; place the effect before the cause.

To learn a foreign language before one can speak one's own language properly is to put the cart before the horse.

Case : AS THE CASE MAY BE. Whichever of several things may happen.

Suppose your son becomes an artist, or a poet, as the case may be ?

CASE-HARDENED. Impervious to emotion ; without a sense of shame. From hardening the surface of iron by heating it in a closed case or box with charcoal.

He became a case-hardened criminal before he was a man.

A CASE IN POINT. See under **Point.**

IN ANY CASE. Whatever may occur.

In any case I shall go.

Cast : CAST ABOUT. Seek for.

I've been casting about for some village in which I can spend a quiet holiday.

CAST ASPERSIONS ON. Comment unfavourably upon ; decry.

She is a woman who always casts aspersions on her friends' characters.

See RUN DOWN (3).

CAST AWAY. I. Discard.

Now I'm rich I shall cast away all my old clothes.

2. Wrecked.

For five months we were cast away on an uninhabited island.

See CAST UP (2).

CAST DOWN. Depressed ; unhappy.

Since he heard of his failure at the examination George has been very cast down.

CAST FORTH ; CAST OUT. Expelled ; ejected.

The traitor was cast forth from their company.

CAST LIGHT UPON. Reveal; exhibit.

Pepys' diary casts a light upon life in England in the seventeenth century.

CAST IN ONE'S LOT. Decide to share the life, the good and bad fortunes, of another person or society.

I decided to cast in my lot with the rebels.

CAST OFF. 1. Nautical. Unfasten the mooring ropes, chains, etc., preparatory to sailing.

The ship cast off from Plymouth in fine weather.

2. Repudiate.

I have cast off my son, and never wish to see him again.

CAST PEARLS. See **Pearl.**

CAST REFLECTIONS ON. Similar to CAST ASPERSIONS ON.

CAST SHEEP'S EYES AT. See **Sheep.**

CAST A SLUR ON. Spoil or stain a reputation.

You have no right to call George a coward, and cast a slur on his character.

See A BLOT ON ONE'S SCUTCHEON.

CAST A SPELL OVER. Bewitch; control by magic.

It was as though her lover had cast a spell over her.

CAST IN ONE'S TEETH. Reproach a person with; sneer at a person for. From the old punishment of knocking out a person's teeth with stones.

His enemies cast in his teeth the fact that his mother was not a white woman.

CAST UP. 1. Add.

Will you kindly cast up these figures.

2. Flung up from a depth.

The body of a whale was cast up by the sea.

CASTING VOTE. A vote given by the chairman of a meeting when the number of votes for or against any proposal are equal. It is the casting vote that then decides the matter.

Caste : LOSE CASTE. Lose one's social position; lose the respect and appreciation of one's equals.

An aristocrat may become a tradesman in these days without losing caste.

Castle : CASTLE IN THE AIR. A dream building; a mere vision of happiness which has no basis in fact.

CASTLE IN SPAIN. The French version (*Château d'Espagne*) of the above, since there are no *châteaux* in Spain.

Cat : A CAT MAY LOOK AT A KING ! Whatever may be our social positions, one person is as good as another.

CAT'S CONCERT. A series of loud, discordant cries, resembling the noises made by cats at night.

CAT-AND-DOG LIFE. A life of continual quarrelling and fighting.

The Browns live a cat-and-dog life, but it seems to suit them.

FIGHT LIKE KILKENNY CATS. Fight desperately with extreme fierceness. From the legend of the two cats of Kilkenny (Ireland) who fought so furiously that presently " instead of two cats there weren't any ".

LET THE CAT OUT OF THE BAG. Allow a secret to escape.

We weren't going to tell my mother we were married, but Mary's wedding-ring let the cat out of the bag.

RAINING CATS AND DOGS. Raining heavily, with the rain being driven in varying directions by the wind.

WHICH WAY THE CAT JUMPS. What events indicate as a probability.

The Prime Minister will not announce anything yet : he is waiting to see which way the cat jumps.

Also WHICH WAY THE WIND BLOWS.

CAT'S PAW. One who is used merely for the convenience of a cleverer or stronger person. Or. Æsop's fable of the monkey who, wanting to eat some chestnuts that were on a hot stove, but not wishing to burn himself getting them, seized a cat and holding its paw in his own, used it to knock the chestnuts to the ground.

The stupid fellow never realized that he was a mere catspaw in the hands of his enemy.

Catch : CATCH-AS-CATCH-CAN. Or. Wrestling. A struggle in which all formalities are ignored.

It was a catch-as-catch-can affair.

CATCH FIRE ; CATCH LIGHT ; CATCH ALIGHT. Ignite ; burn.

The spilt oil caught light, and the house was burnt down.

CATCH BY THE HEELS. Chase and capture.

The thieves ran off, but were soon caught by the heels.

See LAID BY THE HEELS (under **Heel**).

CATCH IT (S.). Receive punishment.

When Father discovers that you've broken his pipe, you'll catch it.

CATCH NAPPING. Lit., Discover asleep. Met., Obtain an advantage through someone being careless or ignorant.

He's a clever swindler, but the police will catch him napping sooner or later.

CATCH ON (S.). Become fashionable or popular.

The new style of hairdressing seems to have caught on.

CATCH OUT. Or. Cricket. Find out ; expose.

He told me he was a hunting man, but was caught out when he spoke of the hounds as " dogs ".

See CATCH TRIPPING.

CATCH A PERSON'S EYE. See under **Eye**.

CATCH TRIPPING. Discover making a mistake. See CATCH OUT.

CATCH UP. 1. Snatch up ; seize suddenly.

He caught up his gun and dashed out.

2. Become level with.

He ran so fast that he soon caught up with me (or caught me up).

Caviare : CAVIARE TO THE GENERAL. Or. Quotation from Shakespeare's *Hamlet*. Beyond the appreciation or understanding of the general public. (Caviare is an expensive preparation made from sturgeon's roe ; it is highly popular in Russia.)

Picasso's art is caviare to the general.

Chain : CHAIN STORE. One of a number of precisely similar stores, controlled by the same company, and selling goods of the same type and price.

Chair : TAKE THE CHAIR. Occupy the chair, i.e. the seat of the chairman. Preside over a meeting as chairman.

Chalk : BY A LONG CHALK ; BY LONG CHALKS (S.). By a great deal ; thoroughly. Or. An ancient custom of recording merit by chalk marks.

The boy will win the race by long chalks.

AS DIFFERENT AS CHALK FROM CHEESE (S.). Totally, utterly different.

> *The music of Strauss is as different from Bach's as chalk from cheese.*

Chance : CHANCE ONE'S ARM (S.). Accept a risk.

> *I'll chance my arm, and offer £10 for the horse.*

AN EYE TO THE MAIN CHANCE. See under **Eye**.

SPORTING CHANCE. A chance, though not a great one.

> *There's still a sporting chance that the horse will win.*

TAKING NO CHANCES. Taking no risks.

> *He has two bolts on every door, and an extra one on the window ; he's taking no chance of burglars getting in.*

Change : CHANGE HANDS. Change owners.

> *That shop has changed hands only once in a hundred years.*

SMALL CHANGE. Coins of small value.

> *I had to give the conductor a ten-shilling note ; I had no small change.*

Chapter : CHAPTER OF ACCIDENTS. A series of accidents or misfortunes.

> *John arrived late, having been delayed by a chapter of accidents.*

CHAPTER AND VERSE. Exact authority for a statement ; details by which the truth of a statement can be checked.

> *It was an astonishing story, but true ; he gave me chapter and verse.*

Character : IN CHARACTER. In harmony with a person's known habits or temperament.

> *Mary gave the poor woman clothes and money ; an action entirely in character.*

OUT OF CHARACTER. The reverse.

REDEEM ONE'S CHARACTER. Cause one's faults to be forgiven ; cancel a bad reputation.

> *He redeemed his character by hard work and honesty.*
> *His character is redeemed by his great kindness.*

Charge : CHARGE WITH. 1. Formally accuse of some crime.

> *I shall charge him with forgery and theft.*

2 (normally used in past tense only). Loaded or filled with something of an explosive character.

> *The bomb was charged with dynamite.*

3 (also normally past tense only). Formally and solemnly given as a task.

On his death-bed my father charged me with the duty of taking care of my sister.

GIVE IN CHARGE *or* CUSTODY. Formally give a person into the charge of a policeman.

The man caught the thief, and at once gave him into custody.

Chartered : CHARTERED LIBERTINE. One allowed by society to break its laws ; an accepted eccentric or fool.

Brummel was abominably rude, but his wit made him a chartered libertine.

Chase : STERN CHASE. Or. Nautical. A pursuit from some distance behind.

The policeman dashed after the robber, but it was a stern chase and the man escaped.

Cheap : CHEAP AS DIRT ; DIRT CHEAP. Extremely cheap ; a bargain. See FOR A SONG.

Cheek : CHEEK BY JOWL. Close together, very near (compare Fr. *tête-à-tête*).

Rich and poor were sitting cheek by jowl in the audience.

Cheer : CHEER UP ! Recover your cheerfulness ! See TAKE HEART OF GRACE (under **Heart**).

GOOD CHEER. Good and rich food and drink.

The table was laden with good cheer.

Cheese : CHEESE IT (S.). Stop ! Equivalent to " Shut up " and a number of other extremely slangy idioms which the foreigner is advised to avoid.

Chicken : CHICKEN-FEED (S.). Or. American. Of small value or use.

Five pounds is mere chicken-feed to a man as rich as he is.

NO CHICKEN (S.). No longer young (almost always applied to a woman).

Miss Jukes is no chicken—she is at least fifty.

CHICKEN-HEARTED. Cowardly ; easily terrified, typical of chickens who run to their mother for shelter at the slightest danger.

COUNT ONE'S CHICKENS BEFORE THEY ARE HATCHED. Make definite plans about profits or advantages before it is certain that you will obtain them.

Or. Æsop's fable about the woman who, on her way to market, reckoned on how much she would get for her eggs and how she would spend the money, and in her excitement dropped the basket and broke them all.

Chime : CHIME IN. Or. The chiming of bells. Add in support of something already said.

> " And Mother," chimed in John, " is certain to agree with Father."

CHIME IN WITH. Harmonize with.

> Those blue curtains will chime in with the carpet.

China : FROM CHINA TO PERU. From one side of the world to the other ; everywhere. A quotation from Dr. Johnson's poem " On the Vanity of Human Wishes " : " Let observation with extended view, survey mankind from China to Peru ! "

> These hats are being worn from China to Peru.

Chip : CHIP OF THE OLD BLOCK. See under **Block.**

Choice : HOBSON'S CHOICE. No choice at all ; the acceptance of what one is offered. Originating in the custom of a Cambridge stable-keeper named Hobson, who insisted on every customer who wanted to hire a horse taking the one nearest the stable door.

Chorus : CHORUS OF APPROVAL, *or* APPLAUSE. General approval.

> The King's decision had been received with a chorus of approval.

Chuck : CHUCK ; CHUCK UP (S.). Stop ; abandon.

> I hear that Bill is going to chuck up his job.

Church : BROAD CHURCH. A term applied to those who think the Church's religious belief should be broad-minded enough to include all variations of ritual.

HIGH CHURCH comprises those who follow the more elaborate ritual in use in England ; those who give a " high place " to the importance of the priests and bishops.

LOW CHURCH is the term applied to those who follow simpler and less-formalized ritual.

(Any detailed analysis of the differences is, of course impossible in so limited a space.)

Circumstance : EXTENUATING CIRCUMSTANCES. Excuses ; causes which make forgiveness possible.

He was terribly rude to his father, but there were extenuating circumstances.

IN ANY CIRCUMSTANCES. See IN ANY CASE (under Case).

IN THE CIRCUMSTANCES. In the present condition or state of affairs ; after consideration of what has happened.

In the circumstances, we have decided to dismiss the secretary.

(*Note.*—Written " under the circumstances " before the recent realization that the phrase was grammatically incorrect.)

Clap : CLAP ON. Old f. Place on energetically and quickly.

He clapped his hat on his head, and ran out of the house.

CLAP-TRAP. Worthless, valueless talk, generally used in an attempt to become popular or appear learned. Lit., A trap to catch applause.

The crowd listened to his clap-trap and cheered loudly.

Clean : CLEAN BILL OF HEALTH. Lit., An official document certifying that a ship has left port with no case of infectious illness on board. Generally used to indicate that there is no risk of infection, or, alternatively, that no illness, infectious or otherwise, exists.

The Smiths have all recovered from measles, and have a clean bill of health.

CLEAN AWAY. Similar to CLEAR AWAY (2).

MAKE A CLEAN BREAST OF. See under Breast.

Clear : CLEAR AWAY. 1. Remove.

Will you please clear away all this rubbish.

2. (*With* GET). Escape completely.

The burglars got clear away with all my wife's jewellery.

CLEAR AS CRYSTAL. Obvious ; absolutely plain.

Jack's reason for going to London is as clear as crystal —it is to meet Mary again.

CLEAR-CUT. Clearly defined.

The girl is pretty, with clear-cut features.

CLEAR THE DECKS FOR ACTION. Or. Naval. **Before a**

sea battle or " action " begins, the deck of each ship is cleared of all unnecessary or impeding objects. Prepare, get ready.

As our visitors are due in ten minutes, we must clear the decks for action.

CLEAR OF. Free from.

The river is clear of weeds, and delightful to swim in.

CLEAR OFF. Go away; depart.

I told the beggar to clear off immediately.

CLEAR OUT. 1. Make clean; remove impurities, etc.

The workmen are clearing out the tank.

2. Similar to CLEAR OFF.

CLEAR UP. 1. Make plain and clear.

I am trying to clear up any misunderstanding.

2. Make tidy by removing or rearranging.

You'll have to clear up the things on the table before we have tea.

3. Become fine.

The weather has cleared up ; we can go out.

CLEAR THE WAY. Remove obstructions, Lit. or Met.

The police cleared the way for the King.

This new law will clear the way for many educational improvements.

Clinch : CLINCH AN ARGUMENT, A DISPUTE *or* THE MATTER. Settle finally and completely, conclude.

He clinched the dispute by producing the old man's will.

(" Clinch " literally means to bend the end of a nail after it has been driven through the wood, making it immovable.)

Clip : CLIP THE WINGS OF. Lit., Cut the wing-feathers of a bird so that it is unable to fly at any height. Met., Limit the powers or authority of a person.

I shall have to clip the wings of my new manager, who behaves as if he owns the business.

CLIPPED SPEECH. Words uttered in short, staccato tones, with the final consonants sharply stressed.

He spoke in the clipped speech of the typical English officer.

Close : BEHIND CLOSED DOORS. Privately; secretly.

We cannot report the discussion, as it took place behind closed doors.

CLOSE IN UPON. Approach and surround.

> *The soldiers fought desperately, but the enemy closed in upon them from all sides, and they finally surrendered.*

CLOSE WITH. Grapple with ; grasp violently.

> *The man tried to escape, but the policeman closed with him, and both fell to the ground.*

CLOSE SHAVE (S.). A narrow escape ; an event which just missed disaster.

> *The bullet missed me, but it was a close shave.*

See A NEAR THING.

(*Note.*—" Close " here is an adjective, not a verb, the " s " being sounded as such, and not like " z ", as in the three previous idioms.)

Cloud : IN THE CLOUDS. Day-dreaming, with one's thoughts elsewhere.

> *I've called Jane to tea, but she's been in the clouds ever since Peter asked her to marry him.*

UNDER A CLOUD. Regarded with disfavour and distrust ; with an injured reputation.

> *The firm has been under a cloud ever since those questions were asked in Parliament.*

Cloven : CLOVEN HOOF. An evil or base personality suddenly revealed.

> *The Minister's speech on the new Nursing Bill has revealed the cloven hoof.*

(The " cloven hoof " is a reference to the Devil, who, however he may disguise himself, can never conceal the fact that he has hoofs instead of feet.)

Clover : IN CLOVER. In a condition of luxury ; very well off. (Cattle particularly enjoy feeding in a clover field.)

> *Henry's new job is very well paid, and the family are in clover.*

Coach : DRIVE A COACH AND FOUR THROUGH. Easily evade or make ineffective. The phrase is applied almost entirely to Parliamentary laws.

> *The Act is so badly worded that any clever lawyer can drive a coach and four through it.*

Coals : HAUL OVER THE COALS. Find fault ; blame for some error. In the Middle Ages money was extorted by the King from rich Jews by hauling or pulling them over a slow-burning fire until they agreed to pay the amount demanded.

I shall have to haul my secretary over the coals for this mistake.

HEAP COALS OF FIRE ON. Or. Biblical. Return good for evil and kindness for unkindness, and so melt the heart of one's enemy and make him ashamed of his conduct.

The man I had called a miser heaped coals of fire on my head by inviting me to dinner.

Coast : THE COAST IS CLEAR. There is no enemy in view ; no probability of interference.

The boys waited till the headmaster was out of sight ; then, when the coast was clear, they ran back to school.

Coat : CUT ONE'S COAT ACCORDING TO ONE'S CLOTH. Limit one's expenses to the money available.

We'd like to go on a cruise to Africa, but we have to cut our coat according to our cloth.

WEAR THE QUEEN'S COAT. Become a soldier. See JOIN THE COLOURS.

Cock : COCK-A-HOOP *or* HOUP. Boastful and triumphant. Or. The almost obsolete sport of cock-fighting. A winning bird erected his *houpe,* the feathered crest on his head.

You needn't be so cock-a-hoop over your victory ; the other man may win next time.

A COCK-AND-BULL STORY. Said to be a corruption of " a concocted and bully story " (" bully " from the Danish *bullen,* exaggerated). A fantastic and unbelievable story.

The girl came home with a cock-and-bull story about seeing a ghost in the lane.

COCK SURE (*more correctly* " COCKY SURE "). Aggressively sure and certain.

He was cock sure that the weather would be fine ; we came home in a tremendous thunderstorm !

COCK OF THE WALK. The chief ; the dominant person. " The Walk " is the name of the feeding-place of poultry, among whom there is always a cock who is master.

He's been cock of the walk since his father died.

LIVE LIKE FIGHTING COCKS. Live on the best and

richest food. Or. Sporting. Fighting cocks were
so fed in order to make them fiercer and stronger.

Cockles : WARM THE COCKLES OF ONE'S HEART (from *cochlea
cordis*, the ventricles of the heart). Make one's
body glow, as with wine.

*Here's a cup of coffee that will warm the cockles of
your heart this cold day.*

Coin : COIN MONEY. Produce riches very rapidly. (Applied
both to individuals and to the means of produc-
tion.)

He's coining money with that new invention.

The shop at the corner is coining money.

PAY BACK IN HIS OWN COIN. Retaliate or retort by the
same method one's enemy uses.

*Last week, when my wife arranged to meet me, she
kept me waiting nearly an hour ; to-day I am
going to pay her back in her own coin.*

Cold : COLD COMFORT. Very slight satisfaction (the phrase
is generally used ironically).

*She refused to marry me, but offered to be a sister,
which was cold comfort.*

Collar : AGAINST THE COLLAR. Fatiguing ; against one's
inclinations (like a horse pressing against the
collar when dragging a cart uphill).

*It goes against the collar to get up early after a late
night's work.*

See AGAINST THE GRAIN (under **Grain**).

OUT OF A COLLAR. Lit., Unharnessed. Met., Without
a regular job.

*I hear that Mrs. Tompson's husband is out of a collar
again.*

Colour : COLOUR-BLIND. Unable to distinguish the colours
correctly, though otherwise possessing normal
sight.

GIVE *or* LEND COLOUR TO. Support ; help to prove.

*The cut on his cheek gave colour to his story that he
had been attacked.*

IN ONE'S TRUE COLOURS. As a person really is, as
distinct from what he pretends or is generally
supposed to be.

For the first time I saw my uncle in his true colours.

JOIN THE COLOURS. Enlist in the Army.

A MAN OF COLOUR. A Negro, or a man possessing
  Negro blood.

OFF-COLOUR (S.). Unwell, without being definitely ill.
  *My wife's been off-colour all this week, but she refuses
  to see a doctor.*

UNDER FALSE COLOURS. Or. Nautical (colours = flags).
  Falsely ; pretending to be what one is not.
  The visitor introduced himself under false colours.

WITH FLYING COLOURS. As a victorious army with its
  flags " flying " or waving ; triumphantly.
  He passed his examination with flying colours.

Come : COME ABOUT. Occur ; happen.
  *And then—I don't know exactly how it came about—
  she promised to marry me.*

COME ACROSS. 1. Lit., Cross.
  He came across the road to speak to me.
  2. Met., Find casually, discover.
  *Yesterday, tidying my desk, I came across some old
  letters of yours.*
  See COME UPON.

COME TO AN ARRANGEMENT. Agree ; mutually arrange.
  *We can soon come to an arrangement about our shares
  of the profits.*

COME-BACK. A return from obscurity to the prominence and success of the past.
  *The old actor made a splendid come-back in the part
  of Lear.*

COME TO BLOWS. Proceed to fight.
  *The brothers began to argue, and presently came to
  blows.*

COME BY. Acquire.
  How did you come by your new car ?

COME CLEAN (S.). Or. American. Similar to MAKE A
  CLEAN BREAST (see under **Breast**).

COME INTO EXISTENCE. Exist ; be born ; function (Law).
  A new spirit has come into existence since the War.
  The regulations came into existence on June 1st.

COME TO GRIEF. Suffer disaster.
  He was learning to skate, but came to grief at the corner.

COME IN FOR. Receive ; inherit.
  He came in for a good deal of blame for his action.
  He'll come in for £20,000 when his aunt dies.

COME INTO FORCE. See under **Force.**

COME OF. Become ; result from.

I don't know what will come of all these war preparations.

COME OFF. Lit., Be removable.

I can't make the lid come off the saucepan.

Met. (S.). Reach a successful result.

The comedian did his best to amuse us, but it didn't quite come off.

COME OFF WELL, BADLY, *etc.* End with credit, discredit, etc.

For over an hour he was examined in court by the lawyer, and came off well.

COME ON. 1. Hasten ! Move more quickly ! COME ALONG is similar. See also HURRY UP.

2. Begin.

It came on to rain soon after midnight.

COME OUT. Take one's place, as a grown-up person, in Society. (*Note.*—This idiom is applied to women only.)

Lady Marian will come out next season.

COME OVER. 1. (S.). Become affected by emotion or illness.

She came over dizzy.

I don't know what came over me.

2. Sound (applied to wireless).

His speech on the radio came over very well.

COME RIGHT. Prove itself to be correct.

I can't make this addition sum come right.

COME ROUND. 1. Recover from a fainting fit.

We splashed water on her face, and she soon came round.

2. Visit someone not far away.

Come round and see us when you've time.

3. Modify one's own account or accept another person's view.

I discussed the subject for an hour before he came round to my opinion.

COME TO ; COME TO ONESELF. Identical with COME ROUND (1).

COME TO TERMS. Reach a formal agreement.

We expect to come to terms about the house very soon.

COME TRUE. Actually happen.

If our hopes come true, we shall be married in the spring.

COME UPON. Encounter. Similar to COME ACROSS (2).

COME UP TO. Reach the level of. Lit. and Met.

The water came up to the top of the bath.

This picture does not come up to the one you showed me yesterday.

COME UP TO THE SCRATCH (S.). See under **Scratch**.

COME UP WITH. Draw level with.

We came up with the travellers at the top of the hill.

COME WHAT MAY. Whatever may happen in the future.

Come what may, I shall always love him.

IT COMES, *or* AMOUNTS, TO THIS. Summarizing the situation; stated briefly.

It comes to this—George can't go to America unless we pay his fare.

Command : AT ONE'S COMMAND. At one's service; available; capable of being used.

We have nearly £1,000 at our command.

WORD OF COMMAND. Or. Military and Naval. A formal order, spoken in public.

At the word of command, the soldiers marched away.

Commit : COMMIT *or* CONSIGN, TO THE GRAVE. Bury.

We committed his body to the grave.

COMMIT TO MEMORY. See under **Memory**.

Common : BY COMMON CONSENT. By general agreement.

By common consent, the meeting was fixed for the following week.

COMMON ORIGIN ; an origin in common. The same beginning.

Many French and English words have a common origin—Latin.

COMMON PARLANCE. Plain, ordinary speech.

Peter, in common parlance, won't work if he possibly can avoid it.

IN COMMON. Shared; possessed by each (or all).

They should be very happy, for they have much in common.

OUT OF THE COMMON. Unusual.

It is a curious old village, quite out of the common

ON SHORT COMMONS. With only a small and insufficient supply of food.

Owing to the heavy snowstorm we are on short commons.

COMMONPLACE BOOK. A book in which the owner writes interesting or amusing extracts from the works of various writers.

Company : PART COMPANY. Separate ; part.

Bill and I have decided to part company.

The strain was so great that the links of the chain parted company.

Compare : COMPARE NOTES. Discuss impressions and opinions.

The American travellers were comparing notes on London.

Comparison : COMPARISONS ARE ODIOUS. Any comparison between two persons or things is almost certain to lead to dissatisfaction and trouble.

INSTITUTE A COMPARISON BETWEEN. Compare.

One might institute a comparison between Ancient Rome and Modern Britain.

Compassion : BOWELS OF COMPASSION. Pity, sympathy with the misfortunes of others. In the past various secretions or organs of the body were supposed to be connected with the emotions ; the bowels were responsible for pity.

Compliment : COMPLIMENTARY TICKETS. Free tickets, given nominally as a compliment to the receiver's position and importance.

COMPLIMENTS OF THE SEASON. Traditional Christmas and New Year greetings, for which the idiom itself has become a synonym.

FISH FOR COMPLIMENTS. Speak deprecatingly of oneself in the hope of being contradicted.

I'm not a very good cook.

Nonsense, you're merely fishing for compliments.

RETURN THE COMPLIMENT. Repay a pleasant speech or a kindly action by another.

My brother and his family spent last Christmas with us ; this Christmas they have returned the compliment and invited us to spend it with them.

Concert : IN CONCERT. Unitedly ; all together.

The audience shouted in concert, " Go home ! "

CONCERT-PITCH. Lit., The pitch (sharpness or flatness) of the musical note to which all instruments in the orchestra are tuned ; the exact and vital note. Met., Perfect fitness, general good health.

I'm not feeling up to concert-pitch this morning.

Conclusion : ARRIVE AT THE CONCLUSION, *or* COME TO THE CONCLUSION.

1. Perceive ; realize after considering all the facts.

I think you'll arrive at the conclusion that Pat is suitable for the job.

2. End ; finish.

The debate came to a conclusion soon after midnight.

FOREGONE CONCLUSION. An end so obvious that one is justified in assuming it.

When Peter came back to England, it was a foregone conclusion that he would become a partner in his father's business.

JUMP TO A CONCLUSION. Assume rashly and without justification.

Ellen jumps to the conclusion that every young man is going to fall in love with her, which is nonsense.

TRY CONCLUSIONS. Test by opposing ; fight against.

You'll be very foolish if you try conclusions with a firm as wealthy and unscrupulous as his.

Conduct : LINE OF CONDUCT. Behaviour.

His line of conduct has, from the first, been that of a man who means to be master.

Confidence : IN STRICT CONFIDENCE. Absolutely privately.

Miss Smith told Miss Robinson that Mrs. Jones had told her in strict confidence that Mrs. Brown drank too much.

Confusion : CONFUSION WORSE CONFOUNDED. Or. Quotation from Milton's " Paradise Lost ". Disorder and confusion made even worse than before.

The Ministers tried to explain the Government's policy. but only made confusion worse confounded.

Conjecture : HAZARD A CONJECTURE. A pompous and formal equivalent of " Risk assuming, or stating ".

I'll hazard a conjecture that your daughter is at the cinema with my son.

Conjunction : IN CONJUNCTION WITH. Added to ; together with.

What you have told me, in conjunction with what I already know, fills me with fear.

Conscience : IN ALL CONSCIENCE. In any imaginable set of circumstances. (There is no exact and literal synonym for this idiom ; it is almost entirely exclamatory.)

He paid me five shillings, little enough in all conscience !

Consequence : OF NO CONSEQUENCE. Totally unimportant.

Don't apologize for breaking the cup—it's of no consequence.

Construction : PUT A FALSE CONSTRUCTION ON. Misinterpret ; assume wrongly.

When I say that I like Joe very much indeed, you must not put a false construction on the statement.

Contact : COME IN CONTACT WITH. Meet ; encounter.

I don't often come into contact with the Smiths nowadays.

Contempt : HOLD IN CONTEMPT. Regard with contempt or scorn.

I hold in contempt anyone who is afraid to fight for liberty.

Contradiction : CONTRADICTION IN TERMS. A statement which contradicts itself.

To say that Jane is stupid, but brilliant at mathematics, is a contradiction in terms.

Contrary : ON THE CONTRARY. The reverse ; the opposite course of action.

I shall go to the concert. On the contrary you will stay at home.

See ON THE OTHER HAND (under **Hand**).

CONTRARY TO EXPECTATION. The reverse of what was expected.

Contrary to expectation, the Queen was not present at the ball.

Convert : CONVERT INTO. Change into.

All the bank-notes were converted into cash.

Conviction : CARRY CONVICTION TO. Convince ; compel belief in.

The story of his sufferings would carry conviction to anyone who heard it.

Cool : COOL AS A CUCUMBER. Completely calm and unexcited.

The boy was as cool as a cucumber throughout the action.

3

COOL CUSTOMER, CARD, HAND. One who demands something to which he has no right, who makes a "cool" or impudent request.

That new gardener is a cool customer—he's asking five shillings an hour for working on Sunday.

Cost : AT ALL COSTS. Whatever may be involved ; whatever efforts or sacrifice may be needed.

We must prevent the fire reaching the gunpowder at all costs.

Counsel : KEEP ONE'S OWN COUNSEL. Remain discreetly silent ; say nothing of one's own plans.

The General heard rumours of mutiny, but kept his own counsel.

Count : COUNT UPON. Rely upon ; be sure of.

We know we can count on your support.

See RECKON ON.

DOES NOT COUNT. Is immaterial ; does not make any difference.

Personal friendship does not count in politics.

Countenance : KEEP IN COUNTENANCE. Encourage ; support morally.

I've an appointment with the lawyers to-morrow— you had better come too to keep me in countenance.

KEEP ONE'S COUNTENANCE. Refrain from laughing.

The poor old chap is so funny that one can hardly keep one's countenance.

See KEEP A STRAIGHT FACE (under **Face**).

PUT OUT OF COUNTENANCE. Confuse ; disconcert.

He was completely put out of countenance when he saw the man he had robbed in court.

Courage : DUTCH COURAGE. Temporary courage created by drinking. In the seventeenth-century wars with Holland, Dutch sea-captains had barrels of brandy placed on deck from which the sailors helped themselves before beginning a fight.

HAVE THE COURAGE OF ONE'S CONVICTIONS, *or* OPINIONS. Be brave enough to speak and act as one really believes.

My father told the manager that the scheme was a swindle : Father has always had the courage of his opinions.

PLUCK UP COURAGE; SUMMON UP COURAGE; BRING ONE'S COURAGE TO THE STICKING-POINT. Succeed in showing bravery in spite of fears.

The old lady plucked up her courage, and asked the burglar what he wanted.

Course : ADOPT A COURSE. Take a certain definite and considered action.

The judge said he would adopt an unusual course, and gave the prisoner another chance.

IN DUE COURSE. Eventually; ultimately; at the appropriate time.

They fell in love, and in due course were married.

EMBARK ON, CONTINUE A COURSE. Or. Nautical. Begin a connected series of actions or words. The "course" is the direction in which a ship travels.

He embarked on a course of extravagant living.

A MATTER OF COURSE; OF COURSE. The normal; the expected procedure.

The sentry saluted, as a matter of course, as the officer approached.

Court : PAY COURT. Old f. Make love to; woo.

The knight paid court to the King's daughter, but she refused to marry him.

Coventry : SEND TO COVENTRY. Disregard completely; refuse to associate with. Or. The dislike the inhabitants of Coventry had at one time for soldiers. Any country woman seen speaking to one was thereafter treated as an outcast and ignored.

If you tell tales about other boys in school, you'll be sent to Coventry.

See COLD SHOULDER (under **Shoulder**).

Cover : UNDER COVER. 1. Lit.,

(a) *We were under cover when the rain fell.*

(b) Covered by a wrapping or envelope.

I am sending you a letter under separate cover.

2. Met., Concealed by a pretence.

Under cover of friendship, he betrayed the King.

Cow : TILL THE COWS COME HOME (S.). An indefinite period; never.

If we wait for Jim, we shall wait till the cows come home.

Crab : CATCH A CRAB. An idiom limited to rowing. To dip one's oar too deeply in the water to recover it in time for the next stroke, and as a result, to be struck by the handle and knocked backwards.

Crack : CRACK OF DOOM. The Day of Judgment, the last day. Commonly used to indicate an infinitely future period.

The house is built to last till the crack of doom.

CRACK UP. Break ; deteriorate. Frequently used in connection with a person's health.

Poor old Peter is beginning to crack up.

Creature : CREATURE COMFORTS. The material things which make life comfortable—good food, warm clothing, etc.

He may be a very spiritually-minded person, but he loves all his creature comforts.

Credence : GIVE CREDENCE TO. Believe.

Don't give credence to half the things she tells you.

Credit : GIVE CREDIT TO. Give praise where it should be given.

I must give credit to my daughter for the decorations.

REDOUND TO ONE'S CREDIT ; REFLECT CREDIT UPON. Be worthy of praise or honour.

The inventor was a poor man, and it redounds to his credit that he never attempted to obtain riches.

Creeps : GIVE ONE THE CREEPS (S.). Cause one to shudder with nervous fear.

The shadows in the old house gave her the creeps.

Crop : CROP UP. Appear unexpectedly above the surface. Lit. and Met.

Weeds always crop up in our flower-bed.

I never expected that our past quarrel would crop up again.

Cropper : COME A CROPPER (S.). Lit., Fall at full length while riding. Met., Meet with sudden disaster.

The lawyer who starts gambling with his clients' money is certain to come a cropper in the end.

Cross : TALK AT CROSS PURPOSES. Discuss from incompatible points of view, owing to a misunderstanding.

We failed to reach an agreement ; from the first it was plain to me that we were talking at cross purposes.

CROSS, *or* PASS, THE RUBICON. Take any irrevocable step. The Rubicon was a small river dividing Ancient Italy from Cæsar's territory, and when he and his army crossed it, he automatically invaded Italy.

I've crossed the Rubicon, and bought the farm I told you about.

CROSS AS TWO STICKS (i.e. two sticks laid one across the other). In an extremely bad temper.

CROSS SWORDS. See MEASURE SWORDS.

Crow : CROW'S FEET. The small wrinkles which age, ill-health or trouble cause to form at the corners of one's eyes.

AS THE CROW FLIES. In a straight line, regardless of obstructions. (A crow flies in a straight line from point to point.)

The villages are ten miles apart as the crow flies, but nearly fifteen miles by road.

CROW OVER. Boast about one's triumph over an opponent.

You need not crow over your victory at tennis to-day ; I shall probably beat you to-morrow.

A CROW TO PLUCK. Identical with A BONE TO PICK.

Cry : CRY DOWN. Decry ; deprecate ; speak slightingly about. See RUN DOWN (3).

He cries down everything his wife does.

CRY OFF. Refuse, or cease, to share in or co-operate.

The Simpsons said they were coming to the picnic, but cried off the day before.

CRY QUITS ; CALL IT QUITS. Agree to end a dispute or transaction, and regard both sides as being equal.

You owe me ten shillings, but I have your watch, so we'll cry quits.

CRY STINKING FISH. Speak unfavourably about one's own profession, trade, family, etc.

He told me there was a great deal of dishonesty in selling antiques—which was crying stinking fish, as he deals in them himself.

CRY WOLF. Cause excitement or anxiety by spreading false news. From Æsop's fable of the shepherd boy who shouted " Wolf " and brought his neigh-

bours from their work so many times that when
a wolf really did attack his sheep no one paid
attention to his cries. See FALSE ALARM.

Cub : UNLICKED CUB. An uncouth, ill-mannered young
person (usually a youth). The reference is to
baby bears, which after birth are vigorously licked
by their mothers until they can stand up and walk.
See LICK INTO SHAPE.

Cudgel : CUDGEL ONE'S BRAINS. Met., beat one's brains (a
" cudgel " is a stick) to compel them to work.
Try to compel one's brain to function, and to
understand or remember.

*I've cudgelled my brains, but I can't recollect where I
put the money.*

See RACK ONE'S BRAINS.

TAKE UP THE CUDGELS. Defend or support the cause
of a friend.

*They all said John was to blame, but I took up the
cudgels for him.*

Cup : ONE'S CUP (OF HAPPINESS) IS FILLED. One's happiness
is absolutely complete.

*With his family around him and no fears for the future,
his cup was filled.*

CUP OF BITTERNESS. The reverse.

CUP THAT CHEERS. Tea. Incomplete and inaccurate
quotation from Cowper. " The cups that cheer
but do not inebriate."

IN ONE'S CUPS. Intoxicated ; drunk.

*The man was quarrelsome, as he always was when in
his cups.*

Cupboard : CUPBOARD LOVE. Affection shown only in the
hope of obtaining something tangible in return.

*My cat follows me everywhere, but it's only cupboard
love—she wants some fish.*

Currency : ACQUIRE, OBTAIN, *or* GAIN CURRENCY. Circulate ; become publicly discussed.

*A rumour that the King may abdicate has acquired
currency.*

Curry : CURRY FAVOUR. Attempt by flattery, bribery, etc.,
to become popular.

*He tried to curry favour with the King by presenting
him with a splendid house.*

Curtain : CURTAIN LECTURE. Admonition—" nagging " by a wife to a husband at bedtime. (The " curtains " are the old-fashioned hangings which used to surround the equally old-fashioned bed.)

Customer : UGLY, AWKWARD, TOUGH, *etc.*, CUSTOMER. A difficult and dangerous person to oppose.

> *My enemy was an ugly customer who looked like a retired prizefighter.*

Cut : CUTS BOTH WAYS. Has a second and compensating effect.

> *Her refusal to meet him cuts both ways—he won't be responsible for maintaining her.*

CUT THE CACKLE (S.). Be brief and to the point ; talk less and deal with the subject under discussion. Incomplete quotation, " Cut the cackle and come to the horses." See CUT SHORT.

CUT CAPERS. Caper ; dance fantastically about ; waste time in irrelevant movements. (To " cut capers " in dancing is to spring upwards, rapidly interlacing the feet.)

CUT AND COME AGAIN. Help oneself freely and repeatedly.

> *There are hundreds of books to choose from ; you can cut and come again.*

CUT A DASH, A FIGURE (S.). Exhibit oneself as a smart or fashionable person.

> *Doesn't Peter cut a dash in his new suit !*

CUT DOWN. 1. Lit.,

> *He cut down a tree.*

2. Met., Reduce.

> *He has to cut down his expenses since his father died.*

CUT AND DRIED. Already arranged or prepared.

> *His plans for leaving the country were all cut and dried.*

CUT FINE. Allow little margin for accident, etc.

> *You may catch the train but you are cutting it rather fine.*

CUT THE GORDIAN KNOT (*or simply* THE KNOT). Take a quick and drastic method of ending a difficulty. Or. The knot tied by Gordius, a peasant who, on being chosen King of Phrygia, dedicated his wagon to Jupiter and tied the yoke to the beam with a knot that no one could untie. Alexander, on being told that whoever untied it would rule the whole of the East, solved the problem by cutting the knot with his sword.

CUT NO ICE (S.). Fail to convince or impress.

The salesman's arguments cut no ice at all.

CUT, *or* CHIP, IN. Interrupt, intervene.

" We're starting to-morrow," I said. " But you can't go till Tuesday," cut in George.

CUT OF ONE'S JIB (S.). Or. Nautical. The face and general appearance. The shape, or cut, of a ship's jib indicates to a sailor what type she is.

I don't like the cut of his jib, and don't want to meet him again.

CUT ONE'S LOSSES. Abandon any further attempts to continue a business or enterprise which has not been profitable, and limit one's losses to those already incurred.

CUT OFF. 1. Sever ; cut.

She is going to cut off her long hair.

2. Separate from.

That remote village will entirely cut her off from her friends.

3. Hurry ; hasten (S.).

Cut off and buy me some cigarettes.

CUT OFF WITH A SHILLING. Bequeath nothing, or practically nothing to a person. From the custom of leaving an unpopular member of the family only a shilling in one's will—the shilling merely being to make it impossible for the recipient to plead that his or her name had been omitted by accident.

CUT OUT. 1. Lit., Cut round, as with a pair of scissors.

2. Met., Old f. Supplant.

George seems to be cutting out Peter in Mary's affections.

3. Designed for, suitable for.

I don't think you're cut out for a soldier.

(*Note.*—This phrase has also an obsolete naval meaning—to separate an enemy vessel from its fleet and capture it.)

CUT *or* WOUNDED, TO THE QUICK. Hurt intensely. " Quick ", A.S. *cwic*, originally meant " living ": hence the part of one's nails which is below the skin, which still has feeling, is called the " quick ".

The old man was cut to the quick when his rich son refused to recognize him.

CUT AND RUN (S.). Hurry away; leave as quickly as possible.

You'll have to cut and run, if you want to catch the train.

See CUT OFF (3). Also CUT ONE'S STICKS and CUT ONE'S LUCKY—both old-f. S.

CUT SHORT. End abruptly.

The preacher cut short his sermon when the church caught fire.

See CUT THE CACKLE (S.).

CUT UP. 1. Lit., Cut into small pieces. 2. Met., Distressed, unhappy.

She was terribly cut up when she heard the bad news.

CUT UP ROUGH (S.). Show excitement and anger.

When I tell Mary we can't go on holiday, she'll cut up rough.

D

Daggers : AT DAGGERS DRAWN. In a state of open and bitter hostility.

Mary and George are at daggers drawn.

LOOK DAGGERS. See under **Look**.

Damn : DAMN WITH FAINT PRAISE. (A quotation from the poet Pope). Praise in so formal and limited a manner that it is an obvious cloak to adverse criticism or dislike, e.g. *Well, one can't deny that she wears elegant shoes.*

Damp : A DAMP SQUIB. A squib is a small firework which sends out showers of sparks and finally explodes. If, however, it is not dry, it will do neither. Hence, a joke or other form of entertainment which has failed is said to have " gone off like a damp squib ".

Dance : DANCE ATTENDANCE. Attend, as an inferior, to every whim or requirement of a person.

The whole court danced attendance on the Queen.

Darby : DARBY AND JOAN. An aged and devoted husband

and wife. (From an eighteenth-century ballad called " The Happy Old Couple ".)

Mr. and Mrs. Brown are a regular Darby and Joan.

Dare : DARE-DEVIL. A daring and reckless person.

George is a young dare-devil who will certainly get into trouble.

Dark : IN THE DARK. In ignorance.

I am completely in the dark concerning his plans.

MAKE DARKNESS VISIBLE. Used in reference to any small light which emphasizes the surrounding darkness.

He lit a match in the cellar, but it merely made darkness visible.

Dash : DASH OFF. 1. Hurry away.

He dashed off for help.

2. Write in great haste.

He dashed off a note to his wife.

DASH ONE'S HOPES. Abruptly destroy one's hopes.

The sudden death of the King dashed her hopes of an heir.

Date : OUT-OF-DATE. Obsolete ; belonging to an earlier period.

Your ideas about the rights of a husband are entirely out-of-date.

Davy Jones : DAVY JONES' LOCKER. A " locker " or box is one used by seamen and others for their personal possessions. " Davy Jones " (a corruption of " Jonah ", who was thrown into the sea) is a legendary character who lives at the bottom of the ocean. " To go to Davy Jones' locker " is therefore to drown.

Day : ALL DAY *or* NIGHT LONG. Continuously ; throughout the day (or night).

All day long wounded soldiers were tramping past the cottage.

See THE LIVELONG DAY.

BROAD DAYLIGHT. Full and complete daylight.

Our house was robbed in broad daylight.

CALL IT A DAY (S.). Consider work on any particular job ended for the day or for the present time.

We've worked till its dark : we'll call it a day.

CARRY THE DAY. See **Carry.**

DARK DAYS. Days of trouble and distress.

DAY AFTER THE FAIR. Too late.

Peter went to call on Lucy. But, as usual, he was a day after the fair; she had left for America.

DAYS TO COME. The future.

In the days to come we shall all travel by air.

DAY OF DOOM. Day on which some terrible or fatal occurrence takes place.

The day of doom approached, and on January 14th the King was beheaded.

DAYDREAM. A reverie or flight of the imagination. Also used as a verb.

Cinderella was daydreaming over her work.

DAY IN, DAY OUT. All day and every day.

Day in, day out we watched for the invaders.

DAYLIGHT ROBBERY. Any form of gross and obvious swindling or profiteering.

Five shillings a pound for chestnuts is daylight robbery.

THE DAY IS WON *or* **LOST.** The battle is won (or lost).

The day is won; order the whole line to advance.

DAYS *or* **HOURS ARE NUMBERED.** Death is inevitable, and is approaching.

The King looked very ill; it was plain that his days were numbered.

DAYS OF OLD *or* **OF YORE.** A long time ago; the remote past.

In days of yore people believed in dragons.

DECLINE OF DAY. The latter part of the day; when the sun declines, or sinks in the sky.

THE LIVELONG DAY. All day; the whole of the time. See **ALL DAY LONG.**

NAME THE DAY. Literally, the day on which a girl wishes to marry. But the phrase is frequently used in the sense of " consent to marry ", no exact date being specified.

A RAINY DAY. An emergency, a period of misfortune for which money, etc., has been reserved.

He had £500 put aside for a rainy day.

SEE BETTER DAYS. Be richer and more prosperous (almost always used in the past tense).

The woman had obviously seen better days.

Dead : This word is commonly used in the sense of " absolute " and " absolutely ", e.g. DEAD CENTRE, DEAD
LEVEL, DEAD STRAIGHT ; DEAD CERTAIN, DEAD
SURE, DEAD HEAT (the last when two competitors
are absolutely equal).

DEAD BEAT. See DEAD TO THE WORLD.

DEAD EARNEST. See under **Earnest.**

DEAD LETTER. 1. Letters, etc., which for any reason
cannot be delivered go to the Dead Letter Office,
which returns them to the senders. 2. A law or
regulation which exists but is never enforced—
e.g. the law compelling people to go to church on
Sunday is said to be a " dead letter ".

DEAD LOSS. Complete or total loss.
The ship broke up and became a dead loss.

WAITING FOR A DEAD MAN'S SHOES. Waiting for an
advantage that may be obtained when someone
dies.
*Simpson will be rich when his uncle dies, but it's
a miserable business waiting for dead men's
shoes.*

DEAD OF NIGHT. The darkest, most silent time of
night.

DEAD TO THE WORLD ; DEAD BEAT (S.). Utterly
exhausted ; sleeping deeply ; or unconscious for
any other cause.
*After working for two days and nights with only an
hour's sleep I was practically dead to the world.*

Deaf : DEAF MUTE. A person who is both deaf and dumb.

Deal : A RAW DEAL (S.). Unfair or unduly harsh treatment.
*The old man was left only the cottage—a raw deal for
one who had worked so hard.*

Death : AT DEATH'S DOOR. On the verge of dying ; desperately, almost hopelessly ill.

IN AT THE DEATH. Or. Hunting. Arriving in time
to see the climax.
*John will not see the beginning of the competition, but
he will be in at the death.*

THE JAWS OF DEATH. Extreme danger or risk of
death.
The firemen rescued the child from the jaws of death.

PALE AS DEATH. As pale as though already dead.

A DEATH-WARRANT. Lit., A legal warrant authorizing execution. Met., Information that one is fatally ill. Also used to indicate general extinction.

The defeat at Culloden was the death-warrant of the hopes of the Jacobites.

TO THE DEATH. Till one combatant is killed. See **War**.

Deduction : MAKE A DEDUCTION. 1. Deduce.

From what the Chairman said, it was easy to make deductions about the future of the firm.

2. Reduce by (with " of " added).

We can make a deduction of ten per cent.

Deliver : DELIVER UNDER HAND AND SEAL. " I deliver this under my hand and seal " is the phrase used when signing and sealing a legal document.

Demean : DEMEAN ONESELF. Humiliate oneself morally or socially.

I would not demean myself by meeting the villain.

Denizen : DENIZENS OF THE DEEP. Old f. Inhabitants of the deep water—fish, crabs, etc.

Depend : DEPEND UPON. Rely upon ; have faith in.

You may depend upon our goods ; they are of the best quality.

DEPEND UPON IT. Be certain ; have no doubt.

Depend upon it, we shall win the war.

Depth : OUT OF, *or* BEYOND, ONE'S DEPTH. Literally, one's " depth " is the depth of water in which one must either swim or drown. Used as an idiom, " out of one's depth " indicates a subject beyond one's knowledge or mental understanding.

The student was out of his depth in discussions on the Middle Ages.

Descend : DESCEND TO PARTICULARS. Cease to talk about generalities, and discuss the subject in detail.

To descend to particulars, just what work do you do every day ?

Deserve : RICHLY DESERVE. " Richly " here means thoroughly, completely.

The boy richly deserves whipping.

Despair : YIELD *or* GIVE WAY TO DESPAIR. Give up hope.

Yielding to despair, she wept bitterly.

Determination : COME TO A DETERMINATION. Definitely decide.

The boy came to a determination to run away from school.

Devil : GIVE THE DEVIL HIS DUE. Admit good, even in someone of whom you disapprove.

To give the Devil his due, old Simpkins, miser though he is, has always been generous to his son.

HOLD A CANDLE TO THE DEVIL. From fear or caution to assist someone of whom we disapprove. From the story of the old woman who lit one candle to St. Michael and another to the Devil he was trampling underfoot, so that whether she went to Heaven or Hell she would have a friend.

PRINTER'S DEVIL. The boy who assists a printer at his work ; formerly one who took the printed sheets from the press, in which work such boys became so smeared with ink that they were said to be as black as devils.

DEVILLING (*Law*). A law student is said to be " devilling " when in order to increase his practical knowledge of the profession he serves as assistant to an established lawyer.

Die : DIE AWAY. Become more and more faint, until the sound cannot be heard at all.

The sound of her father's footsteps gradually died away.

DIE DOWN. Subside ; become calm after violence.

Difference : SPLIT THE DIFFERENCE. Halve the amount in dispute.

You ask twelve shillings, I offer eight ; will you split the difference and accept ten ?

Dilemma : ON THE HORNS OF A DILEMMA. In a position where a choice has to be made between alternatives that are unpleasant in either case ; in a difficult position. " Lemma ", from the Greek, means taken, accepted, taken for granted, and dilemma is a double acceptance—*two* things accepted, a bull with horns that will toss you whichever you grasp.

Ding-dong : DING-DONG FIGHT. One in which the opponents are fighting hard and are fairly evenly matched. (To " ding " is Anglo-Saxon for " bruise ".)

Dint : BY DINT OF. Dint = effort, usually continued.

By dint of much saving, he succeeded in going to college.

Discount : AT A DISCOUNT. Not required, or not fully appreciated.

Books about the war are at a discount just now.

Discussion : OPEN A DISCUSSION. Begin or start a discussion.

The subject was " Is Marriage a Failure ? " and Mrs. Smith opened the discussion.

Distance : KEEP ONE'S DISTANCE. Refrain from becoming familiar or intimate.

The Countess compelled even the oldest servants to keep their distance.

Divine : DIVINE RIGHT. A right supposedly received direct from God, applied chiefly to the right of sovereigns to occupy their thrones regardless of their suitability, or of their subjects' wishes.

Do : DO. 1. Be sufficient or suitable.

A small loaf will do for the family's breakfast.

2. Exert oneself.

I'll do all I can.

3. Swindle. Abbrev. of Do brown (S.).

That man is a cheat—he'll do you if he has a chance.

4. Visit a theatre, etc., as part of a plan.

We did two concerts and the Royal Academy last week.

DO AWAY, *or* MAKE AWAY, WITH. Dispose of, usually by destroying.

DO IN (S.). Kill.

Macbeth decided to do in Duncan.

(*Note.*—" DONE IN " is frequently used in the sense of exhausted—*I was absolutely done in after that long walk.*)

DO TO DEATH. Kill violently ; murder.

Cæsar was done to death by the conspirators.

DOING. Happening.

What's doing at the concert to-night ?

See TAKING PLACE.

DONE. Completely cooked.

The pudding is done.

See note under DO IN.

HAVE DONE WITH. 1. Cease to have any connection with.

I've done with hard work for the rest of my life.

2. Stop. Old f.

Have done with all this nonsense.

IT ISN'T DONE. It is socially forbidden; taboo.

*You mustn't pour your tea in the saucer to cool it—
it isn't done.*

Dog : DOG-DAYS. (Traditionally July 3rd to August 4th.)
The hottest weeks of the summer. So called
because Sirius, or the dog-star, rising with the
sun, combines to add his heat to it.

DOGS-EARED. Applied to pages which, by constant
handling, have become bent or curled at the
corners.

DOG-LATIN. Latin words employed literally, without
regard to correct grammatical construction.

A DOG IN THE MANGER. A person so selfish that he
will not allow people to enjoy something he himself cannot enjoy.

From Æsop's fable of the malicious dog who
barked and snarled in the manger containing the
cows' hay, and refused to let them eat it, though
he did not want it himself.

DOG-WATCH. Or. Nautical. A corruption of " dodge "
watch—two short watches introduced on board
ship (from 4 to 6 and 6 to 8 in the evening) so that
the same men should not be on duty at the same
time every day.

GO TO THE DOGS. Abandon all social standards and
moral restraints.

*That young man has gone to the dogs completely during
the past year.*

HELP A LAME DOG OVER A STILE. Help someone who
is in need of assistance, usually financial.

*I contributed five shillings to the fund for poor Smith ;
he is a lame dog who deserves help.*

LET SLEEPING DOGS LIE. Or. Proverbial. Avoid any
action leading to unnecessary friction or trouble ;
allow matters to remain as they are.

*We'll let sleeping dogs lie, and get married without
asking your uncle's opinion.*

UNDER-DOG. One who is in a helpless or inferior social
or financial position, who has no power to assert
his wishes or authority.

Doldrums : IN THE DOLDRUMS. Depressed and miserable.
Or. Part of the ocean, near the equator, known

as the doldrums, in which the wind is so slight
that sailing vessels are frequently unable to
proceed.

*Poor Mary has been in the doldrums ever since George
sailed for America.*

See DOWN IN THE MOUTH.

Dole : DOLE OUT. Distribute at intervals in small quantities,
with a suggestion of charity.

Don Juan : A dissipated and immoral character, usually one
of the aristocratic classes. (The original was a
fourteenth-century nobleman, upon whose career
Byron's poem " Don Juan " is founded.)

Door : SHOW A PERSON THE DOOR. Lit., Escort him to the
door. Met., Order him to leave the house.

He was so insolent that I showed him the door.

Double : DOUBLE-DEALING ; DOUBLE-CROSSING. Trickery
and deceit ; plotting against one's friends.

DOUBLE-EDGED. Or. A sword or similar weapon
sharpened on both sides. Possessing a double
significance.

*" Anyone could distinguish your plays from Shake-
speare's " is a double-edged statement.*

DOUBLE-QUICK. Extremely quickly.

*I dashed to the door, double quick, but was too late
to catch the thief.*

Doubt : BEYOND A DOUBT ; WITHOUT DOUBT. With absolute
certainty.

The man is dead beyond a doubt.

IN DOUBT. Uncertain ; hesitant.

When in doubt, do what your conscience advises.

MAKE NO DOUBT. Be quite sure ; certain.

Note.—This idiom is used with two slight but definite
shades of meaning :

1. Do what is necessary to make certain.

    Make no doubt that the safe door is locked.

2. Accept as a fact about which there is no
   doubt at all.

    *He'll agree to our offer—make no doubt
    of that.*

SHADOW OF DOUBT. Very slight uncertainty. (Frequently in the negative to indicate complete
certainty.)

The judge said he had no shadow of doubt of the prisoner's guilt.

Down : DOWN ON ONE'S LUCK. Temporarily unfortunate.
Spare sixpence for an honest man who is down on his luck.

DOWN IN THE MOUTH. Depressed-looking ; miserable. See IN THE DOLDRUMS and IN THE DUMPS.

DOWN AND OUT. Or. Boxing. In a state of complete destitution. A boxer is said to be down and out when he has been knocked down and is unable to rise before he is " counted out ".

Dozen : BAKER'S DOZEN. Thirteen. A baker may be fined if his loaves are under the official weight. To ensure that this should not happen, he includes (or used to include) an extra loaf in each dozen.

Drag : DRAG UP *or* IN. Talk about some subject which it is neither tactful nor necessary to discuss.
Why drag up my poor father's suicide ?

Draw : DRAW ASIDE. 1. Lit., Draw as one draws a curtain.
2. Met., Separate a person from others.
The King drew the General aside to discuss the situation.

DRAW AWAY. Withdraw from ; shrink from.
The crowd drew away from the dying man.

DRAW DOWN. Attract, as metal " draws down " electricity from lightning.
The boy's rudeness drew down a rebuke from his schoolmaster.

DRAW TO AN END. Reach the end ; finish.
I shall be glad when the concert draws to its end.

DRAW IN. 1. Shrink ; become shorter. (Applied especially to the period between summer and winter, when the hours of daylight decrease.)
After September the days seem to draw in very quickly.
2. Move to the side of the road, or stop entirely.
The small car drew in to allow the Rolls-Royce to pass.
See DRAW UP (3).

DRAW THE LONG BOW. Exaggerate.
The old sailor says he once swam thirty miles, but he's always drawing the long bow.
See also SWING THE LEAD (under **Lead**).

DRAW, PULL *or* MAKE A LONG FACE. Appear melancholy or distressed.

It's no use drawing a long face because the doctor says you're not well enough to go out to-night.

DRAW NEAR. Approach ; come near.

Draw near—I have news for you.

DRAW OFF. 1. Lit., Cause to flow away.

We must draw off the water from the tank.

2. Met., Cause to depart, to lead away.

The Captain drew off his men.

DRAW OUT. 1. Remove money from a bank or company.

I drew out a hundred pounds last week.

2. Encourage to talk.

The boy was very shy, but we succeeded in drawing him out about his home.

DRAW REIN. Lit., Pull at a horse's rein to compel it to stop ; halt.

The Captain galloped away, and did not draw rein until he reached Bristol.

DRAW UP. 1. Arrange in correct order (applicable both to people and to legal documents).

He drew up an agreement.

The troops will be drawn up on the parade ground.

2. Raise ; pull up.

The women will draw up water from the well.

3. Stop ; halt.

The carriage drew up at the castle entrance.

DRAWN GAME *or* DRAW. Term applied to any match or competition which ends in both sides being absolutely equal.

The contest ended in a draw.

See DEAD HEAT (under **Dead**).

Dribs and Drabs : Unnecessarily small quantities.

The landlady gave us our hot water in dribs and drabs.

Drive : DRIVE AWAY, OFF. 1. Depart, in a carriage, etc.

I must drive away in five minutes.

2. Compel someone or something to leave quickly.

These boys are a nuisance ; please drive them away.

DRIVE HOME. 1. Lit., Hammer a nail, etc., as far as it can go ; all the way. 2. Met., Emphasize.

My father drove home the evils of greed by telling us the story of Midas.

DRIVEN TO THE WALL. See under **Wall.**

DRIVING *or* GETTING AT (S.). Implying ; hinting.

When I mentioned Mary, her father asked me what I was driving at. I told him I wanted to marry her.

Drop : DROP (*a person*). Cease to be friends with.

She has become so rude lately that we've decided to drop her.

(*A subject*). Abandon ; cease to discuss.

DROP A BRICK (S.). Behave tactlessly ; commit a *faux pas*.

I'm afraid I dropped a brick when I asked if your uncle had ever been inside a prison.

See PUT ONE'S FOOT IN IT.

DROP IN. Call casually and informally.

Drop in for tea whenever you're passing.

DROP A HINT. See under **Hint.**

DROP A LINE. Send a short note.

Drop me a line when you are next in town.

DROP IN THE OCEAN *or* BUCKET. A small and inadequate contribution towards what is needed.

The five shillings I contributed was a mere drop in the ocean—they need £10,000.

DROP OFF. Fall asleep.

He closed his eyes, and soon dropped off.

DROP ON. 1. Select for questioning, etc.

The examiner may drop on George.

2. Blame.

I wasn't even there when the accident happened, so why drop on me ?

DROP OUT. Absent oneself ; cease to compete.

Ten runners started, but three soon dropped out.

TAKE A DROP TOO MUCH (S.). Become intoxicated (among many other slang terms, e.g. ONE OVER THE EIGHT ; DEAD TO THE WORLD ; HALF-SEAS OVER ; etc.).

Drug : A DRUG IN THE MARKET. Largely exceeding requirements, and consequently of low value commercially.

Poetry is at present a drug in the market.

Duck : DUCK (*verb*). Jerk one's head downwards to avoid a blow.

MAKE A DUCK, *or* DUCK'S EGG (*cricket only*). Be bowled without making any runs at all.

MAKE DUCKS AND DRAKES. 1. Send small flat stones skimming horizontally over the surface of the sea, a pond, etc. 2. Scatter one's fortune in extravagant living.

> *He soon made ducks and drakes of the money his uncle left him.*

Dumps : IN THE DUMPS. Thoroughly depressed. See IN THE DOLDRUMS ; DOWN IN THE MOUTH.

Durance : DURANCE VILE. Old f. Imprisonment.

Duress : UNDER DURESS. Compelled by moral or physical force.

> *He confessed, under duress, to several crimes.*

Dust : THROW DUST IN THE EYES. Hoodwink ; mislead and confuse.

> *The criminal threw dust in the eyes of the public by giving large sums to charity.*

NOT SO DUSTY (S.). Not so bad ; tolerable.

Duty : IN DUTY BOUND. Compelled by a sense of duty.

> *In duty bound, he went to see his mother.*

Dye : OF THE DEEPEST DYE. Of the most extreme type, usually unpleasant.

> *Judas was a traitor of the deepest dye.*

E

Ear : BOX A PERSON'S EARS. Administer a sharp slap on the side of the head.

> *If you don't go to bed at once I'll box your ears.*

BY EAR. Without any technical knowledge, merely by a natural appreciation of the sounds.

> *She plays the piano entirely by ear.*

COME TO, *or* REACH, ONE'S EARS. Be heard or known.

> *If the news should come to the old man's ears, it would break his heart.*

AN EAR FOR. A natural appreciation for (hearing).

> *Certain animals have an ear for music.*

See AN EYE FOR ; A TASTE FOR.

EAR-SPLITTING. Deafening ; distressingly loud and shrill.

> *He gave an ear-splitting yell.*

GIVE EAR. Old f., meaning " Listen to, and attend carefully ".

Give ear to all that your father is saying.

Also LEND AN EAR.

GIVE ONE'S EARS. Make almost any sacrifice to obtain.

I'd give my ears to visit Venice this spring.

HAVE ONE'S EAR TO THE GROUND (S.). Be aware of, or *au fait* with, what is likely to happen.

George knew of the proposals already ; he always has his ear to the ground.

IN AT ONE EAR AND OUT AT THE OTHER. Without being appreciated or remembered.

Everything we try to teach the boy goes in at one ear and out of the other.

LEND AN EAR. Similar to GIVE EAR.

PRICK UP ONE'S EARS. Listen with sudden attention to something heard unexpectedly. (Animals " prick up " or raise their ears at an unfamiliar sound.)

The prisoner heard his name whispered, and pricked up his ears.

SET BY THE EARS. Involve in ill-tempered arguments and quarrelling.

She is never in the house ten minutes without setting the whole family by the ears.

TURN A DEAF EAR. Refuse to listen.

The gambler turned a deaf ear to all advice.

Earnest : IN EARNEST ; IN DEAD *or* GOOD EARNEST. Serious ; the reverse of joking.

I am in earnest when I say that we are ruined.

Earth : GO TO EARTH. Disappear from the places in which one is usually seen. Or. Hunting. A fox " goes to earth " when it vanishes into its " earth " or burrow.

Ease : PUT, *or* SET, AT EASE. Make unembarrassed and socially happy by friendliness.

The Duke soon put his humble visitors at their ease.

Easy : IN EASY CIRCUMSTANCES. Financially comfortable ; rich enough to be able to live without worrying.

The old man has retired ; he is in easy circumstances.

EASY MONEY. One from whom money is easily obtained, or the money itself.

There is never any difficulty in borrowing from George ; he's always easy money.

Eat : EAT AWAY ; EAT INTO. Penetrate and destroy, as acid or moisture does.

The sea had eaten away much of the shore.

EAT ONE'S CAKE. See under **Cake.**

EAT ONE'S HEART OUT. Grieve continuously, until one's whole life is embittered.

She is eating her heart out because Jim never writes.

EAT HUMBLE PIE. Behave meekly, apologetically as a servant. The word *should* be "umbles", the inferior parts of a deer, which was served as a pie to the servants of a mediæval household, while the host and guests received the better portions.

He began by threatening me, but I told him I knew all about his past life, and he soon ate humble pie.

EAT INTO. See EAT AWAY.

EAT ONE'S HEAD OFF. Eat greedily and unprofitably ; do little or nothing in return for what one receives.

The boy is extremely lazy at present ; he is living at home and eating his head off.

EAT OUT OF HOUSE AND HOME. Eat so much that one's host would be ruined. (Often used jokingly of hungry children.)

That boy will eat you out of house and home.

EAT ONE'S WORDS. Completely and ignominiously withdraw a statement or challenge.

He boasted that he would throw me downstairs, but I made him eat his words.

Edge : EDGE AWAY. Move gradually away (as a boat moves very slowly from the edge of the shore).

ON EDGE. In a state of nervous tension.

We were all on edge to know the news.

EDGE ONE'S WAY. See THREAD ONE'S WAY.

Effect : IN EFFECT. Stated briefly and in other words.

He drank too much, and neglected his wife and children, and was, in effect, a disgrace to the village.

TAKE EFFECT. Operate ; function.

The poison will soon take effect.

Egg : AS SURE AS EGGS IS EGGS (S.). Stated with absolute certainty.

As sure as eggs is eggs it will rain to-morrow.

A BAD EGG (S.). See under **Bad**.

A DUCK'S EGG (*cricket*). See under **Duck**.

PUT ALL ONE'S EGGS IN ONE BASKET. Invest all one's capital, financial or otherwise, in a single enterprise.

He's put all his eggs in one basket, and bought an hotel.

Eke : EKE OUT. Make just sufficient by adding to.

The widow eked out her little income by selling flowers from her garden.

Elbow : ELBOW ONE'S WAY. Push forward by thrusting with one's elbows. Frequently used metaphorically.

They're trying to elbow their way into society.

ELBOW-GREASE (S.). Physical effort and energy.

You'll never clean the floor properly unless you put more elbow-grease into your work.

ELBOW-ROOM. Space in which to move.

We're moving to an office in which we shall have more elbow-room.

Element : IN ONE'S ELEMENT. In a congenial atmosphere and surroundings.

Jim is entirely in his element among a crowd of girls.

OUT OF ONE'S ELEMENT. In an uncongenial atmosphere or surroundings. See A FISH OUT OF WATER.

Eleven : THE ELEVENTH HOUR. The latest possible time before it is too late.

The crew were rescued at the eleventh hour.

Embargo : LAY AN EMBARGO ON. An embargo is a legal prohibition. The phrase is loosely applied to any definite impediment.

The new taxes will lay an embargo on the company's future prosperity.

Enamoured : BECOME ENAMOURED. Old f. variation of " fall in love ".

He became enamoured with the village schoolmistress, and finally married her.

End : AT ONE'S WITS' END. Mentally desperate, and unable to find a solution.

I was at my wits' end to find the money to pay the rent.

TO THE BITTER END. To the extreme end, whatever may happen.

I shall be faithful to you to the bitter end.

NO END (S.). Greatly; very much.

I was no end pleased when I heard of my promotion.

NO END OF A (S.). Superlatively good.

We went to Brighton, and had no end of a time.

ENDS OF THE EARTH. The most distant parts of the world.

She swore that she would follow him to the ends of the earth.

THE END OF ONE'S TETHER. The limit of one's endurance or patience. (Tether = the rope or chain by which a horse or other animal is secured.)

We had been walking all day, and were at the end of our tether.

GO OFF THE DEEP END (S.). Become suddenly and violently angry. Or. The deep end of a swimming-pool, into which one dives from a spring-board. See FLY OFF THE HANDLE.

MAKE BOTH ENDS MEET. Make one's income enough for one's expenses. (More frequently used in the negative.)

I cannot make both ends meet on my salary.

PUT AN END TO. Finish; terminate. Applied to something which has already existed for some time.

The King decided to put an end to the barons' quarrels.

TO NO END *or* PURPOSE. Without effect or result.

The priest tried to obtain the King's pardon, but to no end.

Enemy : HOW GOES THE ENEMY? How is the time (the enemy of man) going? What time is it?

English : MURDER THE QUEEN'S ENGLISH. " Queen's English ", or " standard English " is the English language as spoken by educated people. To " murder " the Queen's English is to use it incorrectly or to speak it with a very bad accent.

Enough : ENOUGH AND TO SPARE. Ample; more than is needed.

Ten yards of carpet will be enough and to spare.

ODDLY ENOUGH. Unexpectedly; surprisingly. ("Enough" here is equivalent to "in the circumstances", "considering the conditions", etc.) Similarly, CURIOUSLY, STRANGELY, REMARKABLY ENOUGH, etc.

We met by chance in Egypt, and a year later, oddly enough, in New York.

Enquiry : IN THE COURSE OF ENQUIRY. While enquiries were being made ; during an investigation.

In the course of an enquiry, it was discovered that he had never been in the Army.

SEARCHING ENQUIRY. Close and thorough enquiry.

The Government promise a searching enquiry into the whole matter.

Enter : ENTER INTO. 1. Comprehend ; understand.

We can enter into your feelings of relief.

2. Occupy oneself with.

We cannot enter into details at present.

The two old men entered into (or upon) a long discussion.

ENTER INTO AN AGREEMENT. Agree ; undertake.

The firm will enter into an agreement to supply five thousand pairs of shoes.

ENTER THE LISTS. Compete. Or. Mediæval tournaments, the lists (plural form) being the place where combats between knights took place.

I hear that John intends to enter the lists as a Parliamentary candidate.

ENTER UPON. Begin.

We are entering upon a new epoch in the history of civilization.

Entrench : ENTRENCH UPON. Lit., Dig a place for oneself. Met., Occupy or possess part of a person's time, money, etc.

I hate to entrench upon your leisure, but can you spare me five minutes ?

Entry : MAKE AN ENTRY. 1. Record in a book.

The secretary made an entry of the arrangement.

2. Enter formally or ceremoniously a town, etc.

The troops made an entry into the city.

Esteem : HOLD IN (HIGH) ESTEEM, HONOUR, *etc.* Regard as deserving.

The young nobleman was held in high esteem by the peasants.

Estimate : FORM AN ESTIMATE. Judge in a general way.

You can form an estimate of her charm when I tell you that her portrait has been painted at least a dozen times.

ROUGH ESTIMATE. A rough calculation ; approximately.

At a rough estimate, he must have walked twenty miles.

Even : EVEN SO. In spite of, even after the circumstances have been considered.

George is a poor man, but even so, there is no reason for him to wear rags.

BE EVEN WITH. Be revenged upon ; pay back an injury.

He's cheated me, but I'll be even with him next time.

Event : AT ALL EVENTS. Nevertheless ; yet.

Our landlady may be mean, but at all events she does not rob us.

See AT ANY RATE.

COMING EVENTS. Events which are expected or planned.

Coming events in the village include a flower-show and a treat for the schoolchildren.

COMING EVENTS CAST THEIR SHADOWS BEFORE. An English proverb. What is going to happen may frequently be guessed from preliminary events.

COURSE OF EVENTS. A succession of events ; a number of events that followed.

The course of events made it necessary for him to go to America.

IN ANY EVENT. Whatever may happen.

I hope to go to-morrow ; in any event I shall go before Saturday.

See IN ANY CASE ; IN ANY CIRCUMSTANCES ; HAPPEN WHAT MAY.

IN THE EVENT OF. If a specified event should take place.

In the event of fire, ring the alarm-bell.

PROPHESY AFTER THE EVENT. State that something was certain to have happened after it has already happened.

BE WISE AFTER THE EVENT. State what should have been done to avert a disaster when it has already occurred.

Ever : EVER AND ANON. Old f. and poetical. At intervals.

Ever and anon the lost traveller studied the stars above him.

FOR EVER AND AYE ; FOR EVER AND A DAY. Old f. and poetical. Always ; eternally.

FOR EVER AND EVER. A more modern version of the above.

I shall love her for ever and ever.

EVER SO ; EVER SO MUCH, MANY (S.). " Ever so " is a popular (but not recommended) form of emphasis, equivalent to " extremely " or " greatly ". Perhaps " THANKS, EVER SO " is the commonest form of this, and the one to be most avoided.

Every : EVERY OTHER. Every alternate. Lit. or Met. Applied only to the singular.

Every other man carried a lighted torch.

She asks questions every other minute.

Evidence : CONFLICTING EVIDENCE. Evidence which is contradictory given in a legal action by two people.

The evidence in the case is conflicting ; Mrs. Smith states that she saw the prisoner in the street at four o'clock ; Mrs. Jones says that she spoke to him in his shop at the same time.

Ewe : EWE LAMB. Or. Biblical (The Parable of the Ewe Lamb). The chief, or a very greatly valued, possession.

She loved her three tall sons, but little Marion was her ewe lamb.

Example : FOR EXAMPLE. To quote as an example.

Some English poems are extremely long—" The Faerie Queene ", for example.

MAKE AN EXAMPLE OF. Inflict punishment on an individual who has done wrong as a warning to others who might behave in the same way.

Exception : TAKE EXCEPTION. Object.

I take exception to your statement that I am bad tempered.

Execution : PUT INTO EXECUTION ; CARRY OUT. Do something already planned or arranged.

They wanted to sell the house and go abroad, but realized that it would be some months before they could put their plan into execution.

Exercise : EXERCISE POWER. Exert power or influence.

The King cannot exercise much political power, though he frequently offers advice.

Explain : EXPLAIN AWAY. Remove uncertainty by persuasive and reasonable explanations.

I didn't believe her at first, but she managed to explain away my doubts.

Extent : TO A CERTAIN (CONSIDERABLE, LARGE) EXTENT. To a limited degree ; partially.

Eye : APPLE OF ONE'S EYE. Loved and prized intensely.

Her son was the apple of her eye.

ARGUS-EYED. Intensely alert and watchful. Or. Mythology. (Argus, who had a hundred eyes, was set by Hera to watch Io, of whom she was jealous.)

That Argus-eyed Mrs. Smith knows just where her husband spends all his spare time.

A BLACK EYE. The result of being struck so violently in the face that the flesh surrounding the eye is bruised and blackened.

Jim got a black eye in his fight with Joe.

CAST IN ONE'S EYE. A squint. " Cast " here is used in the naval meaning of " twist ".

CATCH SOMEONE'S EYE. Meet the gaze of a person for a brief time.

The schoolboy caught his master's eye, and stopped talking.

AN EYE FOR. Natural ability to appreciate (visual).

He has always had an eye for a bargain.

See also AN EAR FOR ; A TASTE FOR.

TO EYE. To glance at, usually with suspicion.

GIVE AN EYE TO ; KEEP AN EYE ON. Watch ; devote a certain amount of attention to.

Cook asked me to keep an eye on the meat while she was away.

HAVE AN EYE TO THE MAIN CHANCE. Be alert for opportunities of personal profit.

Robinson visits his rich uncle every week ; he's always had an eye to the main chance.

HAVE ONE'S EYES ABOUT ONE. Be observant and alert.
A big-game hunter must have his eyes about him.

HAVE ONE'S EYES SKINNED. As above.

IN THE EYES OF. Regarded by.
In the eyes of our grandfathers, Picasso's paintings would have seemed absurd.

EYE OF THE LAW. See under **Law.**

MAKE EYES AT. See CAST SHEEP'S EYES ; MAKE EYES ; and SHEEP'S EYES.

IN ONE'S MIND'S EYE. Mentally ; as a mental vision.
In my mind's eye I can still see my old home, with the roses over the door.

RUN THE EYE OVER. Glance over ; survey quickly.
Do you mind running your eye over these accounts.

SEE EYE TO EYE. Regard in the same way ; agree.
I hope we shall see eye to eye in this matter.

SEE WITH HALF AN EYE. Realize easily, and at once.
One could see with half an eye that he was a gentleman.

UP TO THE EYES, *or* EYEBROWS, IN (S.). Immersed ; completely occupied with.
I found George up to the eyebrows in business.

WITH AN EYE TO. With a definite object in one's mind.
I bought the house with an eye to converting it into a school.

WITH ONE'S EYES OPEN. Fully aware of the circumstances.
He was a poor man, but Jane married him with her eyes open.

EYE-WITNESS. One who actually sees an incident, etc.
According to an eye-witness, it was the car-driver's fault.

F

Face : FACE ; FACE UP TO. Accept and meet a situation without flinching.
We are ruined, and must face up to the fact.

FACE ABOUT. Turn in the opposite direction.
The troops were ordered to face about.

FACE TO FACE. Directly opposite ; confronting one another.
The brothers came face to face in a crowd.

FACE IT OUT. Meet a situation with defiance.

He knew he was in the wrong, but was determined to face it out.

FACE VALUE. Nominal or superficial value.

The face value of the stamp was a penny, but it was worth fifty pounds.

FLY IN THE FACE OF PROVIDENCE. Commit an act which is obviously rash or foolish.

It would be flying in the face of Providence to go out in this weather without a coat.

HAVE THE FACE, THE NERVE TO. Have the effrontery or impertinence to.

I'm surprised that you have the face to ask again for money.

KEEP A STRAIGHT FACE. Remain serious.

George was so funny that it was impossible to keep a straight face.

See **KEEP ONE'S COUNTENANCE**, under **Countenance.**

MAKE FACES. Twist and contort one's features, usually in contempt or dislike.

ON THE FACE OF IT. As it appears ; judging from what has been stated.

On the face of it, you have been very badly treated.

PULL A LONG FACE. Look miserable and depressed.

We've lost a good deal of money, but it's no use to pull a long face about it.

PUT A GOOD, *or* **BOLD, FACE UPON IT.** Behave fearlessly and cheerfully, and as though there was nothing wrong.

Joan Smith has run away from home, but her family are putting a good face on it.

SET ONE'S FACE AGAINST. See under **Set.**

Fact : **IN FACT.** See **IN FINE.**

STUBBORN FACT. A fact which cannot be denied or ignored.

The stubborn fact remains that the man has been in prison for fraud.

Fag : **FAG-END.** (Lat. *facto*, the part added when the rest is finished.)   The latter, the final and inferior part. Lit., The rough end of a piece of cloth.

We spent the fag-end of our holiday on the river.

Faint : FAINT YET PURSUING. Or. Biblical. Weary, but continuing still the pursuit or purpose.

Faint but pursuing, they followed the thief all the way to London.

Fair : FAIR AIM. Careful, deliberate aim (with a weapon).

He took fair aim with his rifle, and fired.

FAIR COPY. A clear copy, unspoilt by corrections.

FAIR DEAL. A transaction which is fair and just to both sides.

My house for your farm would be a fair deal.

See FAIR AND SQUARE.

FAIR FIELD AND NO FAVOUR. Or. Racing. A fair and open opportunity of winning.

I want to marry her, and all I ask is a fair field and no favour.

FAIR GAME. A suitable object of amusement and ridicule.

The country boy is fair game to his smart acquaintance in town.

FAIR NAME. Old f. Honourable reputation.

I will do nothing to spoil the fair name of my family.

FAIR PLAY. Correct and courteous treatment between opponents ; justice according to accepted rule.

The prize fight took place as arranged, and the old boxer was present to see fair play.

FAIR SEX. Women in general. See WEAKER SEX.

FAIR AND SQUARE. Just ; openly honest.

The terms of the contract are absolutely fair and square.

See FAIR DEAL and ON THE SQUARE.

IN A FAIR WAY TO. Likely to ; behaving so that a certain event is probable.

Old Peter is in a fair way to make a fool of himself over the girl.

FAIR-WEATHER FRIEND. One who is a friend only during prosperity, and who ceases to be one when trouble comes.

FAIR WORDS BUTTER NO PARSNIPS. Or. Old proverb. Polite and friendly speeches are of no practical value unless accompanied by kind actions.

Faith : BAD FAITH. Treachery ; dishonesty.

It was an act of bad faith to betray his friend.

(*Note.*—GOOD FAITH (which see) has not the opposite meaning.)

BREACH OF FAITH. A dishonourable action ; a broken promise, given or implied.

It was a breach of faith to reveal the story I told you.

IN ALL GOOD FAITH. Honestly believing.

I told you in all good faith that my husband was dead.

PIN ONE'S FAITH TO, *or* ON. Place one's entire faith in ; believe in.

I pin my faith on that horse winning the Derby.

SHAKE ONE'S FAITH. Make one doubtful of one's previous beliefs.

What you tell me shakes my faith in human nature.

SHATTER ONE'S FAITH. Destroy one's belief completely.

Fall : FALL APART, ASUNDER. Break up in separate pieces.

FALL INTO ARREARS. Fail to pay a sum due at regular intervals.

If you fall into arrears with your rent, your furniture will be sold.

Similar to FALL BEHIND (2).

FALL ASTERN. Or. Nautical. Go more slowly, till instead of being level one is behind.

The damaged vessel fell astern.

See FALL BEHIND (1).

FALL AWAY. 1. Diminish ; dwindle.

Trade always falls away during the summer.

See FALL OFF.

2. Separate from ; desert.

All his old friends fell away from him.

FALL BACK. 1. Retire ; retreat.

The guns began to fire, and the troops to fall back.

2. Make use of in an emergency.

One can always fall back upon condensed milk.

FALL *or* DROP BEHIND. 1. Similar to FALL ASTERN.

2. Similar to FALL INTO ARREARS.

FALL BETWEEN TWO STOOLS. Attempt to combine two plans, and succeed with neither.

He spent half the holiday with his mother and half with his wife—and, falling between two stools, was blamed by both women.

FALL FLAT. 1. Lit., Be prostrate.

The wounded man staggered, and fell flat on the floor.

2. Met., Fail to amuse or interest ; end in an anti-

climax. ("Flat" here is used as the reverse of "sparkling", a term applied to soda-water or other effervescent drink which has been spoilt by exposure to the air.)

What was meant to be a funny story fell completely flat.

FALL FOR (S.). Become an admirer of ; yield to the attractions of.

My son has definitely fallen for your daughter.

FALL FOUL OF. Or. Nautical. Lit., Collide with ; crash into. Met., Quarrel with.

That detestable old woman falls foul of everyone she meets.

FALL IN THE REAR. Or. Military and Naval. Retire to a position behind the rest of one's company, regiment, etc.

The wounded men were ordered to fall in the rear of the column.

FALL INTO A HABIT. Form or acquire a habit.

He's fallen into the habit of coming to tea every Sunday.

FALL IN PLACE. Lit., and Met., Take up the proper and logical place or position.

When he told me his story, all the facts I had known before fell into place.

FALL IN WITH. Encounter ; meet.

On my way from the station I usually fall in with Smith.

FALL ON ONE'S FEET. Be successful as the result of good fortune or luck.

Arriving in London penniless, John, as usual, fell on his feet, and met a friend who offered him a job.

FALL OFF. Deteriorate.

The quality of his painting has fallen off greatly.

FALL OUT. 1. Disagree ; quarrel.

Discussing the Government, the two old friends fell out.

2. Happen ; occur.

It may never fall out that we meet again.

FALL SHORT. Be less than, or below.

My income falls short of my expenditure by five hundred pounds.

FALL THROUGH. Collapse ; fail to happen.

All his plans fell through.

FALL TO. Make a vigorous beginning.

Fall to, men, and we shall soon finish the job (or the meal).

FALL TO ONE'S LOT. Happen to one.

It will probably fall to my lot to die a bachelor.

FALL TO PIECES. Break up completely.

The chair was made so badly that it fell to pieces the first time I sat on it.

FALL UPON. Attack.

The wolf fell on the lamb and devoured it.

FALL UPON A PERSON'S NECK. Embrace (Biblical, now used only facetiously).

Don't expect me to fall on your neck because you've lent me five shillings.

Fancy : FANCY FREE. Or. Shakespeare's *Midsummer Night's Dream.* (" In maiden meditation, fancy free.") Heart-free ; not in love with anyone.

FLIGHT OF FANCY *or* IMAGINATION. Something visualized which is entirely imaginary; unconnected with actual events.

In a flight of fancy, the poor clerk saw himself as the wealthy owner of the business.

TICKLE ONE'S FANCY. Amuse ; divert.

It tickled the millionaire's fancy to recall the time when he had been a servant in this great house.

Far : AS FAR AS IN ONE LIES. As far cr as much as one is capable.

I swear to do my duty as far as in me lies.

FAR AND AWAY, *or* BY FAR. To a much greater extent or degree.

I was far and away happier when I was young and poor.

FAR AND WIDE ; FAR AND NEAR. Many places, both near and distant.

People came from far and wide to hear him preach.

A FAR CRY. A remote connection only ; distant or slightly connected.

It is a far cry from selling cabbages to lecturing on agriculture.

See FAR-FETCHED.

FAR BE IT FROM ME. An apologetic phrase for interfering or criticizing.

*Far be it from me to instruct the nurse in her duties,
but the patient has fallen out of bed.*

FAR-FETCHED.   Exaggerated and over-elaborate.

His story was full of far-fetched similes and metaphors.

FAR GONE.   In a dangerously critical condition ;   *in
extremis.*

I'm afraid he is so far gone that there is no hope.

IN SO FAR.   To the extent or degree.

*I am able to help you, in so far that I can obtain you
a post in a bank.*

Fashion : AFTER A FASHION.   In an amateurish and ineffective way.

He cooked the dinner after a fashion.

Fast : FAST DYE.   " Fast " here is equivalent to " fixed " ;
immovable.   Dye which will not wash out.

PLAY FAST AND LOOSE.   Act irresponsibly, and without
regard to one's duties and responsibilities.

*If you think you can play fast and loose with the
agreement we made, you are mistaken.*

Fasten : FASTEN ON.   1. Lit., Attach.

I can't fasten on this button.

2. Pick out for a particular purpose or as the person
responsible.

*Someone must have broken the plate, but why fasten
on me ?*

Also **Pick** or **Pitch.**

Fat : FAT IN THE FIRE.   Lit., The splutter and flames made
when fat splashes from a frying-pan into the fire.
General excitement, anger, etc., when a sensational
piece of news is made public.

*I told Father that Tom and I were married, and then
the fat was in the fire.*

THE FAT OF THE LAND.   The best and most expensive
food, etc., obtainable.

*Though they haven't much money, they seem to live on
the fat of the land.*

Fate : THE IRONY OF FATE.   An ironic coincidence.   An
event, frequently tragic, which defies or defeats
what has been intended.

*By the irony of Fate, the prisoner died of a broken
heart on the morning he was to have been set free.*

Fault : AT FAULT.   Wrong ; inaccurate.

You were at fault in thinking that he married Mary for her money.

IN FAULT. Not merely wrong, but to be blamed
You were in fault for having been so rude.

FIND FAULT WITH. Grumble at ; complain.
His wife is constantly finding fault with him.

Favour : IN HIGH FAVOUR. Extremely popular.
I hear you're in high favour with the old man.

Feather : A FEATHER IN ONE'S CAP. An honour ; something to be proud of. From the custom of American Indians adding a feather to their headdress for every enemy that they killed.

It's a feather in John's cap to be chosen captain of the cricket team.

FEATHER ONE'S NEST. Gradually acquire extra money, honestly or otherwise, during one's employment. From the habit of birds lining their nests with feathers.

She feathered her nest very thoroughly while she was housekeeper to the old man.

FEATHERED LIFE. Birds in general. See FOWLS OF THE AIR.

IN HIGH FEATHER. Extremely pleased ; elated.
Jim is in high feather at the chance of going abroad.

SHOW THE WHITE FEATHER. Behave like a coward. Or. The old English sport of cockfighting. No pure-bred gamecock has a white feather in its plumage.

Any soldier who shows the white feather in battle will be instantly shot.

Fed : FED UP (S.). Utterly bored and disgusted.
I'm fed up with London and want to go back to Sheffield.

Feel : FEEL FOR. Feel pity for ; sympathize with.
All of us feel for you in your great trouble.

Feeling : FELLOW-FEELING. The sympathy and understanding felt for a sufferer by one who has been through similar trials.

Fellowship : THE HAND OF FELLOWSHIP. The right hand of a friend, clasped as a sign of goodwill and peace.

Fence : SIT ON THE FENCE (S.). Refrain from giving one's support to either side ; remain entirely neutral (usually from motives of cowardice or discretion).

I don't know old Peter's politics ; he's sitting on the fence.

Few : FEW AND FAR BETWEEN. Or. Abbreviated quotation from the poet Campbell, " Like angel visits, few and far between ". Rare, scarce.

My holidays are few and far between.

Field : THE FIELD IS LOST (*or* WON). " Field " here is the field of battle itself. See DAY IS LOST.

KEEP THE FIELD. Remain on the field of battle ; continue to fight successfully.

We will keep the field against all competition.

TAKE THE FIELD. Prepare for battle ; advance against an enemy.

The English took the field with ten thousand troops.

FIFTY-FIFTY. See under **Go.**

Fight : FIGHT SHY OF. Avoid ; keep away from.

Peter fights shy of women : he says they frighten him.

FIGHT TO A STANDSTILL. Fight until both sides are too exhausted to make any further effort.

Figure : CUT A FIGURE. Become prominent, usually for being conspicuously well-dressed.

FIGURE OF FUN. Ridiculous ; absurd.

The old woman looks a figure of fun in that girlish hat.

FIGURES OF SPEECH. Literary forms such as the metaphor, simile, hyperbole, allegory, etc.

File : IN INDIAN FILE ; IN SINGLE FILE. Singly, one behind another. Or. The American Indians used to mislead their enemies as to their number by each man stepping exactly in the footsteps of the man in front of him.

The path was so narrow that we had to walk in Indian file.

Fill : FILL AN OFFICE. Occupy a position or post.

Charles filled the office of general manager for twenty years.

FILL UP, *or* IN, DOCUMENTS. Add details which are required.

If you require a passport, will you please fill up this form.

TAKE ONE'S FILL. Take enough to satisfy, all that one is capable of taking.

We took our fill of the sunshine and fresh air.

Filthy : FILTHY LUCRE. Old f. Or. Biblical. Money; wealth.

Final : FINAL TOUCH. The last detail; that which completes the work.

> *As a final touch to her costume, she pinned a red rose in her hair.*

Find : FIND ONESELF IN. Supply oneself with.

> *We can let you have tea and sugar, but you'll have to find yourself in milk.*

ALL FOUND. Everything provided.

> *We are paying five pounds a week, all found.*

FIND GUILTY. The legal phrase used when an accused person has been tried, and it has been " found " that he committed the crime.

FIND IN ONE'S HEART. See under **Heart.**

Fine : IN FINE. Stated exactly or briefly.

> *In fine, you will have to stay in bed till we know what is the matter with you.*

Also IN FACT.

Fingers : FINGERS ARE ALL THUMBS. Fingers are clumsy, awkward.

> *It's so cold this morning my fingers are all thumbs.*

BURN ONE'S FINGERS. Suffer as a result of some action.

> *If you buy that business, I think you'll burn your fingers.*

HAVE A FINGER IN THE PIE (S.). Be concerned with, or mixed up with some affair.

> *You may be sure that old Bill has a finger in the pie.*

See HAVE A HAND IN THE MATTER.

AT ONE'S FINGER-TIPS. Immediately available. (Applied to information, knowledge, etc.)

> *He has all the information at his finger-tips.*

Finish : THE FINISHING STROKE. 1. The final blow.

> *He was dismissed from his job; it was the finishing stroke.*

See LAST STRAW.

2. The final touch to a work of art.

> *The artist was putting the finishing stroke to the portrait.*

Fire : FIRE AWAY ! (S.). Begin.

> *He hesitated for a time, but I told him to fire away and tell me what happened.*

LINE OF FIRE. Any line crossing the ground over which shots are being fired.

Many men were killed when we crossed the enemy's line of fire.

TAKE FIRE. Lit., Become ignited. Met., Become excited, indignant or enthusiastic.

She took fire at the prospect of going to America.

Similarly, STRIKE FIRE, to arouse enthusiasm.

THROUGH FIRE AND WATER. Through any kind of suffering or discomfort.

I would go through fire and water to make her happy.

First : AT THE FIRST BLUSH, *or* GLANCE. Superficially ; before examining closely.

At first blush it seems an excellent plan.

FROM FIRST TO LAST. From beginning to end ; all the time.

From first to last, he never treated his family as he should.

Fish : A FISH OUT OF WATER. One out of his natural element or surroundings.

Among so many well-dressed and cultured people, the country girl felt a fish out of water.

FISH IN TROUBLED WATERS. Interest oneself in affairs that are likely to lead to trouble and danger.

The man who interferes in South American politics is fishing in troubled waters.

OTHER FISH TO FRY. Other business to occupy the time.

I can't discuss the matter any longer—I've other fish to fry.

PRETTY KETTLE OF FISH. A thoroughly unsatisfactory state of affairs ; general upheaval and excitement ; a mixture of muddle and trouble. " Kettle " is a corruption of " kittle ", which in turn is a corruption of " kiddle ", a basket arranged in river water to catch fish.

A QUEER FISH. An eccentric person ; an unusual type.

That old uncle of yours is a queer fish.

Fit : FIT. In a suitable condition to work, in good health. (Also FIGHTING FIT.)

FIT IN WITH. Co-ordinate with.

Your visit to-morrow will fit in with my cousin's arrival.

FIT UP *or* **OUT.** Prepare an expedition, etc.
The Government is fitting up a new expedition to the North Pole.

IN FITS AND STARTS. Irregularly, in a series of spurts.
He does his work in fits and starts.

THROW A FIT; HAVE A THOUSAND FITS (S.). Be extremely agitated.
Mother would throw a fit if she saw me in these clothes.

Flame : ADDING FUEL TO THE FLAMES. Adding fresh causes for anger.

FAN THE FLAMES. As above.
Everything she said fanned the flames of his anger against her.

AN OLD FLAME. A sweetheart in past days.
I'm told Miss Simpson is an old flame of yours.

Flare : FLARE UP. As a verb; give way to a sudden burst of anger. As a noun; a violent quarrel.
You need not flare up merely because I mentioned your work.
There was a tremendous flare up at the office to-day.

Flash : FLASH IN THE PAN. A brief display producing no useful result. Or. Military. The " flash-pan " of the old-fashioned gun was the place at which a small quantity of powder was exploded to fire the larger quantity in the barrel. If it failed to do this, it merely " flashed " in the pan.
That brilliant poem he wrote when young was a mere flash in the pan ; he has produced nothing since.

Flat : FLAT DENIAL, CONTRADICTION, *etc.* Flat (adjective) (or flatly, adverb) is here in the sense of complete and absolute.
He flatly denied that he had stolen the coat.

FLAT AS A FLOUNDER, *or* **PANCAKE.** Completely flat. A flounder is a flat fish. A pancake is a thin cake made of batter and fried in a pan. See **FALL FLAT.**

Flea : SENT OFF WITH A FLEA IN ONE'S EAR (S.). Dismissed, after receiving a sharp rebuke.
Tom came to borrow some money, but I sent him away with a flea in his ear.

FLEA-BITE, A MERE. A trivial quantity or sum.
He is a rich man ; five pounds is a mere flea-bite to him.

FLEA-BITTEN GREY. A grey horse with small dark spots.

Flesh : NEITHER FLESH, FOWL NOR GOOD RED HERRING. With no definite qualities ; not worth classifying.

He is extremely vague about his profession ; he seems to be neither fish, fowl nor good red herring.

FLESH POTS (OF EGYPT). Or. Biblical. The good things of life ; rich food, etc.

Though nearly eighty, he still yearned for the flesh pots of Egypt.

MAKE ONE'S FLESH CREEP. Horrify ; shock ; frighten with some ghastly story or sight.

What he told us about prisoners of war made our flesh creep.

Flight : TAKE FLIGHT. Retreat ; flee away rapidly.

At the first sight of a white man, all the natives take flight.

Fling : HAVE ONE'S FLING. Indulge freely in one's pleasures.

Every young man likes to have his fling.

See SOW ONE'S WILD OATS.

Float : FLOAT A COMPANY. Organize a public company and issue shares in it.

Flood : FLOOD TIDE. Highest degree of success, misery, etc.

At the flood tide of his success the doctor was earning ten thousand a year.

Floor : WIPE THE FLOOR (S.). Reduce to helplessness or ignominy ; completely overwhelm.

The brilliant young lawyer wiped the floor with the prosecutor.

Flow : FLOW OF SPIRITS. High spirits ; gaiety.

The young couple had a tremendous flow of spirits.

Flowing : FLOWING BOWL. Old f. Intoxicating drinks—wines, spirits, etc.

If you wish to prosper, shun the flowing bowl.

FLOWING WITH MILK AND HONEY. Or. Biblical. Filled with all good things to eat and drink.

The country lad thought London was flowing with milk and honey.

Flutter : Applied to playing card games, betting, etc. A brief period of amusement.

I had a flutter at Epsom, and lost nearly £30.

CAUSE A FLUTTER. Cause excitement, as when a flock

of birds is disturbed. (Similarly FLUTTER THE
DOVECOTES—cause excitement in a society or
community.)

*The announcement of the Duke's marriage caused a
tremendous flutter.*

Fly : FLY AT. Attack violently, physically or verbally.

The dog flew at the tramp.

Don't fly at me because I mentioned Communism.

See FLY OFF THE HANDLE.

FLY IN THE OINTMENT. The flaw, inconvenience or
impediment in an arrangement.

*I'm invited to spend a month with Aunt Agatha, but
there's a fly in the ointment—she won't allow me
to take my dog.*

FLY OFF THE HANDLE (S.) (as the iron head of a hammer
flies off when loose). Suddenly lose one's temper.

*Don't contradict my aunt—she's sure to fly off the
handle.*

See OFF THE DEEP END, under END.

FLY, *or* GO, OFF AT A TANGENT. Abruptly abandon
one subject for another.

*We were discussing politics when Jane flew off at a
tangent to ask what I thought of Mary's baby.*

MAKE THE FUR FLY (S.). Create a violent quarrel or
disturbance, as animals make the fur fly when
fighting.

*When George referred to " our bloodthirsty capitalists ",
the fur began to fly.*

Foam : FOAM WITH RAGE. Lit., To foam at the mouth, as
mad dogs do. Used to indicate a state of extreme
and ungovernable anger.

*Poor father foamed with rage when I told him I would
no longer obey him.*

Fob : FOB OFF. Persuade someone to accept a substitute.

*I asked for butter, and will not be fobbed off with
margarine.*

Follow : FOLLOW ONE'S BENT. Follow one's inclination ; act
in accordance with one's abilities and desires.

*John became a clerk, but if he had followed his bent
he would have been a sailor.*

FOLLOW THE DICTATES OF ONE'S HEART. Obey one's
inward desires and feelings.

She followed the dictates of her heart, and married the poor man and not the rich one.

FOLLOW ONE'S OWN DEVICES. Amuse or divert oneself as one wishes. See GO ONE'S OWN WAY.

FOLLOW SUIT. Or. Card-playing. Behave similarly ; do the same thing.

The thief dashed across the road, and the policeman followed suit.

FOLLOW UP. Continue a process already begun.

The horse kicked furiously and followed this up by trying to bite me.

Fool : FOOL AWAY. Waste (as a fool wastes).

Don't fool away your time in public houses.

A FOOL'S ERRAND. A useless journey.

I was sent to Germany to interview the prisoner ; it was a fool's errand, for the man had died two years previously.

FOOL'S PARADISE. An entirely false conception ; a state of happiness unjustified by the actual facts.

I told young Joe that he was living in a fool's paradise.

FOOL-PROOF. So simple and strong that even a fool cannot use it wrongly or break it.

MAKE AN APRIL FOOL OF. The phrase refers to an old English custom—that of playing harmless practical jokes and deceptions on one's friends on the morning of the first of April.

MAKE A FOOL OF. Cause someone to appear ridiculous or contemptible. See TAKE A RISE OUT OF.

Foot (Feet) : FEET FOREMOST. An elaborate evasion of " dead ".

I shan't leave this house until I'm carried out feet foremost.

FOOT THE BILL. Pay whatever charge is involved.

If the Government grants higher pensions, the people themselves will have to foot the bill.

MISS ONE'S FOOTING. Slip ; stumble.

OBTAIN *or* GAIN A FOOTING. Obtain a status or position (" footing " is constantly used in this sense).

He gained a footing in the firm which made him almost as important as the manager.

ONE FOOT IN THE GRAVE. So old or diseased that life is nearly finished.

Old Jack is very feeble, and has one foot in the grave.

ON FOOT. Walking or running.

We went all the way to Brighton on foot.

ON A FRIENDLY FOOTING. On friendly terms ; friends with.

I like to be on a friendly footing with my neighbours.

PUT ONE'S FOOT DOWN. Take firm and determined action.

When the girl wanted to stay out until past midnight, her father put his foot down.

PUT ONE'S BEST FOOT FORWARD. Proceed as quickly as possible.

We shall have to put our best foot forward if we are to reach London to-night.

PUT ONE'S FOOT IN IT. Make a blunder ; a *faux pas.* See DROP A BRICK.

SET FOOT ON. Step on to.

As the Queen set foot on deck, the band played the National Anthem.

SET ON FOOT. Initiate ; begin any process or action.

The Government intends to set on foot an enquiry into betting.

SET ON HIS, *or* HER, FEET. Help a person to regain a lost position or lost health.

The money we've collected ought to set the old man on his feet again.

Force : COME INTO FORCE. Operate ; function.

The new laws come into force next month.

FORCE A MAN'S HAND. Or. Card-playing. Compel him to show his intentions, or to take definite action.

I did not want to sell the shares, but a financial crisis forced my hand.

JOIN FORCES. Become associated with, or partners with.

The two explorers joined forces, and continued their journey together.

Fore : FORE AND AFT. Or. Nautical. From one end to the other of a vessel.

The boat was filled with cabins fore and aft.

Foreign : FOREIGN SUBSTANCE *or* BODY. Any improper and injurious substance—dust, dirt, etc.

The boy was half-blinded by some foreign substance which the wind had blown into his eye.

Forfeit : FORFEIT THE GOOD OPINION OF. Lose the good opinion of a person by bad or foolish conduct.

If you continue to tell lies, you will forfeit the good opinion of everyone.

Fork : FORK OUT (S.). Pay.

You'll have to fork out five shillings for your dinner.

Forlorn : FORLORN HOPE. Corruption of the Dutch " Verlorenhoop "—lost troop. Hope that is very unlikely to be fulfilled ; a final effort.

As a forlorn hope, we lit matches. Their light was seen in the darkness, and we were rescued.

Forty : FORTY WINKS (S.). A slight, brief sleep. (" Forty " formerly implied an indefinite number, meaning " a few ". Shakespeare so uses it.)

Mother always has forty winks after lunch.

THE ROARING FORTIES. Nautical. Applied to latitude 40 degrees south, where strong winds blow throughout the year.

Foul : FOUL PLAY. Or. Sport. Unfair, unsporting ; frequently applied to criminal action.

The sailor was never seen again ; the police suspected foul play.

Fountain : FOUNTAIN-HEAD. Starting-place ; source.

The fountain-head of all these stories is Miss Jones, the village gossip.

Four : FOUR-SQUARE. Lit., Facing squarely in four directions. Met., Facing the world firmly and without fear.

We stand four-square against our troubles.

Fowls : FOWLS OF THE AIR. Or. Biblical. Birds in general. See FEATHERED LIFE.

Fraught : FRAUGHT WITH. Old f. Laden with ; bearing.

I fear this telegram is fraught with trouble.

Fray : THICK OF THE FRAY. Where the fighting is fiercest.

The sergeant dashed into the thick of the fray.

Free : FREE AND EASY. Unconventional ; not arranged according to any formal plan.

We spent a delightfully free-and-easy evening with the Robinsons.

FREE-HAND (*one word, or with hyphen*). Applied to drawing in which no mechanical help from instruments is employed.

FREE HAND (*two entirely separate words*). Complete freedom of action.

I have been given a free hand in arranging the concert.

FREE-HANDED, *or* FREE. Generous.

He is extremely free-handed with his money.

FREE FIGHT. A general and indiscriminate combat in which anyone may join.

Someone in the audience threw a cabbage at the speaker, and the meeting ended in a free fight.

FREE-LANCE. Political: One attached to no party. Journalistic: One attached to no particular paper.

FREE TRANSLATION *or* RENDERING. A translation which is not literal, but which conveys the general meaning and effect.

MAKE SO FREE AS TO. Old f. Dare to.

May I make so free as to ask you for your autograph ?
See MAKE SO BOLD.

SCOT FREE. Or. Legal. Lit., Tax free (scot = tax). Without any punishment or penalty.

The older thief received five years' imprisonment, but his young companion escaped scot free.

SET FREE. Release.

I opened the cage door, and set the birds free.

Fresh : FRESH AS PAINT *or* AS NEW PAINT. Entirely fresh and unspoilt.

In spite of the dance last night, Mary looks as fresh as paint this morning.

Friend : BOSOM FRIEND. A specially close and intimate friend.

She was my bosom friend at school.

FRIEND AT COURT. Someone with private influence.

Through a friend at court, he was able to obtain plenty of butter during the war.

MAKE FRIENDS (*plural only*). Form friendships ; become friendly.

Peter never made friends easily.

Full : FULL WELL. Very well (adverb only).

He knew full well.

G

Gaff : BLOW THE GAFF (S.). Reveal or betray a secret.

We were going to the theatre without Mother knowing, but George blew the gaff.

Gall : GALL AND WORMWOOD. Extremely and bitterly annoying. (Gall is extremely bitter. Wormwood is a plant said to have sprung up in the path of the serpent as he writhed out of Eden.)

The news of Mary's marriage to John was gall and wormwood to the man she had refused.

MAKE GAME OF. Similar to MAKE FUN OF (under **Make**).

THE GAME'S UP. Further effort is useless. See ALL UP.

Gate : GATE-CRASHING. Entering uninvited to a dance, entertainment, etc. GATE-CRASHER—one who so enters.

Gather : GATHERED TO ONE'S FATHERS. Old f. Dead, and buried. (The phrase originally implied " with one's ancestors.")

He was ninety when he died and was gathered to his fathers.

Gauntlet : RUNNING THE GAUNTLET. Lit., Driven between a row of persons each provided with sticks, ropes, etc., with which to strike the offender. (" Gauntlet " is a corruption of the French *Gauntelope*, itself of Swedish derivation, a passage between two rows of soldiers facing one another.) A former punishment for sailors ; still employed by schoolboys. Met., Subjected to criticism or attack from an organized body of people.

He ran the gauntlet of criticism from every doctor in the country when he published his book.

FLING OR THROW DOWN THE GAUNTLET. Applied to any act of defiance. Or. The Middle Ages, when a knight who wished to fight with another threw down his gauntlet (or hand-armour) as a challenge.

Russia, by invading India, would fling down the gauntlet to the British Commonwealth.

Get at : 1. Contact ; reach.

I should like to get at some of the papers in Uncle Joe's safe.

2. (S.). Influence, usually with a view to giving false evidence.

All the servants swore they had never seen the prisoner before, but someone had obviously been getting at them.

GETTING AT. Identical with DRIVING AT, which see.

GET AWAY. Escape.

I caught three mice, but one got away.

GET ONE'S GOAT ; GET ONE'S MONKEY UP ; GET ONE'S RAG OUT (S.). Make one angry ; exasperate one.

That girl's insolence always gets my goat.

GET GOING. Make a beginning, a start.

It's past seven—we must get going.

GET THE HANG OF (S.). Comprehend ; understand the working of.

The machinery is quite simple: you'll soon get the hang of it.

GET HOLD OF. Grasp, Lit., and Met.

I'll explain, and you'll soon get hold of the idea.

GET OFF (S.). Become friendly and intimate with.

There goes Jane, getting off with the Jones boy.

GET ON. 1. Lit., Mount ; climb on to.

The boy was too small to get on his pony without help.

2. Met., Agree ; be friends with.

I hope Jack and his cousin will get on together.

See HIT IT OFF.

3. Met., Progress satisfactorily.

Jane works so hard at her job that she is certain to get on.

GET OVER. 1. Recover from.

He soon got over the shock.

2. Overcome by persuasion, etc.

He got over her objections to the marriage.

GET OUT ON THE WRONG SIDE OF THE BED (S.). Get up in the morning in a bad temper.

GET RID OF. Dispose of something not desired or needed.

We're going to get rid of our old car.

GET UP. 1. Organize and start (an entertainment, etc.).

Our cricket club is getting up a concert.

2. Rise from one's bed.

At what time do you get up in the morning?

3. Study for a special purpose.

I have to get up Milton's poems for the examination.

GET ONESELF UP. Dress smartly or strikingly.

Dorothy has got herself up in a new costume.

Ghost : GHOST OF A CHANCE. The slightest, the least chance.

That horse hasn't a ghost of a chance of winning the race.

Gift : GIFT OF THE GAB (S.). The ability to speak brilliantly and convincingly. (" Gab " is both Scotch and Danish for " mouth".)

There is no doubt that our candidate has the gift of the gab.

Gilt : TAKE THE GILT OFF THE GINGERBREAD. Take away the charm or advantage. In the Middle Ages small gilded gingerbread cakes were sold at fairs.

The fact that I've got to return to the office in the middle of my holiday takes the gilt off the gingerbread.

GILT-EDGED INVESTMENTS. Investments—mortgages, debentures, etc.—in which there is no risk of losing one's capital.

Gird : GIRD UP ONE'S LOINS. Or. Biblical. Prepare for an ordeal or combat.

We must gird up our loins for the long journey to-morrow.

Give : GIVE A PERSON, *or* THING, THE GO-BY. Ignore ; treat as non-existent.

I shall give the whole scheme the go-by.

GIVE AWAY. 1. Distribute. 2. Reveal a secret or expose a person.

GIVE ONESELF AWAY. Unintentionally reveal one's intentions or emotions.

Mary gives herself away by blushing every time Peter's name is mentioned.

GIVE IN. Surrender.

The enemy is surrounded, and must soon give in.

See GIVE UP and GIVE WAY.

GIVE IT TO (S.). Punish.

I'll give it to you if I find you opening my desk again!

GIVE OUT. 1. Issue ; distribute (information, verbally or in print).

The Government has given out that war is declared.

2. Be finished, all used.

You can't have a hot bath—the water will give out.

GIVE OVER (S.). Stop; cease.

Give over teasing the cat, Charley.

GIVE, *or* YIELD, PLACE TO. Be replaced or superseded by someone or something else.

In the nineteenth century gas gave place to electric light.

GIVE RISE TO. Cause; create.

The sound of guns gave rise to a rumour of invasion.

GIVE AND TAKE. Mutual allowances and concessions.

With a little give and take, we can soon come to an agreement.

GIVE UP. 1. Abandon.

I shall give up smoking.

2. Surrender; cease to fight. See GIVE IN.

GIVE IT UP. Cease to attempt.

The puzzle is too difficult; I shall give it up.

GIVE ONESELF UP. Surrender to authority.

The murderer gave himself up to the police.

GIVE UP THE GHOST. Die; expire. (The ghost or spirit of man is supposed to leave his body at the moment of death.) The idiom is also used (facetiously) in connection with inanimate things.

My old bicycle ran into a cart to-day and gave up the ghost.

GIVE WAY. 1. Yield.

Mary refused at first to marry him, but she gave way at last.

See GIVE IN and GIVE UP.

2. Break; collapse.

The railings gave way, and he fell over the cliff.

Globe : GLOBE-TROTTER. One who travels extensively.

Glory : GLORY IN. Take great pride in.

He glories in the record of his family.

Gloss : GLOSS OVER. Try to minimize by ignoring or excusing.

The lawyer tried to gloss over his client's bad record by saying that his parents neglected him.

Go : (*noun*) (S.). Turn, according to a prearranged plan.

It's my go to throw the ball.

ALL THE **GO** (S.). Fashionable ; popular ; the vogue. (The phrase is now slightly out of date.)

These silk ties are all the go.

GO AFTER. Follow.

Go after George, and ask him for some money.

GO AHEAD. 1. Lit., Go in front, or before.

You go ahead and tell Mr. Jones that we're coming.

2. Met., Proceed at once.

If you think you can solve the problem, go ahead.

GO ALL OUT (S.). Make every possible effort.

We shall have to go all out if we are to win the race.

GO ALONG WITH YOU ; GET AWAY WITH YOU ! Scamper ; run away quickly !

GO BACK ON. Reverse a previous promise or under-taking.

He said he would help us, and then went back on his promise.

GO-BETWEEN. One who acts as a link between two people or groups of people ; a negotiator.

GO-BY. See under **Give.**

GO DOWN (S.). Be believed ; be acceptable.

That argument won't go down with him.

GO FIFTY-FIFTY. Receive fifty per cent each ; share equally.

We'll go fifty-fifty with the profits.

GO FOR (S.). Attack.

I saw your dog go for our cat.

GO FOR NOTHING. Be without value ; have no effect.

All the efforts we have made will go for nothing.

GO HALVES. Same as GO FIFTY-FIFTY.

GO IN FOR. Undertake seriously, as a profession or hobby.

I hear he's gone in for gardening.

GO ON ! An expression which may mean, according to circumstances, an injunction to hurry (*Go on— we shall never get there !*) ; of disbelief (*You saw a ghost ? Go on !*), or Continue ! (*Please go on with the story*).

GO ONE BETTER. Improve upon ; prove more skilful, etc.

Henry's ambition is to be a schoolmaster, but George wants to go one better, and become a professor at Oxford.

GO OUT OF ONE'S WAY. Incur extra trouble.

This hotel-keeper goes out of his way to make his guests happy.

GO OVER THE GROUND. Examine the facts, survey.

It is a difficult problem, and I should like to go over the ground again.

GO PIT-A-PAT. Applied only to one's heart; beat irregularly through fear.

Her heart was going pit-a-pat as she entered the haunted room.

GO THROUGH FIRE AND WATER. Make any sacrifice; endure any sufferings.

Nelson's men would go through fire and water to serve him.

GO THROUGH WITH. Continue to the end.

He has begun to study for a degree, but I don't think he'll go through with it.

GO TO! Obsolete abbrev. of the oath, "Go to the Devil!"

GO TO THE WALL. Be pushed on one side, passed by; ignored (as people in a hurry leave the wall side of the pavement to slower, weaker people).

When a workman becomes old and feeble he goes to the wall.

GO WITHOUT. Be without; lack.

I'm afraid you'll have to go without milk in your tea.

GO WITHOUT SAYING (Fr. *Cela va sans dire*). Be obvious; self-evident.

He'll inherit his father's money—that goes without saying.

NO GO (S.). Impossible; futile; unworkable.

I've tried to persuade your father to come, but it's no go.

ON THE GO (S.). Active; continually busy.

My mother is on the go all day long.

Going : GOING TO HAPPEN; OCCUR, *etc.* "Going to" here is used in the sense "will".

I don't know what is going to happen when Father hears the news.

Golden : GOLDEN MEAN. The ideal "middle course"; that which pleases most people because most moderate.

Good : AS GOOD AS. Equal to.

This coat is as good as new.

BE SO GOOD AS TO. Old f. Will you please.
Be so good as to open the door for me.

FOR GOOD, *or* FOR GOOD AND ALL. Permanently;
always.
You may keep that hat for good.

MAKE GOOD. 1. Repair. See **Make.**
2. Reclaim the past. See **Make.**

A GOOD SAMARITAN. Or. Biblical. The Parable of the
Good Samaritan, St. Luke x. 30–37. One who
helps and relieves a person in need.
*He acted as a good Samaritan, and took the poor woman
to the hospital.*

ON GOOD TERMS. On friendly conditions; in a friendly
way.
We parted on good terms.

A GOOD TURN. A kindness; a friendly action.
*My wife is always ready to do a good turn to a neighbour
in need.*

TO THE GOOD. 1. Profit.
I am a shilling to the good.
2. General advantage.
Peace is all to the good.

Goose : GOOSE-FLESH. A cold and roughened condition of
the skin, resembling that of a plucked goose,
caused by cold or fear. People are said to " go
all goose-flesh " when they are terrified.

SAY " BO " TO A GOOSE. Show courage. (*Note.*—This
idiom is always used in the negative.)

Gorge : MAKE ONE'S GORGE RISE. See under **Make.**

Got : HAVE GOT TO. Must.
I have got to finish this sewing before I go out.

Grace : WITH A GOOD GRACE. Cheerfully; without pro-
testing.
The King listened to my arguments with a good grace.
WITH A BAD GRACE. The reverse.
IN ONE'S GOOD GRACES. Popular with.
*I must keep in the old man's good graces if I want to
marry his daughter.*
See IN ONE'S GOOD BOOKS (under **Book**).

Grade : MAKE THE GRADE (S.). (Of American origin, but
used in England since 1930.) Succeed in some
specified object. The literal meaning of " grade "

is a railroad incline which the engine driver is required to " make " or climb.

He's working very hard for the position, but I'm afraid he won't make the grade.

Grain : AGAINST THE GRAIN. Or. The grain or fibre of wood. Against one's inclination or wishes. See AGAINST THE COLLAR (under **Collar**).

Grass : GRASS WIDOW. A woman whose husband is away for a prolonged period or lives apart from her.

Grate : GRATE ON THE EAR. Sound harsh and unpleasant.

The sounds of quarrelling grated on his ear.

Grave : COMMIT, *or* CONSIGN, TO THE GRAVE. See under **Commit**.

SINK INTO THE GRAVE. Die, after prolonged mental or physical suffering.

Her faithless lover broke her heart, and she gradually sank into the grave.

Grease : GREASE A MAN'S PALM. Bribe.

The innkeeper will tell you the lady's name if you grease his palm.

Green : GREEN-EYED MONSTER. Jealousy. Or. Shakespeare's *Othello* : " Beware of jealousy, it is a green-eyed monster."

GREEN ROOM. The general reception room of a theatre ; It is said that such rooms formerly had their walls coloured green to relieve the strain on the actors' eyes after the stage lights.

Grievance : AIR A GRIEVANCE. See under **Air**.

Grim : GRIM-VISAGED. Grim or stern-looking.

A grim-visaged old woman opened the door.

Grin : GRIN AND BEAR IT (S.). Endure as well as one can.

If Jane won't marry me, I must just grin and bear it.

Grist : ALL'S GRIST THAT COMES TO THE MILL. Everything that is received can be used. (" Grist " is all corn, etc., which is to be crushed in a mill at one time.)

The author writes on any subject ; everything is grist that comes to his mill.

BRING GRIST TO THE MILL. Bring supplies of money.

His knowledge as an art expert brought grist to the mill.

Groove : RUN IN A GROOVE *or* RUT. Function in the same limited and narrow way, or by the same methods.
> *He was a bank clerk, and his whole life ran in a narrow groove.*

Ground : GAIN GROUND. Advance ; progress.
> *He wanted to be more friendly with the girl, but did not seem able to gain ground.*

Grow : GROWN UP. Adult.
> *Young John looks quite grown up.*

GROW ON ONE. Gradually impress its charm and personality.
> *You may not like Brighton at first, but you'll find it grows on you.*

Grub : GRUB UP. Dig up ; reveal ; retrieve from the past.
> *The police have grubbed up many details of the woman's childhood.*

Grudge : BEAR A GRUDGE. See BEAR MALICE.

Grundy : MRS. GRUNDY. A severely conventional character in a play called " Speed the Plough ". " What will Mrs. Grundy say ? " = " What will Society and our neighbours think of this ? " " To offend Mrs. Grundy " is to commit some social crime.

Guard : CATCH OFF ONE'S GUARD. Take advantage of one's opponent when he is temporarily distracted or forgetful.
> *The police, catching the criminal off his guard, arrested him as he was drinking in a public house.*

ON ONE'S GUARD. Alert ; prepared.
> *You must be on your guard against swindlers.*

Gun : BIG GUNS (S.). Important and influential people.
> *George is one of the big guns of his profession.*

BLOW GREAT GUNS. Blow tremendous winds ; a gale.
> *It was blowing great guns when the ship left harbour.*

H

Hail : HAIL FROM. Come from.
> *O'Reilly hails from Ulster.*

HAIL FELLOW WELL MET. On familiar and friendly terms with everybody one meets.

Hair : HAIR STANDING ON END. Indicative of extreme terror and astonishment. (There is a legend of one prisoner whose long grey hair rose and stood stiffly upright, and then gradually sank down.)

Her hair stood on end when the ghost appeared.

SPLITTING HAIRS. Arguing or disagreeing over extremely trivial matters.

There's no need to split hairs over the exact cost of the house.

TO A HAIR. Exactly.

That costume fits you to a hair.

Similar to TO A " T ".

NOT TURN A HAIR. Show no signs of fear or embarrassment.

When the lion leapt out of its cage, the keeper, without turning a hair, drove the animal back.

HAIR'S BREADTH. A minute distance. (A hair's breadth is, in accepted measurements, $\frac{1}{48}$th of an inch). A hair's-breadth escape is a very narrow escape, an event which only just missed disaster.

Halcyon : HALCYON DAYS. A time of happiness and prosperity. From an ancient belief that the kingfisher, called in Greek " halcyon ", laid and hatched its eggs on the sea just before the coming of winter (mid-December), when the waves were smooth and unruffled.

Half : HALF-BAKED (S.). Half-witted ; silly ; mentally deficient.

HALF-AND-HALF. Divided into two exactly equal parts or portions.

They drank whisky and water, half-and-half.

See GO HALVES ; GO FIFTY-FIFTY.

HALF-HEARTED. Without energy or enthusiasm.

He made a half-hearted effort to stop her, but failed.

HALF-SEAS OVER (S.). Intoxicated.

HALFWAY HOUSE. Half the distance.

His socialism is a halfway house to Communism.

Hallmark : Or. The official marking (after testing) of all gold and silver goods with the " hall " or standard mark as a guarantee of purity. The word is used met. in connection with conduct, taste, manners, etc.

The young man's manners had the hallmark of good breeding.

Hammer : HAMMER AND TONGS. With much noise and vigour.

The husband and wife were quarrelling hammer and tongs.

HAMMER OUT. Arrive at a decision or solution by examining and discussing every detail of the subject.

We spent all day hammering out our plans for the holiday.

UNDER THE HAMMER. By public auction, the reference being to the auctioneer's hammer (technically a " gavel ") with which he raps on his table each time an object is " knocked down " to a buyer.

Hand : ALL HANDS TO THE PUMPS. Assistance from everyone concerned. Or. Nautical. When a ship is leaking so badly that she is likely to sink, all " hands " (members of the crew) are summoned to work the pumps.

They'll need all hands to the pumps if the business is to be saved.

AT FIRST HAND. Directly ; straight from the person concerned.

I heard the story of the wreck first hand from the captain.

AT HAND ; CLOSE AT HAND. Near ; available.

I want you to be at hand during my interview with the police.

CARRY OFF WITH A HIGH HAND. Behave arrogantly, as one in a superior position.

The prisoner, charged with begging, carried it off with a high hand.

Also HIGH-HANDED (*adjective*).

CHANGE HANDS. Pass from the ownership of one person to that of another.

The property has recently changed hands.

CLEAN HANDS. Innocently ; honestly ; without fraud.

I can at least say that I made my fortune with clean hands.

COME TO HAND. Arrive ; be delivered. (A formal commercial phrase.)

Your parcel should come to hand to-morrow.

GIVE ONE'S HAND TO. Marry (used of females only).
She gave her hand to a good-looking young sailor.

HAND IN GLOVE. In partnership; intimately associated.
The criminals and the police are hand in glove in this swindle.

HAND IN HAND. Lit. Clasped hands. In close association.
The two firms work hand in hand.

HAND TO HAND. One person to another.
The document was passed from hand to hand.

HAND-TO-HAND FIGHTING, STRUGGLE, etc. Close and desperate fighting, without artillery.

HAND TO MOUTH. From day to day, without any provision for the future.
Old Brown has always lived from hand to mouth.

HAND OVER. Surrender; formally give to someone else.
The General handed over the keys of the fortress.

HAND OVER HAND, *or* FIST. Or. Naval. Rapidly.
He's overtaking us, hand over fist.

HAVE A HAND IN. Take a part or share in.
George would like to have a hand in arranging the entertainment.

HAVE ONE'S HANDS FULL. Be completely occupied, very busy.
We shall have our hands full when the visitors arrive.

HAVE ON ONE'S HANDS. Be responsible for; have to dispose of.
When the house is sold I shall have the furniture on my hands.

IN HAND, *or* WELL IN HAND. 1. Under one's control.
There was a little rioting, but the police soon had the situation in hand.

2. In one's possession.
When all our debts are paid, we shall have over £10 in hand.

KEEP IN HAND. Retain; keep under control.
We are keeping £10 in hand.

LEND A HAND. Help.
All the packing has to be done; perhaps you'll lend a hand?

LIFT *or* RAISE ONE'S HAND AGAINST. Strike; attack.
A gentleman would never lift his hand against a woman.

OFF-HAND. See **Off**.

AN OLD HAND. A person with considerable experience.
Let me help—I'm an old hand at chopping wood.

ON ALL HANDS; ON EVERY HAND. Universally.
It was agreed on all hands that the evening was a success.

See IN EVERY QUARTER.

ON THE OTHER HAND. Otherwise; alternatively.
We may leave London; on the other hand, we may remain.

See ON THE CONTRARY.

OUT OF HAND. Uncontrollable; beyond restraint.
The crowd became so excited that it was soon completely out of hand.

SHOW ONE'S HAND. Reveal one's real intentions. Or. The "hand" of cards held by a player.
Then, by accident, the King showed his hand, and his people realized for the first time the sort of man he was.

SLEIGHT OF HAND. See under **Sleight**.

STAY ONE'S HAND. Refrain from action.
The policeman was going to arrest the man, but was persuaded to stay his hand.

TAKE A HAND. Share; play a part in.
The State ought to take a hand in building new houses.

See HAVE A HAND.

TAKE IN HAND. Take immediate charge of; assume responsibility for.
The State will take in hand the problem of juvenile crime without further delay.

THE UPPER, *or* WHIP, HAND. The chief power; the real control.
Grumbling is useless; the villain has the upper hand.

THROW IN ONE'S HAND. Or. cards. Abandon any further effort.
I'm so disgusted with the whole thing that I'm going to throw in my hand.

TRY ONE'S HAND AT. Attempt; test one's powers.
Have you ever tried your hand at cooking?

WASH ONE'S HANDS OF. Have no further connection with; refuse to accept any further responsibility for.

If you disobey my orders, I shall wash my hands of you!

Handle : Deal with; direct.

I think Jones is the best man to handle this affair.

A HANDLE TO ONE'S NAME. A title.

I knew Sir John long before he had a handle to his name.

Handsome : DO THE HANDSOME, *or* HANDSOME THING; COME DOWN HANDSOME (S.). Old f. Treat liberally.

When we're married, I expect my rich uncle will do the handsome.

Hang : HANG BACK. Hesitate to proceed; show reluctance to agree or assist.

I asked him to come home with me, but he hung back.

HANG FIRE. Fail to produce results when expected. Or. A gun or pistol in which the cartridge fails to explode " hangs fire ".

We were going on a holiday with the Smiths, but somehow the scheme has hung fire.

HANG ON (S.). Cling to; persevere in spite of discouragements.

The business hasn't paid yet, but we mean to hang on till Christmas.

HANG ONE'S HEAD. Appear embarrassed and ashamed.

I asked the boy if he had been to school; he hung his head and did not answer.

HANG OUT (S.). Live; lodge.

I hang out in North London.

HANG BY A THREAD. Be in an extremely delicate and precarious state. Or. The story of the sword of Damocles, which see under **Sword.**

The life of the injured man hangs by a thread.

HANG TOGETHER. Collaborate closely; support one another.

Members of the Cabinet are traditionally expected to hang together.

HANG UPON. Depend upon.

My future will hang upon this interview with the chief tomorrow.

Hanky-panky (S.). Fraud; dishonest and untruthful dealing.
>   *The business is hanky-panky from beginning to end.*

Happen : HAPPEN *or* COME WHAT MAY. Old f. Whatever may occur.
>   *We'll go to London to-morrow, happen what may.*
>   See IN ANY EVENT.

Happy : HAPPY-GO-LUCKY. Careless; gaily reckless; relying on good luck for help out of difficulties.
>   *He was of a gay, happy-go-lucky disposition.*

Hard : GO HARD WITH. Involve severe punishment or suffering.
>   *It will go hard with Mary if John leaves her.*

>   HARD BY. Old f. Near.
>   *Hard by the cottage stood an oak.*

>   HARD DRINKER. One who drinks beer, wine, etc., frequently and in large quantities.
>   *The farmer was a hard drinker, and his family never had enough food or clothes.*

>   HARD-FEATURED. Severe-looking; grim.
>   *A hard-featured woman of fifty.*

>   HARD LINES, *or* LUCK. Harsh; undeservedly severe.
>   *Robinson has lost his job. It is hard lines on his family.*

>   HARD UP. With insufficient money.
>   *The student was so hard up that he had to sell his books.*

>   HARD WORDS. See **Word**.

>   See also PLAIN SPEAKING (under **Speak**) and NOT TO MINCE MATTERS (under **Mince**).

Hare : HARE-BRAINED ; SCATTER-BRAINED. Foolish and irresponsible.
>   *It was a hare-brained thing to spend the night on the mountain.*

>   MAD AS A MARCH HARE. See under **Mad**.

Harness : IN HARNESS. Actively engaged in regular work.
>   *The old man died suddenly in harness.*

Harp : HARP ON ; HARP ON THE SAME STRING. Talk about the same subject until the listener becomes bored or irritated.
>   *He is one of those who harp on their bad luck.*

>   JEW'S HARP. Corruption of " Jaw's harp ", a small musical instrument played by vibrating a piece of metal between the teeth.

Hash : A PRETTY HASH (S.). A "hash" in cookery is a mixture of small pieces of meat, previously cooked, and vegetables. In this sense it means a general state of confusion, the "pretty" being ironic. An appalling muddle.

A pretty hash you've made of this sewing !

See PRETTY KETTLE OF FISH.

SETTLE ONE'S HASH (S.). See **Settle.**

HASH UP. Bring forward again a matter previously seen or discussed.

Hat : PERFORM THE HAT-TRICK. Or. Cricket. A bowler is said to do this when he dismisses three consecutive batsmen in three consecutive balls. Loosely used in connection with any similar triple success.

Miss Smith performed the hat trick at Wimbledon by winning three sets of tennis without her opponent scoring a point.

TAKE OFF ONE'S HAT TO. Met., Express unusual approval of some action of another's.

I take off my hat to the police for the way they managed the crowds on Derby Day.

Hatch : " HATCHES, MATCHES AND DESPATCHES." A facetious name for the column in the daily papers in which the births, marriages and deaths are recorded.

Have : TO HAVE ANYONE (S.). To deceive or swindle.

If you paid a shilling for that, you've been had.

HAVE ANYTHING, *or* NOTHING, TO DO WITH. Be concerned or connected with.

He's the kindest person I've ever had to do with.

Have nothing to do with him—he doesn't play fair.

HAVE DONE. Old f. Finish ; stop.

Have done with your quarrelling.

HAVE IT OUT. 1. Have extracted.

I'll have this tooth out to-morrow.

2. Discuss a subject openly and frankly.

I am going to have the whole thing out with Mary.

Hay : MAKE HAY OF. Ruin ; render confused and muddled.

This new plan of yours will make hay of our arrangements for the holiday.

MAKE HAY WHILE THE SUN SHINES. Take advantage of a good opportunity, or a specially suitable occasion.

Peter, making hay while the sun shone, asked her to marry him.

Haywire : GO HAYWIRE (S.). Behave as though one had become crazy and mentally unbalanced.

Owing to the splendid news, the whole family has gone haywire.

See GO TO ONE'S HEAD (under Head).

Hazard : HAZARD AN OPINION *or* GUESS. (Rather old f. and formal.) Risk expressing an opinion or view.

I'll hazard the opinion that we'll have rain to-morrow.

Head : COME, *or* ENTER, INTO ONE'S HEAD. Occur to one.

The idea had just come into my head.

GO TO ONE'S HEAD. Excite ; intoxicate ; make irresponsible. See HAYWIRE.

HANG ONE'S HEAD. See under **Hang.**

HAVE A HEAD ON ONE'S SHOULDERS. Possess intelligence and common sense.

The boy has a head on his shoulders, and will make a first-class lawyer.

HAVE HIS HEAD. Or. Riding and driving. Go his own way without any interference. To let a horse " have his head " is to allow him to travel at his own speed unrestrained by the reins.

I'm going to let Peter have his head in the business, hoping that he'll be more successful than I've been.

HAVE ONE'S HEAD SCREWED ON THE RIGHT WAY. Be intelligent and shrewd.

Jack is farming in Canada ; he's young, but he has his head screwed on the right way, and I think he'll make a success of it.

HEAD AND SHOULDERS ABOVE. Far above or superior to.

George's intelligence is head and shoulders above Peter's.

HEAD OFF. Intercept ; prevent escaping.

One of the boys ran away from school an hour ago ; we are hurrying to the station to head him off.

See CUT OFF.

HEAD ON. Directly ; frontally.

The two cars collided head on.

HEAD-OVER-EARS (*in love, debt, etc.*). Utterly and completely.

The boy is head-over-ears in love with my daughter.

HEAD-OVER-HEELS. Turned upside down : complete inversion.

HEADS OR TAILS. A coin is frequently " tossed " (or thrown in the air) by one person to decide which of two alternatives shall be followed. The other competing person " calls " either " heads " or " tails " ; if what he calls falls uppermost, he is considered the winner. If not, the one who tossed the coin succeeds.

HEADS I WIN, TAILS YOU LOSE. An arrangement which ends in the challenger remaining the winner, whatever happens ; a hopelessly unfair agreement.

You want me to do all the work and take all the responsibility while you take most of the profits—a clear case of heads you win, tails I lose.

See HEADS OR TAILS

KEEP ONE'S HEAD ABOVE WATER. Live within one's income ; avoid bankruptcy.

Jenkins has a wife and six children to support; I don't know how he manages to keep his head above water.

LOSE ONE'S HEAD. Momentarily lose self-control ; behave wildly and senselessly.

Confronted by his victim's brother, the murderer lost his head and confessed all.

MAKE HEAD OR TAIL OF. Understand ; comprehend. (Always used in the negative.)

I cannot make head or tail of Mary's letter.

OFF ONE'S HEAD. Mentally weak ; unbalanced ; mad ; or so excited as to be entirely irresponsible.

Jack is off his head with delight at the prospect of going to America.

ON ONE'S OWN HEAD. One's own personal responsibility. (The phrase is generally used as a warning.)

If you insist, it will be on your own head.

A PRICE ON ONE'S HEAD. A reward for one's capture or death.

The murderer has escaped, and there is a price on his head.

PUT INTO ONE'S HEAD. Suggest.

The boy says he wants to be a sailor; our seaside holiday must have put it into his head.

PUT ONE'S HEAD INTO THE LION'S MOUTH. Deliberately take great risks.

The thief, putting his head in the lion's mouth, stopped a policeman to ask him the time.

PUT, *or* LAY, OUR (*or other applicable adjective*) HEADS TOGETHER. Consult together; discuss.

We put our heads together and formed a plan.

TAKE INTO ONE'S HEAD. Take a sudden and unexpected action.

The boy took it into his head to run away to sea.

TOSS ONE'S HEAD. Raise it with a jerk of pride or contempt.

She tossed her head, and said she would never marry a mere tradesman.

TURN ONE'S HEAD *or* BRAIN. Render one vain and self-conscious.

The admiration the girl received completely turned her head.

TWO HEADS ARE BETTER THAN ONE. It is an advantage to have a second person's opinion; collaboration is valuable.

Find out what your brother thinks about the matter: two heads are better than one.

Headway : MAKE HEADWAY. Progress; go forward.

They made considerable headway in sorting the papers.

Heap : STRUCK ALL OF A HEAP (S.). Overcome; overwhelmed.

I was struck all of a heap to see Phyllis pushing a pram.

Hearing : HARD OF HEARING. Partially, but not completely deaf.

You'll have to shout—the old lady is hard of hearing.

LOSE ONE'S HEARING. Become completely deaf. See STONE DEAF.

OUT OF HEARING. Too far away to be heard.

Though the lovers could be seen, they were out of hearing.

Heart : AFTER ONE'S OWN HEART. Such as one could like and appreciate.

It is a house after my own heart.

DO ONE'S HEART GOOD. Make one happy and pleased.
It did one's heart good to see the children's delight.

FIND IT IN ONE'S HEART ; HAVE THE HEART TO. Be firm or hard-hearted enough (usually used in the negative).
I could not find it in my heart to refuse the boy's request.

HAVE AT HEART. Be personally concerned or interested in.
Her parents naturally have the girl's happiness at heart.

HAVE ONE'S HEART IN ONE'S BOOTS (S.). Be intensely depressed.

HAVE ONE'S HEART IN ONE'S MOUTH. Be in a state of extreme nervousness.
My heart was in my mouth when I passed the policeman.

A HEART OF FLINT *or* STONE. Hard-hearted, without pity ; unmoved by suffering.
The miser, who had a heart of flint, drove the old beggar woman away.

HEART IN THE RIGHT PLACE. In spite of imperfections, possessing good and sensible ideas.
He's rough and uneducated, but his heart is in the right place.

HEART'S CONTENT. Complete satisfaction ; as much or as long as one desires.
We can swim in the river to our heart's content.

HEART-TO-HEART. Frank and intimate.
We had a heart-to-heart talk.

KNOW BY HEART. Know, literally and every word.
I knew the verses by heart.

LEARN BY HEART. Memorize.

LOSE HEART. Become too depressed to continue.
Don't lose heart ; there's still a chance of winning the race.

LOSE ONE'S HEART TO. Fall in love with ; be charmed.
My sister has lost her heart to that good-looking young actor.

SET ONE'S HEART UPON. Desire intensely.
My mother's set her heart on my becoming a doctor.

TAKE HEART. Be encouraged.
We may take heart from the fact that the fever has left him.

See CHEER UP.

TAKE HEART OF GRACE. Or. Biblical (" My grace is
    sufficient for thee "). Take courage ; do not be
    discouraged.
Take heart of grace—all is not lost.
TAKE TO HEART. Take very seriously ; become de-
    pressed.
She has taken her father's death greatly to heart.
WEAR ONE'S HEART ON ONE'S SLEEVE. Exhibit one's
    intentions for all to see ; be completely and
    childishly frank. Or. The old custom of a lover
    tying a ribbon given him by his sweetheart on
    his sleeve.
*She found it difficult to let him know how much she
    cared ; she was never one to wear her heart on
    her sleeve.*

Heel : HEEL OF ACHILLES. See ACHILLES' HEEL.
COME TO HEEL. Obey humbly and completely, as a
    dog comes obediently to the heels of his master.
DOWN-AT-HEEL. Shabby and untidy, like one whose
    heels are worn down.
I've just seen old Brown ; he looks terribly down-at-heel.
    See OUT-AT-ELBOWS.
KICK ONE'S HEELS. Waste time.
*I had to kick my heels for an hour in the office before
    he would see me.*
    See LEFT TO COOL ONE'S HEELS and TWIDDLE ONE'S
    THUMBS.
LAID BY THE HEELS. Arrested.
The thief was laid by the heels before he reached London.
LEFT TO COOL ONE'S HEELS. Kept waiting, usually by
    a superior.
ON THE HEELS OF. Immediately behind, or very soon
    afterwards.
George arrived on the heels of William.
SHOW A CLEAN PAIR OF HEELS. Run away from and
    escape.
*The pickpocket was chased, but managed to show a
    clean pair of heels to the police.*
TAKE TO ONE'S HEELS. Run away.
The boy broke the window and took to his heels.
TURN ON ONE'S HEEL. Turn sharply away.
She turned on her heel, and disappeared in the crowd.

Hell : HELL BROKE LOOSE. A tremendous uproar, a riot, ensued.

Someone opened a bottle of whisky, and hell broke loose.

Help : HELP ONESELF TO. Select and take away without formality or waiting to ask permission.

The guests helped themselves to the refreshments at the buffet.

Helter-skelter : Hurriedly and in confusion.

They dashed helter-skelter out of the room.

Hem : HEM IN. Restrain ; restrict.

The enemy's troops were hemmed in between the mountains and the river.

Here : HERE AND THERE. Scattered ; distributed.

They looked down upon fields and woods, with a farmhouse here and there.

(*Note.*—Also used in a more literal and slightly different sense to mean " in this direction, here, and that direction, there ". See HITHER AND THITHER.)

HERE TO-DAY AND GONE TO-MORROW. Merely temporary ; staying for a short time in any place.

NEITHER HERE NOR THERE. Immaterial to a discussion, etc.

I would rather stay, but that's neither here nor there.

Herod : OUT-HEROD HEROD. Or. Shakespeare. To be excessively wicked.

The villain out-Heroded Herod in the crimes he committed.

Hide : HIDE HIS DIMINISHED HEAD. Exhibit shame ; admit inferiority.

When you see what your sin has done you will hide your diminished head.

HIDE UNDER A BUSHEL. Or. Biblical (" Neither do men light a candle and put it under a bushel "). Conceal one's talents or virtues through modesty. The phrase is generally used in the negative.

He was never one to hide his cleverness under a bushel.

High : HIGHDAYS, HOLIDAYS AND BONFIRE NIGHTS. An old-f. facetious phrase applied to celebrations in general.

It's a dress I wear on highdays, holidays and bonfire nights.

HIGH-FALUTIN'. High-flown ; absurdly elaborate and fantastic (generally applied to speech).

Stop talking that high-falutin' nonsense.

HIGH JINKS (S.). A gay time.

They tell me you had high jinks at the village hall last night.

HIGHLY (PROBABLE, *etc.*). Idiomatically used to indicate to a great extent.

He was highly annoyed at her rudeness.

HIGH-SOUNDING. Pompous ; magnificent.

Though he possesses high-sounding titles, he is a very poor man.

HIGH SPOT Outstanding attraction.

The high spot of the revue was Miss Smith's dancing.

HIGH TABLE. The end table, usually at right-angles to the others and raised, at which the masters and other important personages of a college dine.

HIGH TEA. An evening meal which combines meat or some similar extra dish with the usual tea.

HIGH TIME. Fully time ; applied to an event already due, if not overdue. See HIGHLY.

Look at the clock ; it's high time you went to bed.

Highway : QUEEN'S HIGHWAY. All public roads and thoroughfares along which the public has a right to travel (but, legally, only to travel, not to linger upon, or to obstruct).

Hint : BROAD HINT. A stressed, an obvious hint.

He received a broad hint that we did not want him to call again.

DROP, *or* THROW OUT, A HINT. Hint in a casual manner.

I'm tired of fish for dinner—you might drop a hint to the cook.

Hit : HIT IT OFF. Agree.

It is unfortunate that Charles and Mary don't hit it off.

See SEE EYE TO EYE and GET ON.

HIT THE (RIGHT) NAIL ON THE HEAD. Guess or judge correctly.

Angela's father hit the nail on the head when he said that her chief fault was vanity.

HIT UPON. Discover (usually unexpectedly).

I've hit upon a new method of extracting salt from sea-water.

Hither : HITHER AND THITHER. Here and there; in this direction and in that direction.

We searched hither and thither, but could not find her.

Hoary : HOARY AGE. Age when one's hair has turned white, or hoary; very old.

He died at the hoary age of ninety.

(*Note.*—Hoary is frequently used as the equivalent of very old in connection with other matters, e.g. *a hoary joke.*)

Hocus-pocus : The words traditionally uttered by a conjuror as he performs a trick; hence, a cheat, a swindle. Or. Either the name of a famous French conjuror—*Ochus Boshus*, or the Welsh *Hocca pucca*.

I think the whole thing is complete hocus-pocus.

Hoist : HOIST WITH ONE'S OWN PETARD. Beaten with one's own weapons; caught in one's own trap. Or. The mediæval "petard", an engine designed, when filled with gunpowder, to blow in a city gate. There was extreme risk of those who fired it being destroyed too.

Hold : HOLD ALOOF. Remain deliberately apart; isolated.

I asked Joe for his political views, but he said he preferred to hold aloof.

HOLD CHEAP. Regard as having little value.

All his expressions of sorrow I hold cheap.

HOLD FORTH. Discourse; orate.

The preacher held forth for an hour on the wickedness of Man.

HOLD GOOD. Remain unaffected and unaltered.

My promise to visit you next summer holds good.

HOLD, *or* STAND, ONE'S GROUND. Not yield.

It was a hard struggle, but we held our ground, and won in the end.

HOLD IN. Restrain.

I'm trying to hold in the horses.

HOLD ON. Continue one's grasp.

If you can hold on a little longer, you'll be saved.

HOLD ONE'S OWN. Maintain successfully one's opinion, argument, or position.

Young George can generally hold his own when discussing politics.

HOLD OUT. 1. As HOLD ON. 2. Extend, offer.

I can hold out no hope of the invalid recovering.

HOLD OVER. 1. Keep back; reserve.

I have some more news, but I will hold it over for my next letter.

2. Use some knowledge as a threat.

The woman discovered he had once been in prison, and was constantly holding it over him.

HOLD TOGETHER. Remain undivided; not separated.

I've tied up the parcel with string, but I am afraid it won't hold together.

HOLD UP. Delay.

The train was held up for an hour by the accident.

HOLD WATER. See **Water.**

HOLD WITH. Concur; agree with.

I don't hold with whipping little children.

Hole : HOLE-AND-CORNER. Furtive; secret.

Their meeting was a hole-and-corner affair.

Homage : PAY, *or* GIVE, HOMAGE TO. Show respect and reverence.

They came to pay homage to the old musician on his birthday.

Home : AT HOME. Formal social idiom generally used by servants to indicate that the mistress of the house is out or is not prepared to receive a visitor.

" I am sorry, sir, but her Ladyship is not at home." See also **Out** (2).

BRING A THING HOME TO A PERSON. Compel him to realize it.

The cold and empty house brought the tragedy home to the old man.

GO TO ONE'S LAST HOME. Old f. Be buried.

Poor George went to his last home a month ago.

MAKE ONESELF AT HOME. Behave informally, as though the house was one's own.

Do sit down by the fire and make yourself at home.

Honour : AN AFFAIR OF HONOUR. Old f. A duel.

A DEBT OF HONOUR. A debt which cannot be legally enforced—e.g. a gambling debt, or one which is purely moral.

She was very kind to me when I was a child, and I consider it a debt of honour to help her now.

DO THE HONOURS. Act as host (or hostess).

As Mother was away, Aunt Mary did the honours at the party.

A POINT OF HONOUR. Conduct arising from one's own particular sense of honour or fitness.

It was a point of honour with the old man to walk a mile every day.

Hook : BY HOOK OR BY CROOK. By any method, right or wrong ; without scruples.

He swore to obtain the money by hook or by crook.

HOOK IT ! (S.). Old f. Depart.

SLING ONE'S HOOK (S.). Old f. As above.

Sling your hook, or I'll thrash you !

Horizon : ON THE HORIZON. Met., Used for something planned for the remote future.

We've all sorts of schemes on the horizon.

Horn : DRAW IN ONE'S HORNS. Withdraw or abandon plans. Or. A snail's " horns ", which are drawn in if it senses danger.

Owing to shortage of money, the ambitious young architect has had to draw in his horns considerably.

Hornet's nest : STIR UP A HORNET'S NEST, *or* PUT ONE'S HAND IN A HORNET'S NEST. Create trouble by interfering unwisely.

If you try to stop Peter calling there, you'll stir up a hornet's nest.

Horse : A DARK HORSE. Or. Racing. A person whose qualities and possibilities are unknown.

Smith is very frank and friendly, but Simpson seems to be a dark horse.

HOBBY-HORSE ; *usually abbrev. to* HOBBY. Originally a vehicle like a roughly-shaped horse, on which the rider sat and propelled himself along. The spare time subject in which one is specially interested and occupied.

HORSE LAUGH. A loud, vulgar laugh.

LOOK A GIFT HORSE IN THE MOUTH. Examine too critically anything which is a present. Or. The proverb, " Never look a gift horse in the mouth." (A horse's age is judged by the condition of its teeth.)

ON ONE'S HIGH HORSE Assuming a haughty or superior attitude.

It's no use your being on your high horse because you've got a rich father.

Also TRYING TO RIDE THE HIGH HORSE.

Hot : HOT STUFF (S.). Exceptionally brilliant, daring, unconventional, etc.

I spent an exciting evening with young George ; he's hot stuff.

HOT WATER. See under **Water**.

Hour : IN AN EVIL HOUR. On an unlucky occasion.

Then, in an evil hour, the girl met that good-looking young scamp.

IMPROVE THE SHINING HOUR. Abbrev. quotation from child's poem, " How doth the little busy bee improve each shining hour ". Employ time as one wishes ; take advantage of an opportunity.

Jane's mother went out, and Jane improved the shining hour by talking to the boy next door.

ONE'S LAST HOUR ; ONE'S HOUR. The final moments of life.

The unhappy wretch, realizing that his last hour had come, did not defend himself.

THE SMALL HOURS. The early hours of the morning, i.e. between 1 and 4 a.m.

THE WITCHING HOUR. Old f., poetical. Midnight ; the time when witches are said to exercise their powers.

We'll meet by the church at the witching hour.

House : BRING DOWN THE HOUSE. Give a tremendously popular performance, not necessarily in a theatre, of any type. Or. Theatrical, to receive so much applause that the building shakes.

She brought down the house with her humorous recitations after dinner.

HOUSE-WARMING. A dinner-party, etc., given to celebrate the settling down in a new house, a return after a long absence, or any similar occasion.

KEEP OPEN HOUSE. Welcome visitors, without invitation, at any time.

The Montagues are rich enough to be able to keep open house.

How : HOW ARE YOU ? Same as HOW DO YOU DO ?,
HOW COMES IT ? ; HOW IS IT ? How or why does it
happen ?

How comes it that you are always late on Monday?

HOW DO YOU DO ? The usual formal greeting. (" Do "
should be " du " from the Anglo-Saxon " dugan ",
" to go ".)

HOW GOES IT ? (S.). How are you and your affairs
progressing ?

HOW IS —— ? Abbrev. for How (= in what state)
is the health of —— ?

How is the invalid this morning?

Hue : HUE AND CRY. Or. Legal. (Fr. *huer*, to shout after.)
Applied to a body of people in pursuit of a criminal,
or suspected criminal.

They raised a hue and cry, but the thief escaped.

Hug : HUG THE SHORE. Or. Nautical. Keep close to the
shore.

*The ship hugged the shore, to escape the fury of the
storm.*

Hum : HUM AND HAW. Hesitate ; procrastinate.

*He hummed and hawed so long when I asked him to
come out that I finally went alone.*

Humour : OUT OF HUMOUR. Irritable ; depressed and unre-
sponsive. See also **Temper.**

*The old man was obviously out of humour, and scarcely
spoke at all.*

Hunt : HUNT DOWN. Hunt or persecute until the victim is
finally caught or overcome.

The police are trying to hunt down the burglar.

HUNT UP. Search for.

You'll have to hunt up the word in the dictionary.

Hurl : HURL DEFIANCE. Openly and loudly defy. Frequently used facetiously.

The small kitten hurled defiance at the big dog.

Hurly-burly : Tumult ; the noise and struggle of crowds.

We left London to escape the hurly-burly of City life.

Hurry : HURRY ON WITH. Hasten.

Please hurry on with your work.

See HURRY UP ; LOOK ALIVE, etc.

HURRY UP. Hasten, move more quickly.

Hurry up, or we shall miss the train.

Husband : HUSBAND ONE'S RESOURCES. To " husband " is
to take care of, to use economically. " Resources "
are all the capital one has.

I

Idea : FIXED IDEA (Fr. *idée fixe*). A belief that no argument
will alter.
He has a fixed idea that he's universally popular.

Ilk : THAT ILK. The same name.
*He's called Snook, and he lives in a village of that
ilk.*

Ill : ILL-ASSORTED. Incompatible ; badly matched.
They were an ill-assorted couple.

ILL-AT-EASE. Uncomfortable ; in a state of embarrassment.
*The boy was ill-at-ease in the presence of the head-
master.*

ILLS THAT FLESH IS HEIR TO. The troubles of human
life. (A common misquotation from *Hamlet*,
which should read " the thousand natural *shocks*
that flesh is heir to ".)
She seems to suffer all the ills that flesh is heir to.

Image : THE IMAGE ; THE VERY IMAGE ; THE SPIT AND
IMAGE. Exactly like.
The baby is the very image of his father.

Imagination : FLIGHT *or* STRETCH OF IMAGINATION. Imaginative effort.
*The account of his adventures in Africa is a sheer
flight of imagination.*
*By no stretch of the imagination can I see George as
a successful tradesman.*

Impression : GIVE *or* CREATE A FALSE IMPRESSION. Mislead
by a statement or action.
*The story she has told gives a totally false impression
of what really happened.*
MAKE A GOOD IMPRESSION. Behave in a manner which
will create admiration and respect.
*Jones made a very good impression when he applied
for the job.*

In : IN FOR IT (S.). Involved.

> *When the door opened and a clerk called my name, I realized that I was in for it.*

IN WITH. On intimate or friendly terms.

> *I may be able to get you the job, as I'm in with the Chairman's family.*

Inch : EVERY INCH. Completely ; entirely.

> *John looks every inch a soldier.*

Incline : BE INCLINED TO. Have a tendency to ; be in favour of.

> *I am inclined to forgive him because of his youth.*

Incumbent : INCUMBENT UPON ONE. An essential duty for one.

> *It is incumbent upon you to provide for your parents.*

Inference : DRAW AN INFERENCE. Assume ; infer.

> *From his manner, we drew the inference that he was satisfied with the result of his visit.*

Infernal : THE INFERNAL REGIONS. Hell or Hades.

Influence : UNDER THE INFLUENCE. In full, " under the influence of intoxicating liquor ". The legal equivalent of " intoxicated " or " drunk " (for which there are innumerable slang terms).

Iniquity : SINK OF INIQUITY. Any place with a peculiarly vile reputation or where the lowest characters meet. (Frequently used facetiously.)

> *If you're going to the Club to play bridge, I'll join you in that sink of iniquity later on.*

In-laws : The relations of one's husband or wife—MOTHER-IN-LAW, SISTER-IN-LAW, *etc.*

> *Three of my in-laws are visiting us next week.*

Ins-and-outs : THE INS-AND-OUTS. All the details.

> *I haven't heard all the ins-and-outs of the story yet.*

Instance : FOR INSTANCE. As an example ; to explain or elaborate one's meaning.

> *What would you do if you met a wild animal—a lion, for instance ?*

See FOR EXAMPLE.

Intercourse : HOLD INTERCOURSE WITH. Talk to, or communicate with.

> *I don't want to hold any further intercourse with you or your family.*

Interest : OUT AT INTEREST. Invested ; lent at a fixed rate of interest.

I've put £500 out at four per cent.

Interim : IN THE INTERIM. From now until some specified event occurs.

We leave for Paris next week ; in the interim we shall be visiting our friends.

See FOR THE TIME BEING.

Interval : AT INTERVALS. At irregular periods of time.

The discussion continued ; at intervals the speakers stopped for refreshment.

Iota : ONE IOTA. The smallest possible quantity. Or. The iota is the smallest letter of the Greek alphabet.

I don't care an iota what the result may be.

(*Note.*—This idiom is always used in the negative.)

Irons : IRONS IN THE FIRE. Matters of immediate interest or importance which may also prove profitable.

Even if I don't get the job, I have other irons in the fire.

THE IRON ENTERING ONE'S SOUL. Suffering mental torture, agony of mind. Or. mediæval instruments of torture which pierced the body.

His own son had betrayed him, and at the knowledge the iron entered into his soul.

PUT IN IRONS. Chained ; fettered.

The drunken seaman was so violent that the captain had to put him in irons.

(*Note.*—The phrase is now used almost entirely in connection with crime at sea.)

STRIKE WHILE THE IRON IS HOT. Act promptly, and while the conditions are in one's favour.

The old man was so friendly that I decided to strike while the iron was hot, and ask his consent to my marrying his daughter.

IRONBOUND COAST. A coast of granite or similar hardness, disastrous to wrecked ships.

Issue : CONFUSE THE ISSUE. Confuse the final analysis or result ; bring forward irrelevant arguments.

To talk about politics is merely to confuse the issue.

FORCE AN ISSUE. Compel a decision to be reached.

The King, determined to force the issue, threatened to abdicate unless Parliament admitted his supreme authority.

JOIN ISSUE. Disagree with.

On the question of Kipling's genius I join issue with you.

J

Jack : JACK OF ALL TRADES (AND MASTER OF NONE). One capable of undertaking a variety of jobs, but who is expert at none of them.

JACK O' LANTERN. Another name for the will-o'-the-wisp, the misleading light that shines above swamps and marshes.

BEFORE YOU CAN SAY JACK ROBINSON (S.). Extremely quickly.

He knocked, and before you could say Jack Robinson the door opened.

Also BEFORE YOU CAN SAY KNIFE.

Jail : JAIL-BIRD. A man or woman who has undergone a considerable period of imprisonment ; a professional criminal.

Jaundice : VIEW WITH A JAUNDICED EYE. Regard with jealousy, envy and distrust. Jaundice is a disease which turns the skin temporarily yellow, and yellow is the colour associated with jealousy.

Jiffy : IN A JIFFY, *or* HALF A JIFFY. Very soon ; almost immediately. (The origin of this word is unknown.) Also **Moment** and **Tick.**

Job : JOB'S COMFORTER. Or. Biblical. One who comes nominally to console and comfort a person, but who actually adds to his distress by being pessimistic and reproachful.

Jim is a regular Job's comforter ; he pointed out that my misfortunes had probably only just begun.

Jog : JOG ALONG. To " jog " is to proceed at a slow, regular pace. Used almost always metaphorically to indicate quiet and unexciting progress.

When we are married, I expect we shall jog along as happily as most people.

JOG-TROT. Progress as above.

JOG A PERSON'S MEMORY. Remind, in order to prevent something being forgotten.

Join : JOIN THE GREAT MAJORITY. Join the dead ; die.

Joke : CRACK A JOKE. Make a joke ; tell a humorous story.
They seem to spend most of their time cracking jokes.

Jot : JOT OR TITTLE. " Jot " is a corruption of " iota "
(which see) ; " tittle " means something tiny.
Jot or tittle, like iota, is always used negatively.
I don't care a jot or tittle what you think of my conduct.

JOT DOWN. Note briefly and quickly.
I will jot down all your instructions.

Judgment : SIT IN JUDGMENT. Formally judge.
You've no right to sit in judgment on my actions.

Jump : JUMP AT. Take a quick advantage of ; seize an
opportunity.
*The house is a bargain, and you should jump at the
offer.*

AT ONE JUMP. Instantly.
He realized the position at one jump.

Justice : DO JUSTICE TO. Treat justly or fairly ; appreciate
fully (used frequently in reference to food).
Our guests did justice to my wife's excellent cooking.

K

Keep : KEEP ABREAST OF. Keep level with.
*We do our best to keep abreast of modern improve-
ments.*
See KEEP PACE WITH.

KEEP ALOOF. Remain distant from, physically or in
manner. See KEEP ONE'S DISTANCE.

KEEP COMPANY. 1. Associate with.
A man is known by the company he keeps.

2. Old f. The working-class equivalent of affianced
or engaged.
*Bill and Jane have been keeping company for nearly
a year.*

KEEP DARK. Conceal ; refrain from mentioning.
*I'm going out with David to-night, but please keep it
dark.*

KEEP ONE'S COUNTENANCE. See under **Countenance.**

KEEP ONE'S COUNSEL. Remain silent and reticent.

KEEP ONE'S DISTANCE ; KEEP AT ARM'S LENGTH. Maintain one's correct and formal attitude.

The servant was too familiar, and I told him to keep his distance.

KEEP AN EYE ON. Watch ; act as temporary guardian to.

I would be glad if you'd keep an eye on the garden while we're away.

KEEP GOING ; KEEP ABOUT. Continue at one's work or routine.

He looks terribly ill ; I don't know how long he'll be able to keep going.

KEEP GUARD. Watch ; act as sentinel.

You keep guard, while I go and find a policeman.

KEEP ONE'S HAND IN. Continue to practice, in order to retain one's skill.

I've retired from " The Daily Record ", but I still write an occasional article to keep my hand in.

KEEP HOUSE. Act as the manager of a household.

When his wife died his sister went to keep house for him.

KEEP IN WITH. Remain on good terms with, usually with some definite motive.

Brown is rich and successful, and I want to keep in with him.

KEEP IT UP. Continue in the same manner.

I've been working twelve hours a day, but shall not be able to keep it up.

KEEP AS A HOLIDAY, *etc.* Set aside ; dedicate.

We keep January the first as a holiday.

KEEP ON. Persist in ; repeat one's present actions.

Don't keep on asking silly questions.

KEEP OUT OF THE WAY. Absent or efface oneself.

When father's angry we keep out of his way.

KEEP A STIFF UPPER LIP. Not allow one's lip to tremble with emotion ; be firm and brave.

Always keep a stiff upper lip, whatever your trouble.

KEEP PACE, *or* KEEP UP, WITH. Move at an equal speed.

KEEP THE PEACE. Maintain peace.

The mother did her best to keep the peace between her quarrelsome sons.

KEEP SECRET. Similar to KEEP IT DARK.

KEEP IN TOUCH WITH. See **Touch.**

KEEP UP. Continue.

We wrote frequently at first, but I had not time to keep up the correspondence.

KEEP UP WITH. Similar to KEEP PACE WITH, lit. and met.

I can't keep up with you—you walk too fast.

It is difficult to keep up with all these new inventions.

IN KEEPING WITH. (Negative form—OUT OF KEEPING WITH.) Appropriate to; suitable to.

The mourners wore black, in keeping with the sad occasion.

Kick : KICK THE BUCKET (S.). Die.

Our poor old cat has kicked the bucket.

See also PASS AWAY; GO WEST (under **West**).

KICK UP A ROW, SHINDY *or* RUMPUS (S.). Cause a violent disturbance; quarrel.

If I refuse to go to the theatre, my wife is sure to kick up a row.

Kind : KIND OFFICES. Old f. and formal. Friendly exertions or efforts.

I shall be grateful if you will use your kind offices on my behalf.

KILL WITH KINDNESS. Overwhelm with too much kindness.

His parents were so glad to see the boy that they almost killed him with kindness.

Kiss : KISS THE BOOK, "The Book" being the Bible, which witnesses, unless of a non-Christian faith, are required to touch with their lips when taking the oath in a court of law.

KISS HANDS. Part of the formal ceremony of accepting an office.

KISS THE ROD. Old f. Submit meekly to punishment.

Knight : KNIGHT ERRANT. In mediæval days, an armed knight who roamed about the countryside, prepared to defend oppressed and helpless maidens. The phrase is to-day applied to any chivalrous man who, without expecting reward, helps and protects a weak or helpless person.

Knit : KNIT ONE'S BROWS. Frown ; regard in a puzzled way. (" Knit " in this idiom means to draw towards one another.)

He knitted his brows over the difficulty of getting home.

Knock : KNOCK ABOUT. 1. Wander, gaining experience in the process.

I've knocked about the world for forty years.

2. Injure physically.

Her husband was a brute, and used to knock her about cruelly.

KNOCK DOWN. Strike a person so violently that he falls.

KNOCK-DOWN ARGUMENT. A final and overwhelming argument.

KNOCK DOWN TO. Sell to a person who has made a final bid at an auction sale. (An auctioneer gives a sharp rap with his hammer (more correctly " gavel ") when the highest and final bid has been made, and the article or " lot " is then legally the property of the bidder.) See UNDER THE HAMMER (under **Hammer**).

KNOCK OFF (S.). Cease work for the day.

We knock off at one o'clock on Saturday.

KNOCK ON THE HEAD. Lit., Kill.

George, poor fellow, was knocked on the head during the war.

Met., Destroy.

We'll soon knock his scheme on the head.

KNOCK OUT. Or. Prizefighting. Verb. Render incapable of further fighting.

He was knocked out in ten minutes.

Noun and adjective (with hyphen). 1. Lit., The blow which officially ends a fight.

Jones received the knock-out in the fifth round.

2. Met. (S.). An astonishing or startling object.

Jenny's new hat is a knock-out.

KNOCK OVER. Overturn ; upset. Met. (S.). Completely overwhelm.

The family was completely knocked over at the news.

Also KNOCK ALL OF A HEAP (S.).

KNOCK UP. 1. Rouse from sleep by knocking at the door. 2. (S.). Make ill or unfit.

Mary has been knocked up by the news.

Knot: TIE THE (NUPTIAL) KNOT. Old f. and formal for "marry".
The parson will tie the knot at one o'clock on Tuesday.

Know : KNOW THE ROPES. See under **Ropes.**

KNOW A THING OR TWO (S.). Be shrewd ; possess worldly wisdom.
Bert is a smart lad ; he knows a thing or two.
See KNOW ALL THE ANSWERS (under **Answer**).

Knuckle : KNUCKLE UNDER, *or* DOWN. Surrender. Lit., Kneel for pardon. (" Knuckle " here means the knee. There is also said to be a custom of striking the under side of the table with one's knuckles when beaten in an argument.)

RAP ON THE KNUCKLE. See **Rap.**

L

Labour : LABOUR OF LOVE. Work performed from affection or regard, and without expectation of payment.
It was a labour of love to help her father.

LABOUR A POINT. Over-stress a point in one's argument.
I realise that I am an alien—you need not labour the point.

LABOUR UNDER AN AFFLICTION. Suffer from some handicap or inconvenience, usually permanent.
She laboured under the affliction of having a drunken husband.

LABOUR UNDER A DELUSION, ILLUSION, ERROR, MISTAKE. Be influenced by some false idea.
If he thinks Susan will marry him, he is labouring under a delusion.
Emily labours under the illusion that half the young men in the village want to marry her.

Lady : LADY BOUNTIFUL. A generous and kindly woman ; one who looks after the poor in a village.

LADIES' MAN. One who makes special efforts to charm or please women.

Laid : LAID UP. 1. In bed through illness or accident.
I've been laid up all the week with influenza.
2. Nautical. In harbour for repairs, etc.
The Captain has a month's holiday ; his ship is laid up at Portsmouth.
See LIE UP.

LAID BY THE HEELS. Captured.

Land : SEE HOW THE LAND LIES. Discover the state of affairs ; make discreet enquiries.

> *Marion is calling on her father first, to see how the land lies.*

Land-slide (*political*). A sudden complete change of political popularity and, as a result, political power in an election.

Lap : LAP OF LUXURY. Extreme luxury.

> *The Princess had lived in the lap of luxury all her life.*

Large : AT LARGE. Free after escaping.

> *Two lions from the Zoo are at large.*

See AT LIBERTY.

Last : AT LAST. Eventually ; after a long time has passed.

> *At last we are together again.*

AT LONG LAST. As above, but more emphatic.

AT ONE'S LAST GASP. In an utterly exhausted, or almost dying, condition.

> *The explorers were at their last gasp when they were rescued.*

ON ONE'S LAST LEGS. Almost, though not quite, exhausted. (The idiom is also applied to any affair, etc., which is on the verge of failing.)

> *Their business is on its last legs through bad management.*

Late : LATE LAMENTED. Old f. Deceased. The phrase was once commonly used in funeral notices, epitaphs, etc.

Laugh ; Laughter : CONVULSED WITH LAUGHTER. Laughing so excessively that one is practically helpless.

LAUGH IN ONE'S SLEEVE. Be secretly amused, hear with secret contempt.

> *The Duke's singing was loudly applauded, but most of his audience were laughing in their sleeves.*

LAUGH ON THE WRONG SIDE OF ONE'S MOUTH *or* ON THE OTHER SIDE OF ONE'S FACE. Be the reverse of amused ; be depressed or unhappy.

> *You'll laugh on the wrong side of your mouth when I tell your father.*

LAUGH TO SCORN. Scorn openly and contemptuously.

> *The earl laughed them to scorn when they offered to buy his castle.*

Launch : LAUNCHED INTO ETERNITY. Old f. Suddenly killed ; executed. (The phrase is usually applied to hanging.)

LAUNCH OUT, *or* EMBARK. Or. Naval. Depart from one's normal habits or occupation.

He launched out in an extravagant way of living.

Laurels : WIN LAURELS. Acquire honour. Or. The Roman custom of crowning a victor with laurel wreaths.

The boy won laurels on the cricket field, as well as in his studies.

Law : ARM OF THE LAW. Criminal law, personified by the police.

The arm of the law stopped him as he was escaping to France.

THE EYE, *or* EYES, OF THE LAW. From a legal standpoint.

In the eye of the law, you are a trespasser here.

HAVE THE LAW (S.). Prosecute in a court of law.

If you write any more such libellous letters, I'll have the law on you.

A LAW UNTO HIMSELF. One who follows his own inclinations, regardless of custom.

George is a law unto himself where manners are concerned.

LAW-ABIDING. One who obeys the law.

I've been law-abiding all my life.

LAW OF THE MEDES AND PERSIANS. An unalterable rule. Or. Any law passed by the rulers of the Medes and Persians could never be changed or repealed.

I should like to go out, but it's a law of the Medes and Persians that the house should not be left unoccupied.

SET THE LAW AT DEFIANCE. See under **Set.**

TAKE THE LAW INTO ONE'S OWN HANDS. Ignore the legal method of obtaining justice, and act entirely as one considers suitable and just.

I took the law into my own hands, and gave the young scoundrel a thrashing.

Lay : LAY ABOUT ONE. Strike out violently in every direction.

The captured man laid about him with his stick.

LAY, *or* PUT ASIDE ; LAY BY. 1. Abandon, usually for a short time.

She laid aside her household work to entertain the visitor.

2. Put away for future use.

I've laid aside £20 for the wedding.

LAY A BET. Place a bet or wager.

LAY AT ONE'S DOOR, *or* TO ONE'S CHARGE. Place the blame or responsibility.

The death of the patient was laid at the doctor's door.
You cannot lay that crime to my charge.

LAY DOWN ONE'S ARMS. Surrender one's weapons as a conquered person.

LAY DOWN THE LAW. Make any statement with an air of authority and as one who does not expect to be contradicted.

LAY ONE'S HANDS ON. Obtain possession of, or (in the case of a person) arrest.

The police hope to lay their hands on the murderer.

LAY OUR HEADS TOGETHER. See under **Head.**

LAY IN, *or* LAY UP. Store for future use.

Preparing for the siege, the population laid in a large store of provisions.

(Note the slight but definite difference between LAY BY and LAY IN.)

LAY ON THICK (S.). Exaggerate greatly, either praise or blame ; but usually praise or flattery.

Jim says Mary is lovely, but you might be sure that he would lay it on thick.

LAY ONESELF OPEN TO. Expose oneself to ; lead to an unfavourable assumption.

His foolish actions laid him open to a charge of stealing.

LAY OUT. Spend systematically, often on stock, or as an investment.

I'm going to lay out £500 in fittings for my shop.

LAY STRESS ON. Emphasize.

The Chancellor laid stress on the need for economy.

Lead : LEAD TO THE ALTAR. Old f. Marry. (The "leading" is invariably done by the bridegroom.)

LEAD A DANCE (S.). Cause considerable trouble and activity of a trivial type.

The chicken led us a dance before we caught it.

LEAD BY THE NOSE (S.). Control a person as completely as if he were a horse being led by a rope.
That terrible Mrs. Juggins leads her wretched husband by the nose.

LEAD OFF. Act as the leader in beginning any function : dancing, singing, etc. ; start.

LEAD THE WAY ; TAKE THE LEAD. Similar to LEAD OFF, but also frequently used in the literal sense of going first to point the way.
The inspector led the way to the scene of the crime.

LEAD UP THE GARDEN PATH (S.). Mislead ; deceive.
Don't let that fellow lead you up the garden path.

LEAD UP TO. Progress gradually towards.
I tried tactfully to lead up to our marriage.

TAKE THE LEAD or LEADING PART. Act as leader or chief person.
George always takes the lead when we're arranging an entertainment.

LEADING-STRINGS. Lit., Strings by which children were formerly supported while learning to walk. To-day used met. to indicate complete moral control and guidance.
She kept her son in leading-strings until he was married.

NOTE. In all the above instances, LEAD is pronounced LEED.

Lead : SWING THE LEAD (S.) (pron. " led "). Exaggerate ; invent stories.
He told me he once shot ten lions in one day, but I'm certain he was swinging the lead.
See also DRAW THE LONG BOW.

Leaf : TAKE A LEAF OUT OF A PERSON'S BOOK. Copy ; take as an example.
I wish you'd take a leaf out of Peter's book, and get up early.

TURN OVER A NEW LEAF. Alter ; change ; make a fresh and better beginning.
She has promised to turn over a new leaf, and to be more punctual.

Leap : BY LEAPS AND BOUNDS. With extreme rapidity.
Our sales are increasing by leaps and bounds.

A LEAP IN THE DARK. An action the result of which is uncertain or unknown.

Their marriage on his small income was a leap in the dark, but it proved a complete success.

Learn : LEARN BY HEART. See under **Heart.**

See COMMIT TO MEMORY.

Least : AT LEAST. As the minimum.

If you can't give me ten shillings, at least you can pay my fare home.

LEAST SAID, SOONEST MENDED. The less one says, the better.

We shan't see the scoundrel again, and the least said soonest mended.

TO SAY THE LEAST OF IT. To minimize ; express as mildly as possible.

His rudeness was, to say the least of it, unlikely to make him popular.

Leave : BEG LEAVE. Old f., formal. Ask permission.

May I beg leave to remind you that it is nearly noon.

LEAVE BEHIND. 1. Forget.

John has left his spectacles behind ; he'll be half blind.

2. Deliberately discard.

I've left my umbrella behind ; it isn't going to rain.

LEAVE IN, *or* OUT IN, THE COLD. Ignore ; take no notice of, or interest in.

I am anxious that my country cousin shall not feel left out in the cold at the party.

See SEND TO COVENTRY.

LEAVE IN THE LURCH. Abandon in circumstances of danger and difficulty. Or. The card-game called cribbage, in which the " lurch " is a hopeless position.

George ran away, leaving me in the lurch.

LEAVE OFF. 1. Cease to wear a garment (transitive verb).

I've left off my overcoat.

2. Cease ; stop what one is doing (intransitive verb).

The children are making too much noise ; tell them to leave off.

LEAVE OUT. Omit.

We can leave out the third sentence.

LEAVE A PERSON TO IT. Leave a person alone to continue in his own way.

If you think you can finish cleaning that picture, I'll leave you to it.

See LEAVE TO ONESELF.

LEAVE AT THE POST. Or. Racing. See under POST.

LEAVE TO ONESELF. Leave in solitude, without interference.

If you leave him to himself, he'll be quite happy.

(Very similar to LEAVE A PERSON TO IT.)

LEAVE WORD. Leave a message, verbal or written.

TAKE FRENCH LEAVE. Abandon one's work or post without obtaining the necessary permission from one's superior.

The servants have taken French leave and gone to the dance.

TAKE LEAVE. 1. Venture.

I take leave to differ from you.

2. Depart; say farewell to.

The boy took leave of his mother, and caught the train to London.

Leeway: MAKE UP LEEWAY. Or. Nautical. Compensate for time which has been lost. "Leeway" is the distance which a ship has drifted from the position in which she should have been.

The train was late, and we had an hour's leeway to make up.

Left: LEFT-HANDED COMPLIMENT. One which is the reverse of complimentary.

Jim paid me a left-handed compliment when he said he liked talking to a girl who wasn't particularly clever.

Leg: GIVE A LEG-UP (S.). Lit., Help a person to mount his horse. Help generally.

We'd better give Tom a leg-up with his work, or it won't be finished.

LEG IT; LEG IT ALONG (S.). Walk steadily; go forward at a good pace.

We must leg it along if we are to get there before dark.

See PUT ONE'S BEST FOOT FOREMOST.

NOT A LEG TO STAND ON. Having nothing effective in support of an argument.

George is sure that England will become a republic, but he hasn't a leg to stand on.

Legion : THEIR NAME IS LEGION. Or. Biblical, " My name is legion, for we are many ". The phrase is applied to a vast number.

As for the homeless, their name is legion.

Length : AT LENGTH. After considerable time ; eventually.
At length the wanderers reached their home.

GO TO ANY LENGTHS ; STOP AT NOTHING. Ignore every impediment, legal or otherwise, that may get in one's way.

He would go to any lengths to be revenged.

Let : LET ALONE.   1. Refrain from interfering with
Let that bottle alone.

2. In addition to being (or having).
She was ugly, let alone old.

LET BE. Same as LET ALONE (1).

LET DOWN. Betray ; fail to support when support was needed.

My brother promised to give evidence for me, but he let me down.

LET FALL *(applied to speech)*. Remark casually.
He let fall a hint of trouble.

LET FLY.   1. Lit., Propel swiftly.
He let fly an arrow.

2. Met., Abandon control.
He lost his temper, and let fly.

LET GO. Release one's hold.
He let go of the rope, and crashed to the ground.

LET SOMEONE IN.   1. Admit.
John knocked, and I let him in.

2. Involve a person without his knowledge or consent, make responsible for.

The swindler let me in for nearly £50.

LET OFF.   1. Allow to go free and unpunished.
The prisoner was let off with some good advice.

2. Explode.
We let off fireworks on November 5th.

LET ON (S.). Tell; make public.
I'm going to the circus to-night—don't let on.
See LET OUT (2).

LET OUT. 1. Release; set free.
I'll open the cage and let out the bird.

2. Disclose; reveal. (Similar to LET ON, except that it always has an object.)
I'll tell you a secret, but you mustn't let it out.

LET PASS. Ignore.
I will let your rudeness pass.

LET WELL ALONE. Refrain from interfering, because it may do more harm than good.
See LET SLEEPING DOGS LIE.

Letter : TO THE LETTER. Exactly; precisely.
His recital was correct to the letter.
(*Note.*—The idiom always follows the statement.)

THE LETTER OF THE LAW. Exactly in accordance with the rules and regulations of the law. Its opposite is THE SPIRIT OF THE LAW.

BREAD-AND-BUTTER LETTER. One written when a visit is over, thanking one's hostess.

Level : DO ONE'S LEVEL BEST. Do one's utmost; use all one's efforts.
I'll do my best to be at the concert.

KEEP A LEVEL HEAD. Remain calm and sensible.
In these exciting times, it isn't always easy to keep a level head.

Liberal : LIBERAL EDUCATION. One planned on broad principles. The phrase is entirely non-political, "liberal" here meaning "ample, abundant". (A liberal education implies also one which includes subjects taught at the Universities.)

Liberty : AT LIBERTY. Free; unrestrained.
You are at liberty to wander anywhere in the park.
See under **Set free.**

TAKE THE LIBERTY. Old f. and formal. Act as though one possessed a right which in fact one does not; presume.
I have taken the liberty to re-arrange the books in your library.

TAKE LIBERTIES (*not* the plural form of the above).

Go beyond the normal limits of convention or good manners.

She was one of those who invariably take liberties in a friend's house.

Lick : LICK INTO SHAPE. Discipline, socially or otherwise. Or. The licking by its mother of a new-born bear or similar cub. See UNLICKED CUB, under **Cub.**

Lie : GIVE THE LIE TO. Completely deny ; disprove.

His story will give the lie to the rumours we have been hearing.

LIE AT ONE'S DOOR. Become one's responsibility.

The child's death will lie at your door.

LIE TO. Or. Naval. Rest in harbour or dock.

LIE UP. 1. As above.

2. Lie in bed as the result of an illness or accident.

Mother has strained her back, and has had to lie up.

(*Note.*—The passive form of this idiom is *laid*. See LAID UP.)

WHITE LIE. A harmless lie told only with the object of helping or comforting someone.

Lieu : IN LIEU OF. Instead of ; in place of.

He gave me his watch in lieu of my own, which had been stolen.

Life : AS LARGE AS LIFE. This idiom is used in a general rather than an exact and literal sense, as emphasis.

There stood George, as large as life.

BREATH OF LIFE. Absolutely essential.

Liberty is the breath of life to every Englishman.

COME TO LIFE. Become alive ; give an indication of being alive.

The motionless figure opened its eyes and came to life, and we realized that it was a real person.

FOR THE LIFE OF ME. Lit., " Even if what I am saying meant the loss of my life." An idiom used merely for emphasis.

For the life of me I can't understand what you're worrying about.

NEW LEASE OF LIFE. Fresh possibilities of continued existence.

My grandfather has recovered, and seems to have taken a new lease of life.

PRIME OF LIFE. The most fully-developed period of life (usually about forty).

SELL ONE'S LIFE DEAR. Fight fiercely to the last.
The knight determined to sell his life dear, and killed five of his enemies before he was struck down.

TO THE LIFE. Exactly; with complete realism.
The boy can imitate his old schoolmaster to the life.

Lift : LIFT UP, *or* RAISE, ONE'S VOICE. Or. Biblical. Speak or sing loudly, to praise, worship, etc.
Lift up your voices and praise God.

LIFT ONE'S HAND AGAINST. See under **Hand.**

Light : COME TO LIGHT. Be revealed, exposed.
His marriage came to light after his death.

THE LIGHT FANTASTIC. A gay dance. Abbrev. quotation from Milton's " L'Allegro "—" Come and trip it as you go On the light fantastic toe."

LIGHT-FINGERED. Thievish. "Light-fingered gentry " is a common phrase for pick-pockets.

LIGHT-FOOTED. Capable of moving lightly and quickly.

LIGHT O' LOVE. A prostitute.

LIGHT UPON. Discover by chance.
In an old bookshop I happened to light upon a volume belonging to my grandfather.

SHED, *or* THROW (A FLOOD OF) LIGHT ON. 1. Lit., Light brilliantly.
The searchlight threw a flood of light on the sea.
2. Met., Make clear and plain.
The article in the paper throws a flood of light on the position in China.

STRIKE A LIGHT. Ignite, e.g. a match, by friction.
Give me your box of matches, and I'll strike a light.

Like : LIKE ; THE LIKE. A similar object ; anything strongly resembling another of the same class.
We shall not meet his like again.
Apples, pears, and the like.

NOTHING LIKE. 1. Emphatic form of " unlike ".
That portrait is nothing like him.
2. Not nearly.
There were nothing like as many people as we expected.

Likelihood : IN ALL LIKELIHOOD. Very probably.
In all likelihood the missing boy has run away to sea.
See IN ALL PROBABILITY.

Likely : LIKELY ENOUGH. Fairly probable.
It is likely enough we shall meet at the station.
See ENOUGH.

Limit : THE LIMIT (S.). As far as one can go. (Used idiomatically as an expression of exasperation or disgust.)
George's rudeness is the limit !

Line : ALL ALONG THE LINE. Or. Military, the "line" being the line of battle. In every way ; completely.
I agree with you all along the line.

Lion : THE LION'S SHARE. The greatest or most valuable portion.
The comedian, as usual, received the lion's share of applause.

Lips : SMACK THE LIPS. Lit., Make an appreciative noise with the lips while eating. Met., An indication of intense enjoyment.
John smacked his lips at the prospect of going to Paris.

Liquor : IN LIQUOR. Intoxicated.

Little : LITTLE BY LITTLE, INCH BY INCH, *etc.* A small amount or distance, repeated until a large total is reached.
Little by little the servant stole his master's property.
LITTLE-GO. The preliminary or entrance examination at Cambridge University.

Live : LIVE DOWN. By good conduct enable one's neighbours to forget some past scandal or tragedy.
Many years ago she went to prison for stealing, but she has completely lived it down.
LIVE UP TO. Prove oneself worthy of.
These are magnificent furs ; I must try to live up to them.

Lo ! : LO AND BEHOLD ! An exclamatory introduction. ("Lo" is a shortened form of *loke*, Anglo-Saxon for "look".)
And lo and behold, the crown was on his head.

Loaves : LOAVES AND FISHES. Or. Biblical, from the Miracle of the Loaves and Fishes. Material possession ; wealth.
The bishop has always had a liking for the loaves and fishes.

Lock : LOCK, STOCK AND BARREL. Or. Military. Entirely ; wholly. A gun or pistol consists of three principal parts—the lock, containing the mechanism ; the stock, or wooden portion ; and the barrel.

I've bought the business, lock, stock and barrel.

Loggerheads : AT LOGGERHEADS. Disagreeing ; quarrelling.

Arthur and his wife are always at loggerheads.

Long : IN THE LONG RUN. At the end ; after a number of other things have happened.

In the long run, honesty is always recognized.

LONG AGO. A long time ago ; in the distant past.

LONG ARM OF COINCIDENCE. Applied to coincidences in general, the " long arm " referring to the surprising and abnormal way in which they occur.

John and Ellen separated. But the long arm of coincidence brought them together again in Paris a week later.

LONG-DRAWN. Long continued or sustained.

A long-drawn cry sounded across the sea.

LONG DURATION (*or* SHORT DURATION). A long (or short) period during which some event endures or continues.

Their journey was not, however, of long duration.

LONG ODDS. Or. Betting. Unfavourable chances ; an improbable event.

It is long odds against Peter winning the scholarship.

See under **Odds.**

THE LONG AND THE SHORT OF IT. The whole position or situation briefly stated.

The long and the short of it is that you won't work.

See IN SHORT.

LONG SHOT. Or. Shooting. See under **Shot.**

LONG-SPUN. Lengthy ; unnecessarily drawn out.

We listened to George's long-spun stories of the war.

LONG-STANDING. Existing for a long time.

I am keeping a long-standing engagement this evening.

LONG-SUFFERING. Patient and enduring.

His long-suffering parents saw with relief the boy depart for America.

LONG-TERM PLANS. Plans which extend a long way into the future.

LONG-WINDED. Verbose ; wearingly talkative.

He is one of the most long-winded preachers I have ever met.

Look : LOOK ABOUT ONE. Study one's surroundings and prospects.

I want to look about me for a week or two before I start work.

LOOK AFTER. Take care or charge of.

We promised to look after the cats while the family was abroad.

LOOK ALIVE, LIVELY *or* SHARP (S.). Hurry ; hasten.

Look alive, or we shall miss the train.

See HURRY UP.

LOOK BACK. Contemplate the past.

If we look back, we realize the changes war has made.

LOOK DAGGERS. Regard fiercely and bitterly ; look at with fury and hatred.

She looked daggers at her husband when he invited the actress to dinner.

LOOK DOWN UPON. Scorn ; regard with contempt.

The rich man looked down on his poorer neighbours.

LOOK FOR. 1. Search for.

She looked for the missing money.

2. Expect.

I look for civility from the tradesmen.

LOOK FOR A NEEDLE IN A HAYSTACK. Look for a small object in a large place, or for one person among many.

I tried to find John in the crowd, but it was like looking for a needle in a haystack.

LOOK FORWARD TO. Regard some future event with pleasure.

I look forward to your visit next week.

LOOK A GIFT HORSE IN THE MOUTH. See under **Horse.**

LOOK INTO. Examine ; scrutinize.

He promised to look into my father's affairs.

LOOK ON THE BRIGHT SIDE. Regard cheerfully ; see the best in any situation.

However bad his luck may be, Edward always looks on the bright side.

LOOK THE OTHER WAY. Met., Turn one's head ; refrain from noticing.

When the lovers kissed, I tactfully looked the other way.

LOOK OUT! (*exclamation*). Beware; be careful!
Look out, or you'll be run over!

LOOK OUT; KEEP A SHARP LOOKOUT FOR. Watch for.
Look out for George, or we shall miss him.

LOOK-OUT (with hyphen). Affair; concern; business.
Joan has decided to go to South America. What happens there is her own look-out.

LOOK OVER. 1. Lit.,
He looked over the wall.

2. Met., Scan; examine superficially.
I shall be glad if you'll look over these letters.

LOOK TO IT. Note; take careful action.
Look to it that you don't offend the old man.

LOOK UP. 1. Refer to books, etc., to ascertain some fact.
I'll look it up in the Encyclopædia.

2. Visit an acquaintance whom one hasn't seen for some time.
It's time I looked up old Bill again.

3. Improve; appear more cheerful.
The business is beginning to look up.

LOOK UP TO. Regard with awe or respect.
I shall always look up to my old schoolmaster.

LOOKER-ON. Spectator; observer.
I'm not an expert chess-player, but a mere looker-on.

Loose : ON THE LOOSE (S.). Unattached, and in search of enjoyment, with no particular object in view.
John has gone out on the loose, and won't be back till late.

AT LOOSE ENDS; AT A LOOSE END. Idly; with no definite object.
For a week the returned traveller wandered about the city at loose ends.

Lord : LORD AND MASTER. Husband.

LORDS OF CREATION. Mankind in general.
(*Note.*—Both the above are generally used ironically.)

LORD IT OVER. Behave arrogantly, as a person of importance.
The head of the department lords it over the assistants.

Lose : LOSE OR WIN THE DAY. See under **Day.**

LOSE GROUND. Suffer loss by degrees of reputation, health or position.
The invalid is steadily losing ground.

LOSE ONE'S HEARING. See **Hearing.**

Loss ; Lost : AT A LOSS. 1. For less than the cost price.
I sold the goods at a loss.

2. Temporarily unable to act or reply ; undecided.
I was at a loss to answer him.

MEET WITH A LOSS. Lose ; be deprived of.
*He met with a heavy loss ; over a hundred pounds was
stolen from his shop.*

A LOST CAUSE. A movement or agitation which has
no longer any chance of becoming effective—
e.g. the restoration of the Stuarts to the English
throne.

LOST IN ADMIRATION. So overcome with admiration
that one cannot express one's emotions.
One is lost in admiration at the wonder of Niagara.

LOST TO SHAME, DECENCY, *etc.* Without possessing
such a virtue in any degree whatever.
*The woman was so lost to shame that she sold her
child's clothes to buy drink.*

Lot : THROW *or* CAST IN ONE'S LOT WITH. See under
Cast.

DRAW LOTS *or* CAST LOTS. Decide by throwing dice or
by some similar method of chance.
*We cast lots, and George was the one who had to walk
home.*

Lothario : GAY LOTHARIO. Same as DON JUAN, which
see.

Love : CALF-LOVE. Adolescent love ; a young man's first
love affair, usually not very serious.

NO LOVE LOST. Dislike, unfriendliness.
There's no love lost between the two sisters.

Low : AT A LOW EBB. Lit., a condition existing when an
ebbing tide has left the water in a river at its
lowest point. Feeble, almost exhausted.
Our cheerfulness, like our money, was at a low ebb.

Luck : RUN OF LUCK. Or. Gambling. A series of lucky
events or *coups*. Used also in the opposite sense—
A RUN OF BAD LUCK.

TAKE POT LUCK. Accept impromptu hospitality without a definite invitation. Dine on whatever
happens to be cooking in the pot.
*Come to dinner at any time, if you don't mind taking
pot luck.*

Lump : A LUMP IN ONE'S THROAT. A sense of pity, producing a desire to weep.

He told a story of suffering that brought a lump to my throat.

LUMP IT (S.). Endure ; suffer.

If you don't like it, you can lump it.

LUMP SUM. The whole amount at once.

They paid him in a lump sum all that was owing.

LUMP TOGETHER. Merge.

If we lump all our money together, we shall have over £5.

Lustre : CAST, *or* THROW, LUSTRE UPON. Bring credit or fame to.

The Battle of Waterloo cast lustre upon the name of Wellington.

Lynx : LYNX-EYED. Having especially keen sight, such as the lynx is supposed to possess.

M

Mad : DRIVE, *or* SEND, MAD. Cause to become mad.

Her daughter's conduct drove the mother mad.

LIKE MAD (S.). With tremendous energy.

He ran like mad.

MAD AS A MARCH HARE. Utterly and completely mad. Hares are supposed to be particularly wild and shy during March, their mating-season.

Maiden : MAIDEN NAME. The surname of a woman before she was married (Fr. *née*).

MAIDEN SPEECH. The first speech made in Parliament by a member.

MAIDEN VOYAGE. The first voyage made by a vessel in the sea or air.

(*Note* that in all the above cases " maiden " is used in the sense of " first ".)

MAIDEN OVER. Or. Cricket. An " over " (or six consecutive balls) in which no runs have been made.

Main : IN THE MAIN. Chiefly.

The letters, in the main, were from her mother.

MAIN CHANCE; HAVE AN EYE TO THE MAIN CHANCE. See under **Eye.**

MAIN FORCE. Physical force or energy.
The police stopped her by main force.

Majority : JOIN THE GREAT MAJORITY. Die. See SLEEP WITH ONE'S FATHERS, *etc.*

Make : MAKE AFTER. Follow quickly.
The thief ran, and the policeman made after him.

MAKE AS IF. Pretend.
The troops will make as if to retire, and then suddenly attack.

MAKE AWAY WITH. Destroy; kill.
We were afraid the wretched woman would make away with herself.

MAKE-BELIEVE. Pretence.
The old man's anger was only make-believe.

MAKE THE BEST OF IT. Accept misfortune or discomfort cheerfully.
We have lost the train, but we must make the best of it.

MAKE BOLD. Old f. Be bold enough.
I decided at last that I would make bold to take the girl in my arms and kiss her.

MAKE A CLEAN BREAST. See under **Breast.**

MAKE A CLEAN SWEEP. See under **Sweep.**

MAKE A DEAD SET AT. Concentrate upon, frequently with a view to marrying.
Miss Gibbs is making a dead set at the Vicar.

MAKE DO. Use as the best substitute available.
We hadn't time for luncheon, but we made do with sandwiches.

MAKE THE ECHOES RING. Make sounds loud enough to produce an echo—by singing, cheering, etc.

MAKE EYES AT. Gaze at lovingly or longingly.
He's one of those fools who makes eyes at every pretty girl.

MAKE FAST. Secure; fasten firmly.
They made fast the boat to the pier.

MAKE FOR. 1. Set out, usually quickly, in a particular direction.
The ships made for the harbour because of the storm.
2. Help to make or maintain.
The minister's speech does not make for peace.

MAKE FREE WITH. Use freely, without asking permission.

Who told you to make free with my property?

MAKE FUN OF. Ridicule; joke about.

It is cruel to make fun of a cripple.

MAKE A FUSS OF. Treat with unusual and excessive courtesy and kindness.

The family made a tremendous fuss of John when he came back from the war.

See MAKE MUCH OF.

MAKE GOOD. 1. Repair; put back something that has been destroyed; restore.

The carpenter will make good the broken chair-leg.

2. Recover a lost reputation.

The young man has learnt a lesson, and will make good.

MAKE ONE'S GORGE RISE. Lit., Make one wish to vomit, the " gorge " being the passage to the stomach, and situated in the throat. Met., Disgust and infuriate.

The rudeness of present-day servants makes one's gorge rise.

MAKE HEADWAY, *or* HEAD AGAINST. Or. Nautical. Proceed, usually in spite of any difficulties or obstructions.

The building has made considerable headway, though workmen were difficult to obtain.

MAKE HEAD OR TAIL OF. See under **Head**, and MAKE NOTHING OF (2).

MAKE IT UP. 1. Become friendly again after a quarrel, or agree after a dispute.

The two brothers made it up, and shook hands.

2. Reach a total amount.

I owed him fifteen shillings, and spent another five, which made it up to a pound.

3. Compose.

The story he told was untrue; he made it up himself.

See MAKE UP.

MAKE LIGHT OR LITTLE OF. Treat as something of little importance.

The soldier made light of his injury.

MAKE THE MOST OF. Put to the best use possible.

We must make the most of the fine weather.

MAKE MUCH OF. Make special efforts to please; treat with conspicuous kindness and respect.

They made much of their distinguished visitor.

Very similar to MAKE A FUSS OF.

MAKE NO BONES. Show no hesitation or fear of the consequences.

Her husband made no bones about her leaving for America.

MAKE NOTHING OF. 1. Treat as trivial or of no importance. Similar to MAKE LITTLE OF. 2. Completely fail to understand.

I can make nothing of these figures.

WHAT DO YOU MAKE OF IT? What do you deduce from it?

A curious painting; what do you make of it?

MAKE OFF. Run away (usually as the result of some guilty act).

He made off with all the old man's savings.

MAKE ONESELF SCARCE. Disappear quickly; efface oneself.

We decided that it would be tactful to make ourselves scarce.

MAKE OUT. 1. Comprehend; decipher.

I can't make out these letters.

2. Inscribe, write.

Please make out a bill for these goods.

3. Imply; indicate.

The scoundrel tried to make out that I had swindled him.

MAKE OVER. Make a formal gift of property.

I have made over the farm to my son.

MAKE A SPLASH. See under **Splash.**

MAKE UP. 1. Noun as well as verb. Cosmetics (rouge, powder, etc.).

Susan uses far too much make-up.

2. Invent; originate. Similar to MAKE IT UP (3).

He made up the story he told you.

3. Complete.

He made up his set of Dickens' works.

4. Compensate for.

I gave the child a chocolate to make up for his disappointment.

See MAKE IT UP.

MAKE UP TO. 1. Flatter, attempt to please, in order to obtain favours.

I hate the way you make up to that detestable Mr. Tompkins.

2. Increase, with a definite object.

See MAKE IT UP (2).

MAKE A VIRTUE OF NECESSITY. Treat something one is obliged to do as if it were being done from choice.

Making a virtue of necessity, Peter invited his mother-in-law to stay to dinner.

MAKE WAY FOR. Move away to allow something else to fill the place.

The French Revolution made way for Napoleon.

Makeshift : MAKESHIFT. One word, as a noun or adjective. An inferior or temporary substitute.

We will put up a makeshift roof till the other is mended. Two words, as a verb.

We have no saucers, but we can make shift with plates.

Man : EVERY MAN-JACK (S.). A more colloquial form of TO A MAN.

A MAN OF LETTERS. An author ; one whose profession is that of a writer.

A MAN OF STRAW. A worthless person, with no social position or reputation.

A MAN OF HIS WORD. One who is truthful and trustworthy, who does not break promises.

A MAN OF THE WORLD. One with worldly knowledge and experience.

Dr. Johnson, as a man of the world, did not expect too much from humanity.

MAN'S ESTATE. The age—twenty-one—at which a young person legally becomes a man.

TO A MAN. Everyone, without exception.

The regiment fought bravely, and was killed to a man.

Manner : BY NO MANNER OF MEANS. See under **Means.**

Many : MANY A LONG DAY. A long time.

I have not seen him for many a long day.

ONE TOO MANY. Too clever or too strong.

We struggled, but he was one too many for me.

Mare : THE GREY MARE. (Abbrev. for " The grey mare is the better horse ".) A wife who dominates her husband and household.

MARE'S NEST. Something which does not exist; a *canard,* a mere effort of the imagination. (A mare—female horse—has obviously no nest.)

SHANKS'S MARE, *or* **PONY (S.).** One's legs.

I came all the way from London on shanks's mare.

Mark : BESIDE THE MARK. Unconnected with the subject being discussed.

Your comments are beside the mark.

MAKE ONE'S MARK. Establish an outstanding reputation.

Peter is a boy who will make his mark.

A MARKED MAN. One who has become, and is, notorious through his connection with some particular incident.

Since acting as leader in the strike I have been a marked man.

MAN OF MARK. A prominent man.

Simpson is a man of mark in the grocery trade.

MARK MY WORDS. Take particular note of what I am saying.

Mark my words, we shall have rain to-morrow.

MARK TIME. Or. Military. Deliberately wait, without progressing. At the command "Mark time" soldiers raise and lower their feet as if marching, but do not move forward.

We shall have to mark time at the factory until we receive definite orders from the Government.

UP TO THE MARK. In a normal state of health ; well.

Poor old Smith isn't looking up to the mark this morning.

(This idiom is generally used in the negative.) See also **Par.**

WIDE OF THE MARK. Very inaccurate.

His guesses were all wide of the mark.

Master : MASTER OF ONESELF. Capable of self-control ; able to think and act coolly and logically.

MASTER-STROKE. An exceptionally shrewd or clever action.

Matter : MATTER OF COURSE. An affair of normal routine ; regularly.

He reached his office as a matter of course at ten o'clock.

MATTER-OF-FACT. 1. Adjective (with hyphens). Commonplace; ordinary.

He spoke in a matter-of-fact voice.

2. Noun (without hyphens). Preceded by "as". A plain, literal statement of fact.

As a matter of fact, he died yesterday.

A MATTER OF LIFE AND DEATH. Of vital and extreme importance.

It's a matter of life and death for me to get the job.

THE MATTER IN QUESTION. The affair being discussed or referred to.

The matter in question must be referred to the Chairman.

NO MATTER. 1. In spite of.

I shall go, no matter what the weather may be.

2. Immaterial; having no importance.

I had something to say, but it's no matter (it doesn't matter).

Meal : SQUARE MEAL. A full, complete meal.

We haven't had a square meal for a week.

Mealy : MEALY-MOUTHED. Applied to one who is both a hypocrite and a coward, and is afraid to speak honestly.

Means : BY ALL MEANS. 1. Indication of cordial assent.

Shall I ask him to come in ? By all means.

2. By exerting every effort.

Try by all (or every) means to persuade him to come.

BY ALL, *or* NO, MANNER OF MEANS. Indicating emphatic assent or dissent.

Are you calling at the house ?
By no manner of means.

BY NO MEANS ; NOT BY ANY MEANS. Elaborated forms of " not ".

He was not by any means a villain ; she was by no means happy.

BY WHAT MEANS ? By what method ? How ?

By what means are you going to travel to-night ?

MEAN WELL. Possess good intentions.

Most husbands are stupid, but nearly all mean well.

MEANS TO AN END. An action merely leading to one's real object.

He rang the bell and asked if he might inspect the telephone, but it was only a means to an end— he intended to rob the house.

Meantime ; meanwhile : IN THE MEANTIME ; MEANWHILE.
  1. The period during which an event has occurred ;
  while this was happening.
  *Wellington began the battle of Waterloo ; in the mean-
  time Blücher was marching to help him.*
  2. For the present.
  *We may get richer soon ; in the meantime we'll
  carry on.*
  See FOR THE TIME BEING (under **Time**).

Measure : BEYOND, *or* OUT OF, ALL MEASURE. Beyond
  reckoning or estimating.
  He loved his son beyond all measure.
  IN A GREAT MEASURE. Greatly, very much ; to a great
  extent or degree.
  *The King's foolishness was in a great measure to blame
  for the French Revolution.*
  MEASURE ONE'S LENGTH. Fall flat.
  He staggered, and measured his length on the pavement.
  MEASURE SWORDS. Or. Duelling. Lit., The act of
  measuring the swords of duellists to ensure that
  the weapons are of the same length. Met., Meet
  in public opposition either by writing or by
  discussion.
  *The Prime Minister and Mr. Jones. M.P. for Stack,
  measured swords over conscription.*

Meed : MEED OF PRAISE. " Meed " means a share, the
  measure of what is due. A meed of praise is
  the credit received or due for something one has
  done.

Meet : IT IS MEET. An old f. phrase meaning " It is fitting,"
  " It is appropriate."
  It is meet that we should honour great men.
  MEET WITH. 1. Receive.
  He met with great kindness at Elizabeth's Court.
  2. Be received with.
  The President hoped his plans would meet with approval.
  (*Note* the shade of difference between the active and
  the passive use of this idiom.)
  MORE THAN MEETS THE EYE, *or* EAR. Something
  suppressed or hidden.
  *There's more than meets the eye in George's visits to
  London.*

Melt : IN A MELTING MOOD.   In a gentle, yielding condition.
Jane was in a melting mood, and allowed him to kiss her.
MELT DOWN.   Reduce to a single mass by heating until
it becomes fluid, and then allow to harden.
The gold candlesticks were sold and melted down.

Memory : BURDEN ONE'S MEMORY.   Cause to become a
weight or burden on one's memory.
*I don't want to burden your memory with too many
instructions.*

COMMIT TO MEMORY.   Learn, as one learns a lesson in
school.   See LEARN BY HEART (under **Heart**).

Mention : NOT TO MENTION.   In addition to ; distinct from.
*I've all these apples to carry, not to mention some
pounds of potatoes.*

DON'T MENTION IT.   A polite dismissal of apology or
thanks.
I am sorry to have troubled you.   Don't mention it.

Mercy : AT THE MERCY OF.   Dependent upon ; controlled
by ; in the power of.
The ship was at the mercy of the waves.

Merry : MAKE MERRY.   I. Rejoice.
All Christendom makes merry at Christmas-time.
2. Laugh or jeer at.
The boys made merry at the old man's queer clothes.
MERRY AS A GRIG, *or* GRIGG.   Thoroughly happy and
joyful.   A grig is a grasshopper ; also a small eel.
Incidentally, the word " merry " meant originally
" famous, honoured ".

MERRY-MAKING.   Rejoicing and festivities upon some
special occasion, e.g. Christmas.

Metal : BASE METAL.   Metal which, when melted, has dross
or scum on the surface (copper, tin, zinc).
PRECIOUS METAL.   Metal which, on the contrary, has
no dross (gold, silver, platinum).

Mete : METE OUT.   Distribute ;   give out.   (Frequently
applied to justice, punishment, etc.)
*The judge will mete out fitting punishment for the
criminals.*

Mettle : ON ONE'S METTLE.   Roused to the use of one's best
efforts ;   prepared to do one's utmost.
George did well at the examination ;   he was on his mettle.

Micawber : MICAWBER-LIKE.   In a state of irresponsible

hopefulness. (Mr. Micawber, a character in Charles Dickens' *David Copperfield*, was always expecting something to "turn up" and rescue him from his troubles.)

Mid : MID-CHANNEL. Lit., the middle of the English Channel, halfway between England and France. Frequently used in a general sense of halfway.

They had planned a month's holiday, but it was wrecked in mid-channel.

Midsummer : MIDSUMMER MADNESS. Lit., Temporary madness, brought on by the conjunction of the full moon at midsummer and the heat of the season. Applied to any sort of crazy idea or plan.

To think of flying alone to the North Pole is sheer midsummer madness.

Midway : Halfway ; half the distance.

He started to cross the road, but stopped midway.

Might : MIGHT AND MAIN. All one's powers or strength.

He struggled with might and main to escape.

Mild : DRAW IT MILD ! (S.). Don't exaggerate !

I've had dinner with dozens of dukes.

Oh, draw it mild, Peter !

Milk : MILK-AND-WATER. Feeble ; weak.

The King has made only milk-and-water plans for dealing with the rebellion.

Also **Wishy-washy.**

MILK OF HUMAN KINDNESS. Genuine and natural kindness towards one's fellow-creatures.

MOTHER'S MILK. A term applied to anything that meets an elementary or essential need.

Whisky is mother's milk to old Jock.

Mince : NOT TO MINCE MATTERS, *or* WORDS ; WITHOUT MINCING. Not to speak tactfully or politely ; to be plain and direct.

I told him, without mincing matters, that I never wished to see him again.

(The phrase is generally used in the negative.) See PLAIN SPEAKING (under **Speak**) and HARD WORDS (under **Word**).

MAKE MINCEMEAT OF (S.). "Mincemeat" consists, lit., of ingredients chopped (or minced) into very small pieces for cooking. The phrase is used met. to indicate the destruction of a person's arguments.

The Professor made mincemeat of the young man's foolish theories.

Mind : APPLY, *or* GIVE, ONE'S MIND TO. Consider carefully ; concentrate one's attention upon.

She will never succeed until she gives her mind to her work.

BEAR, *or* KEEP, IN MIND. Retain in one's memory ; remember.

Please bear in mind the instructions I've given you.

CAST ONE'S MIND BACK. Recall the past.

If you cast your mind back, you will remember that an oak-tree used to grow here.

GIVE ONE'S MIND TO. See APPLY ONE'S MIND.

GIVE A PIECE OF ONE'S MIND. Blame ; express one's opinion candidly and adversely.

The boy is late again ; I shall give him a piece of my mind when I see him.

IN ONE'S RIGHT MIND. Sane. Generally used negatively, an alternative being OUT OF ONE'S MIND.

John couldn't have been in his right mind when he struck his wife.

KNOW ONE'S OWN MIND. Have clear and fixed opinions.

Mary always knows her own mind.

MIND.   1. Take into one's care or charge.

The mother asked the girl to mind the baby for an hour.

2. Show care about ; be careful of.

Mind the wet paint.

3. Regret ; object to.

I hope you won't mind my going out.

MIND ONE'S EYE (S.). Be specially careful ; cautious.

If you go into partnership with that young man you'll have to mind your eye.

MIND ONE'S P'S AND Q'S (S.). Be especially careful and exact in one's behaviour. (The or. of this idiom is doubtful, but one suggestion is that it arose from the custom in alehouses of marking up " p " for pint and " q " for quart in keeping customers' accounts.)

If you call on the Duke, you'll have to mind your p's and q's.

A MIND TO. Old f. A liking or desire to.
Having a mind to visit London, I caught the bus.

OF ONE MIND. Having the same opinions.
Most of the electors seemed to be of one mind.

OUT OF ONE'S MIND. See IN ONE'S RIGHT MIND.

PRESENCE OF MIND. Mental alertness and an immediate response to an emergency.
The burglar produced a pistol; with great presence of mind the old lady struck him on the wrist, and the weapon fell to the ground.

PREY ON ONE'S MIND. Cause deep and prolonged mental distress.
The injustice he had suffered so preyed on his mind that he became insane.

SINGLE-TRACK MIND. A mind capable of considering only one subject at a time; a narrow and limited mentality.
She could talk only about her son's success; she had a single-track mind.

Mint : MINT OF MONEY. A very large sum of money. (The Royal Mint is where English coins are made.)
James spent a mint of money during his holiday in London.

Mischief : MAKE MISCHIEF. Intentionally cause discord and unhappiness by spreading gossip and mischievous stories.
That hateful Mrs. Robinson makes mischief wherever she goes.

Mistake : AND NO MISTAKE ! An idiom used entirely for emphasis, usually ironic.
You're a pleasant companion, and no mistake !

THERE'S NO MISTAKING. It is impossible to mistake.
There's no mistaking Mrs. Smith for Mrs. Brown.

Moment : UNGUARDED MOMENT. A moment in which one has forgotten to be careful in speech or action.
In an unguarded moment he admitted that he had been to prison.

IN A MOMENT ; HALF A MOMENT (frequently abbrev. to HALF A MO ! (S.). Similar to IN A JIFFY.

Money : HUSH-MONEY. Money paid to prevent a shameful secret being revealed.
Blackmailers flourish on hush-money.

PIN-MONEY. Money supplied for minor feminine pleasures and amusements. Pin-money was the term originally applied in the Middle Ages to money supplied to women to purchase the very elaborate and beautiful pins that jewellers were allowed to offer for sale on the first two days of the year.

POCKET-MONEY. Small sums given to children, usually each week, for their personal expenditure.

Monkey : GET ONE'S MONKEY UP (S.). See GET ONE'S GOAT, etc.

Month : MONTH OF SUNDAYS (S.). A long and completely indefinite period.

I don't expect to see you again for a month of Sundays.

Moon : MOONSHINE. Unreal ; a fantastic and untrue statement.

The story he told was all moonshine.

MOON-STRUCK. Dazed, incapable of thought, as though under the influence of the moon.

He stared at me, moonstruck.

See THUNDERSTRUCK.

Morning : MORNING COFFEE. Coffee drunk halfway through the morning, i.e. about eleven o'clock. Compare MORNING TEA.

MORNING DRESS. Official and formal clothing worn by men during the day (as opposed to evening dress), i.e. black coat with short " tails ", black waistcoat and dark grey trousers.

MORNING TEA. Tea drunk in one's bedroom before dressing in the morning. Compare MORNING COFFEE.

Most : AT THE MOST ; AT MOST. At the highest ; as the limit.

You'll get £5, at the most, for that bicycle.

FOR THE MOST PART. In most circumstances ; usually

For the most part, we are a cheerful race.

Mother : MOTHER O' PEARL. The shining inner lining of oyster and similar shells, extensively used for ornamental purposes.

MOTHER-TONGUE. The language spoken in one's native land.

I can speak French fluently, but English is my mother tongue.

Mount : MOUNT UP. Increase ; accumulate.

I'm afraid our expenses are mounting up rather fast.

Mountain : MAKE A MOUNTAIN OUT OF A MOLEHILL. Make much out of very little ; greatly exaggerate.

He made a mountain out of a molehill in describing his quarrel with Smith.

Mouth : BY WORD OF MOUTH. By speech ; orally.

We received the news by word of mouth.

DOWN IN THE MOUTH. Depressed ; despondent.

Move : GET A MOVE ON (S.). Take immediate action ; proceed at once.

We'd better get a move on if we are to reach London to-night.

MAKE A MOVE. 1. As above.

2. Depart from one place to another.

Last year they made a move from Brighton to Sydenham.

3. Alter the position of a chessman or draughtsman.

Smith made a move, and his opponent's position became hopeless.

MOVE HEAVEN AND EARTH. Make every possible effort ; use every available means.

Joe is moving Heaven and earth to come home for Christmas.

MOVE OFF. Depart.

The troops moved off at dawn.

MOVE ON. This, curiously enough, means practically the same thing as the above. A policeman invariably tells a crowd to " move on " when he means " proceed ". See PASS ALONG.

Mow : MOW DOWN. Cut, with wide sweeping strokes, as wheat, etc., is cut with a scythe. Gun-fire is frequently said to " mow down " advancing troops.

Must : IT MUST NEEDS BE. It will inevitably be.

It must needs be some weeks before we receive a reply from Australia.

NEEDS MUST WHEN THE DEVIL DRIVES. If this is inevitable, I must accept it as such.

I don't want to undertake the work, but needs must when the Devil drives.

Myrmidon : MYRMIDON OF THE LAW. An old-f. phrase, now used only facetiously, for any legal servant —policeman, bailiff, etc. A " myrmidon " is any rough and inferior servant. Or. Classical. Myrmidons were a brutal and savage race who followed Achilles at the siege of Troy.

N

Nth : TO THE NTH DEGREE. To any extent, without number. N in mathematics stands for number, *any* number.

I believe in him, and I'll support him to the nth degree.

Naboth : NABOTH'S VINEYARD. Or. Biblical. The story (I Kings, xxi.) of the vineyard belonging to Naboth and coveted by Ahab. Something comparatively trivial intensely desired by one far richer and more powerful than the owner.

I won't sell the cottage, though it's a regular Naboth's vineyard to the squire.

Nail : HIT THE NAIL ON THE HEAD. See under **Hit.**

NAIL IN ONE'S COFFIN. Something that will shorten life —drink, anxiety, etc.—or destroy one's reputation.

We have just heard that Brown cheated at cards last night—another nail in his coffin.

NAIL ONE'S COLOURS TO THE MAST. Or. Naval. Refuse to surrender or modify one's opinions or principles. During a battle the colours, or flag, of a ship were in the past frequently nailed to the mast to make it impossible to lower them as a signal of surrender.

ON THE NAIL (S.). Promptly ; immediately.

He pays his debts on the nail.

Namby-pamby : Feeble ; effeminate. Or. The seventeenth-century poet Ambrose (sneeringly nicknamed " Namby " as a baby would pronounce it) Phillips. He wrote verses for children.

Nap : CATCH NAPPING. See under **Catch.**

Narrow : A NARROW ESCAPE ; A NARROW SQUEAK. (S.). An escape which very nearly did not take place.

I had a narrow escape from being run over by a bus this morning.

See ESCAPE BY THE SKIN OF ONE'S TEETH.

A NARROW MARGIN. Very little (space, etc.).

John passed the examination by a narrow margin.

Nature : STATE OF NATURE. A nude condition.

The natives go about their work in a state of nature.

Near : NEAR BY, *or* NEAR AT HAND. Close ; a short distance away.

NEAR THE MARK. Nearly or approximately correct.

You are near the mark when you say that King John was our worst monarch.

A NEAR, *or* A CLOSE THING. A success which was very nearly a failure.

I ran all the way and caught the train, but it was a near thing.

Necessity : MAKE A VIRTUE OF NECESSITY. See under Make.

UNDER THE NECESSITY OF. Compelled ; forced to.

I am under the necessity of selling my house.

Neck : NECK AND CROP. Entirely. (The " crop ", or gorge, is the lower part of a bird's neck.)

The cabinet was thrown out, neck and crop.

NECK AND NECK, *or* NECK-TO-NECK. Or. Racing. Side by side ; level.

The horses ran neck-to-neck.

It was a neck and neck race.

NECK OR NOTHING. Or. Racing. Desperate ; risking everything. To win by the length of the horse's neck, or not at all.

Needful : THE NEEDFUL (S.). Money ; cash. (The one thing needful or required in life.)

I would have taken Phyllis to the theatre, but I hadn't the needful.

See SINEWS OF WAR, THE WHEREWITHAL.

DO THE NEEDFUL (S.). Do what is necessary.

Aunt Agatha wants a taxi : will you do the needful ?

Negative : IN THE NEGATIVE. No.

I asked her if her father was at home. She answered in the negative.

Neither : NEITHER HERE NOR THERE. See under Here.

Nerves : GET ON ONE'S NERVES. Irritate by the repetition of some annoying action, usually slight.

George's continual sniffing gets on my nerves.

Nest : FEATHER ONE'S NEST. See under Feather.

NEST EGG. Lit., An artificial egg left in the nest to

encourage the hen to further laying. Met., **Money** saved for one's old age or for some specific purpose in the future.

Never : NEVER SAY DIE ! Never give up hope of success.
Never say die ; you'll eventually persuade her to marry you.

New : NEW BROOM. A newcomer who is anxious to prove his efficiency. Or. The proverb " A new broom sweeps clean ".
Our latest assistant is doing very well, but of course she's a new broom.

NEW-FANGLED. A contemptuous term applied to any new invention or method, usually of a minor type.
I detest this new-fangled way of arranging one's hair.

Next : NEXT DOOR TO. Lit., In the adjoining house. Met., Any form of nearness.
Her statements are next door to lying.

NEXT TO NOTHING. Practically nothing.
The duke left next to nothing when he died.

Nicety : TO A NICETY. Precisely ; exactly.
The coat will fit you to a nicety.

Nick : IN THE NICK OF TIME. Just in time ; at the right and vital moment. Or. The old custom of marking long sticks with " nicks " or notches at intervals to indicate numbers.
In the nick of time we were saved from drowning.

Nigger : THE NIGGER IN THE WOODPILE (S.). The concealed object or aim ; the hidden intention behind a statement or action.
He said he wanted to study art in Paris, but I guessed that Mary was the nigger in the woodpile.

Night : OVERNIGHT. Lit., The period between one day and the next. Met., In a very brief time.
By shrewd speculation, the ruined man became rich again overnight.

Niminy-piminy *or* **Nimini-pimini :** Irritatingly affected and trivial.
I have no time to listen to this niminy-piminy nonsense. Tell me plainly what you want.

Nine : NINE DAYS' WONDER. See under **Wonder.**

Nines : UP TO THE NINES. Magnificently ; gorgeously. Or. The Oriental regard for the number nine as indicative of the highest splendour and generosity, e.g. presenting a guest with nine camels, nine cases of jewels, etc.

Here comes Pamela, dressed up to the nines for the ball.

Nip : NIP IN THE BUD. End any project before it has a chance of maturing.

He intended to go to Canada, but the family soon nipped that idea in the bud.

No : NO ONE ELSE. No other person.

NO SUCH THING. An emphatic negative.

He said I had promised to go, but I told him I had done no such thing.

Noise : NOISE ABROAD. Cause to be widely known.

The end of the war was soon noised abroad.

Nose : CUT OFF ONE'S NOSE TO SPITE ONE'S FACE. Commit, through revenge or spite, some foolish action which injures oneself.

To annoy his mother, Bill married that stupid widow— cutting off his nose to spite his face.

LEAD BY THE NOSE. See under **Lead**.

PAY THROUGH THE NOSE. Pay far too much ; pay extortionately.

You'll have to pay through the nose if you stay at that hotel.

PUT ONE'S NOSE OUT OF JOINT (S.). Supersede ; supplant in position or affection.

I hope the new baby won't put young Peter's nose out of joint.

TURN UP ONE'S NOSE AT. Sneer at ; scorn.

Jane turns up her nose at a seat in the gallery nowadays.

UNDER ONE'S NOSE. A near and obvious place.

The cat stole the fish from under my nose.

Not : NOT IN THE LEAST ; NOT A BIT. Not to any degree whatever.

I was not in the least afraid.

NOT SO. No ; a general negative.

You will apologize ?
Not so.

Note : NOTE OF HAND. A formal written promise to repay a debt.

Nothing : NOTHING TO CHOOSE BETWEEN THEM. Practically equal.

Both brothers are clever workmen ; there is nothing to choose between them.

NOTHING FOR IT. No option ; no other choice.

If I fail to get this job, there'll be nothing for it but to emigrate.

NOTHING MORE NOR LESS ; NOTHING SHORT OF. Completely ; absolutely.

The affair was nothing more nor less than an insult.

Notice : AT SHORT NOTICE. At the end of an unexpectedly short period.

We have to leave for America at short notice.

Now : JUST NOW. Almost, but not quite at the present time.

George was here just now.

Null : NULL AND VOID. Or. Legal. Non-existent and consequently non-effective.

Almost every new law makes some old one null and void.

Number : NUMBER ONE (S.). Oneself.

A fellow can't expect to be a success if he doesn't look after Number One.

Nut : A HARD NUT TO CRACK. A difficult problem to solve or matter to decide.

What finally became of the diamonds is a hard nut to crack.

OFF ONE'S NUT (S.). Crazy ; mad.

Nutshell : IN A NUTSHELL. Stated very briefly.

In a nutshell, we are getting married to-morrow.

O

Oar : PUT IN ONE'S OAR. Intervene ; interfere.

I am settling the matter—you need not put in your oar.

Oats : SOW ONE'S WILD OATS. Commit the usual follies of youth.

The boy certainly wastes his time and money, but we must expect him to sow his wild oats.

Obligations : DISCHARGE ONE'S OBLIGATIONS *or* DEBTS. Repay what is due.

He discharged his obligations at the inn, and journeyed on.

UNDER AN OBLIGATION. Morally in debt.

Your kindness puts me under an obligation.

Oblivion : SINK INTO OBLIVION. Become completely forgotten.

Shenstone was a popular poet whose works have sunk into oblivion.

Occasion : HAVE OCCASION. Have need.

Captain Blank is dismissed the Army, his Majesty having no further occasion for his services.

ON OCCASION ; AS OCCASION AROSE. Sometimes ; when necessary.

I have on occasion rebuked the boy for his bad manners.

Occupy : OCCUPY ONE'S TIME, ENERGIES, TALENTS, *etc.* " Occupy " here used in the sense of " employ ", " use ".

I wish that you'd occupy your leisure more profitably.

Occur : IT OCCURS TO ME ; IT HAS JUST OCCURRED TO ME. The idea has come to me ; I have just realized.

It occurs to me that if we go to the concert to-night we shall probably meet the Robinsons.

Odds : The " ODDS " represent the terms upon which one may bet upon a particular horse. " LONG ODDS " mean that the chances of its winning are considered slight, and the phrase is used to indicate improbability.

It's long odds against Arthur coming home from Australia this year.

" THE ODDS ", on the other hand, may imply the reverse, a probable event.

The odds are that Jim will be able to come.

NO ODDS. Similar to NO CONSEQUENCE.

WHAT'S THE ODDS ! What does it matter !

ODDS AND ENDS. Small, unclassified objects ; what remains when more important things have been dealt with.

I have tidied your workbasket ; the odds and ends are in this box.

Odour : IN BAD ODOUR. Unpopular ; regarded unfavourably.

I fear that his lordship is in bad odour with the King.

Off : BADLY OFF. Poor. The opposite in both senses, of WELL OFF, which see.

BE OFF. 1. An imperative order to depart.

Be off, or I'll call the police!

2. Depart.

I must be off to catch my train.

3. Be unfit to eat or drink ; stale.

Don't eat that meat—it was bought last week, and must be off by now.

4. Be unavailable ; off the menu, all supplies being exhausted.

I'm afraid apple-pie is off.

OFF ONE'S FEED, *or* OATS (S.). Or. Racing, etc. Disinclined to eat ; without an appetite.

Poor old Joe seems off his feed to-day.

OFF ONE'S GUARD. Or. Fencing. In a state of relaxation and unawareness.

Taken off his guard, the prisoner admitted his guilt.

OFF-HAND. 1. Without preparation ; impromptu.

I can't give you the figures off-hand ; I shall have to look them up.

2. Casual and irresponsible.

I dislike the young man's off-hand manner.

OFF-SCOURINGS. The scum ; the residue left in saucepans, etc., after cooking. Applied, met., to criminals, beggars, etc.

The slums of Marseilles contain the off-scourings of humanity.

OFF-SHOOT. A branching-off ; a lesser concern or business which has developed from the original one.

Simpson's Cleaning Agency is an offshoot of Simpson's Stores Limited.

WELL OFF. 1. Rich.

The family is very well off ; their grandfather speculated successfully in land.

2. In comfortable and satisfactory circumstances.

You shouldn't grumble about the house ; you don't realize when you're well off.

Oil : BURN THE MIDNIGHT OIL. Sit up late at night to work or study.

You'll have to go to bed earlier and burn less midnight oil.

POUR OIL ON TROUBLED WATERS. Or. Naval. Speak

or act soothingly and tactfully in order to bring a quarrel to an end. It is stated that a young eighth-century priest was given by his bishop a bottle of oil to pour on the sea if it became rough, and actually calmed the waves by this means. (It has been proved that oil sprayed upon the surface does calm a high sea.)

The two men were shouting abuse, but she did her best to pour oil on the troubled waters.

Ointment : FLY IN THE OINTMENT. See under **Fly.**

Old : OF OLD. Belonging to the distant past.

In the days of old people believed in giants and fairies.

OLD AS THE HILLS. Very old indeed. Frequently applied to an out-of-date object.

I can't wear that hat—it's as old as the hills.

OLD MAID. Old f. An elderly spinster, or one with fixed habits.

Susan has never married ; she's always been a typical old maid.

Olive : OLIVE-BRANCH. 1. A child (the olive-tree grows very rapidly and profusely).

We're married, and have five olive-branches.

2. A gesture of peace. (The olive-branch was also, in the past, a symbol of peace.)

After a long war, the exhausted enemy held out the olive-branch.

On : ON AND OFF. Intermittently ; occasionally.

We visit them on and off.

See ONCE IN A WAY.

Once : ONCE AND FOR ALL. Finally.

She told him, once and for all, that she would not marry him.

ONCE IN A BLUE MOON. Very rarely. See A MONTH OF SUNDAYS.

ONCE IN A WAY. Occasionally, but not often.

Once in a way we visit the theatre.

See ON AND OFF.

One : ONE AND ALL. Everyone.

The entertainment was greatly enjoyed by one and all.

ONE-HORSE (S.). Or. American. Insignificant ; primitive.

Jimmy lives in a one-horse town somewhere in Canada.

ONE-SIDED (AGREEMENT, TREATY, *etc.*). Made from one point of view and for the advantage of one party only. (Present-day official equivalent, " unilateral ".)

We could not agree to such a one-sided arrangement with a European power.

HAVE ONE OVER THE EIGHT. (S.). Become intoxicated.

Open: OPEN AND ABOVE-BOARD. Entirely frank and candid.

He was entirely open and above-board in his statements.

See ABOVE-BOARD.

OPEN A DISCUSSION, PROCEEDINGS. Begin a discussion, meeting, etc.

OPEN THE DOOR TO. Lead to ; encourage ; result in.

These innumerable minor regulations open the door to innumerable minor crimes.

OPEN SECRET. A fact supposed to be secret, but known to everybody ; no secret at all.

OPEN SESAME. Any simple and miraculous method of solving a problem. From the story of " Ali Baba and the Forty Thieves ", in which a cave containing immense treasure could be entered only by the utterance of those words.

The Chancellor apparently thinks that taxing the rich is the open sesame to universal prosperity.

Opinion : BE OF THE OPINION. Believe ; consider.

I am of the opinion that there will be no kings or queens a hundred years hence.

GOLDEN OPINIONS. Very great admiration ; general praise.

The new President has already won golden opinions, even from his political opponents.

PASS AN OPINION. Express an opinion or view.

I don't know enough about paintings to pass an opinion on this landscape.

Opportunity : TAKE *or* SEIZE THE OPPORTUNITY. Make use of a particular moment.

May I take this opportunity to express my gratitude for your kindness.

Opposition : MEET WITH OPPOSITION. Be opposed.

Any attempt to tax bachelors would meet with strong opposition.

Order : ORDER (*singular only*) OF THE DAY. The current
fashion.

> *Fifty years ago high, stiff collars were the order of the
> day for men.*

ORDERS OF THE DAY. Or. Parliamentary. The daily
prearranged and official order in which the Bills,
etc., are dealt with. Loosely applied to any
definite plans for a particular day.

IN ORDER. 1. In succession ; according to a prearranged plan.

> *The candidates will be interviewed in order of
> arrival.*

2. Tidy, neat.

> *Please see that this room is in order when the visitors
> arrive.*

3. Officially correct.

> *You will be in order if you speak after the chairman.*

OUT OF ORDER. 1. The reverse of IN ORDER (2).

> *All these papers are out of order.*

2. The reverse of IN ORDER (3).

> *You will be out of order if you interrupt the Chairman.*

TAKE ORDERS FROM. Obey orders given by.

> *You will take orders from Mr. Sullivan, the
> manager.*

TAKE (HOLY) ORDERS. Become a clergyman.

> *The new bishop took orders thirty years ago.*

Ordinary : ORDINARY RUN OF THINGS, *or* COURSE OF EVENTS.
Events which may be expected to happen normally.

> *In the ordinary run of things I go home nearly every
> week-end.*

OUT OF THE ORDINARY. Unusual ; exceptional.

> *In our grandfathers' time it was quite out of the
> ordinary for a woman to go to college.*

Other : THE OTHER DAY. Recently ; not long ago.

> *The other day I met your brother.*

Out : BE OUT. 1. Be mistaken in one's judgment.

> *We were out in thinking him an honest man.*

2. Not at home.

> *I am sorry we were out when you called.*

HAVE IT OUT. See Have.

OUT-AND-OUT. Thoroughly, completely.

> *The man is an out-and-out villain.*

OUT-AT-ELBOWS. Shabby; wearing torn and ragged clothes. See DOWN-AT-HEEL. (Under **Heel**)

OUT OF. 1. From.

He did it out of kindness.

2. Without any (applied to something which would normally be available).

The grocer was out of coffee.

See OUT OF STOCK.

3. Having no share or part in.

He was feeling rather out of the fun.

OUT OF BREATH. Breathless.

I reached the station completely out of breath.

OUT OF CONDITION. 1. As OUT OF SORTS, but applying particularly to animals. 2. Unfit for special exertion, because untrained.

I'm not likely to win this race, being out of condition.

OUT-OF-DATE. Belonging to the past; unfashionable.

The costume she wore was completely out-of-date.

See BEHIND THE TIMES.

OUT OF DOORS. In the open air; exposed to the weather.

We'll go out of doors when the rain stops.

As an adjective (with hyphen).

She's always been an out-of-doors (or outdoor) girl.

OUT OF JOINT. Restless, uncomfortable, and generally unsatisfactory.

The political situation is out of joint.

OUT OF PLACE. See under **Place**.

OUT OF POCKET. See under **Pocket**.

OUT OF PRINT. Term applied to a book of which all copies are sold.

OUT OF SORTS. See under **Sort**.

OUT OF THE QUESTION. See **Question**.

OUT OF STOCK. Not available, owing to supplies being exhausted.

I am sorry, but that brand of cigarettes is out of stock.

Similar to OUT OF (2).

OUT OF TRAINING. Similar to OUT OF CONDITION (2).

OUT OF THE WAY. 1. Unusual.

It was an out-of-the-way request.

2. Remote.

The house was in an out-of-the-way village.

OUT OF THE WOOD. Freed from one's trouble and difficulties.

He has worked hard to pay his debts, and is now out of the wood.

OUT OF WORK. Without employment.

Outrun : OUTRUN THE CONSTABLE (S.). Old f. Spend more than one possesses or can afford.

John is so extravagant that he is constantly outrunning the constable.

Over : ALL OVER. See under **All.**

OVER AND ABOVE. In addition to ; extra to.

I gave the cabman five shillings over and above his legal fare.

OVER AND OVER AGAIN. Repeatedly ; many times.

I've told you over and over again to close that door.

OVERSHOOT ; OVERSHOOT THE MARK. Go too far ; exceed ; exaggerate.

He overshot the mark when he said there were a thousand people present.

Owe : OWE IT TO ONESELF. Consider it necessary to one's self-respect or happiness.

I owe it to myself to explain how it all happened.

OWING TO. Because of.

Owing to competition, his business failed.

Own : ON ONE'S OWN (S.). By oneself ; without companionship or assistance.

I've been living on my own since February.

OFF ONE'S OWN BAT. On one's own initiative or responsibility.

I've written to the Prime Minister off my own bat.

P

Pace : KEEP PACE. Keep level ; go at the same speed (Lit. and Met.).

I can't keep pace with your plans.

See **Keep.**

PUT THROUGH ONE'S PACES. Or. Horsemanship. Discover a person's knowledge or ability. A pur-

chaser of a horse "puts it through" its various
"paces"—walking, trotting, etc.

*He told me he had been a soldier in India. I put him
through his paces, and found he was lying.*

Packed : PACKED LIKE SARDINES. Crowded as closely
together as sardines are in the tins in which they
are sold.

We were packed like sardines in the train to London.

Paddle : PADDLE ONE'S OWN CANOE (S.). Manage one's own
affairs without help or interference.

Since my father died I have had to paddle my own canoe.

Pains : BE AT PAINS TO. Take trouble to.

I was at great pains to make the dinner a success.

GET FOR ONE'S PAINS. Receive for one's exertions or
trouble.

All he got for his pains was ingratitude and suspicion.

Palm : BEAR THE PALM. Be above all others ; be pre-eminent.
For sheer beauty, the view from Naples bears the palm.
See TAKE THE CAKE.

PALM OFF ON. Or. Conjuring. Substitute something
of inferior value. (A conjurer "palms", or conceals in the palm of his hand, a card or other small
object he does not wish the audience to see.)

I asked for butter, but they palmed off margarine on me.

PALMY DAYS. Times of great prosperity.

*In the palmy days of gold-mining, many rough and
uneducated men became millionaires.*

Pan : PAN OUT (S.). Or. Mining. Work out ; finally result.
Our investment didn't pan out satisfactorily.

Paper : COMMIT TO PAPER. Write, with the special object of
keeping a record.

*I shall commit to paper all that you have said, and shall
ask you to sign the document later.*

Par : UP TO, *or* BELOW, PAR. Lit., "Par" represents the
full nominal value of a company's shares.

The insurance shares you mention are below par.

Met., "Up to par" means up to the level of one's
normal health ; "below par", unwell.

I'm feeling a good deal below par this morning.

Parallel : DRAW A PARALLEL. Compare to indicate similarity.
*We can draw a parallel between the fate of the Kaiser
and that of Napoleon.*

Parcel : PARCEL OUT. Divide and distribute in portions.

Napoleon parcelled out among his friends the territories he had conquered.

Pare : PARE DOWN. Reduce by degrees. (" Pare " is to peel or shave off the surface.)

We have pared down expenses to the limit.

Parlour : PARLOUR TRICKS. Minor social accomplishments—amateur singing, playing, etc.

Peter is a plain, uneducated man, with no parlour tricks.

Parrot-fashion : As a parrot talks ; from memory, with little or no regard to the real meaning.

The boy repeats his prayers parrot-fashion.

Part : PART AND PARCEL. An essential and necessary part.

The invitation to dinner was part and parcel of the villain's plans.

PARTS OF SPEECH. The eight divisions—nouns, verbs, etc.—into one of which every word in the language is classified.

Parthian : A PARTHIAN SHOT. A parting retort or sneer. (The Parthians used to fire arrows as they galloped away from their enemies.)

" And anyway, you're only a girl ! " was Bill's Parthian shot.

Partial : BE PARTIAL TO. Old f. Like ; enjoy.

I am partial to duck and green peas.

Pass : MAKE A PASS. Make a threatening movement or gesture towards.

The dog, as he rushed away, made a pass at the man.

PASS (*at cards*). Refrain from playing at that particular moment of the game.

PASS ALONG. The traditional phrase used by policemen and other officials in dispersing a crowd ; move or walk further along the path, passage, etc. Similar to MOVE ON.

PASS AWAY, OVER. Formal and rather old-f. phrase for " die ".

The old lady passed away yesterday.

PASS BY. Pass.

I passed by your house yesterday.

PASS ONE'S COMPREHENSION. Be more than one can understand.

Why Jim married her passes my comprehension.

PASS JUDGMENT. Express a final and definite opinion.
It is difficult to pass judgment on the affair when we know so little about what happened.

PASS MUSTER. Or. Military. Be regarded as up to the necessary standards ; just good enough. (Soldiers are " mustered " and examined for correctness of uniform, etc., before going on parade.)
Your clothes aren't smart, but they'll pass muster in a crowd.

PASS OFF. 1. Ignore ; treat as if it were unimportant.
She hated his familiarity, but passed it off as a joke.
2. Intentionally convey a false impression concerning some person or object.
The boy was nearly four, but his mother passed him off as a baby.
3. Disappear by degrees or stages.
There was a thick mist, at first, but it soon began to pass off.

PASS OUT. Faint.

PASS OVER. 1. Ignore.
I shall pass over the first paragraph, and not read it.
2. Forgive ; excuse.
His father passed over the boy's foolish crime.
3. See PASS AWAY.

A PRETTY PASS ! A fine state of affairs ! (Always used ironically.)
Things have come to a pretty pass when a husband has to ask his wife for sixpence !

PASS A REMARK. Utter ; make a remark.
George passed a remark about the weather, but his wife was not listening to him.

PASS, *or* WILE, AWAY THE TIME. See **Wile.**

Passing : PASSING RICH, FAIR, *etc.* More than.
The Vicar was passing rich on £400 a year.

Past : PAST-MASTER. An expert ; a highly experienced person. (A past-master in any guild or Association is one who has in the past achieved the position of Chairman or Master.)
My husband is a past-master in the art of growing strawberries.

Patch : NOT A PATCH ON. Not worthy to be compared with.
Their baby isn't a patch on ours.

PATCH UP A QUARREL. Become friendly again for a time but not permanently or cordially.

I hear the Johnsons have patched up their quarrel with the Jacksons.

Patience : OUT OF PATIENCE ; HAVING LOST PATIENCE. With no patience left ; exasperated.

The old woman became completely out of patience with the children.

Paul Pry : One who makes a hobby of spying upon his neighbours and gossiping about them ; an inquisitive meddler in other people's affairs. Or. The chief character in an old comedy, by John Poole, called *Paul Pry.*

Pave : PAVE THE WAY TO. Lead to ; result in.

I believe this treaty will pave the way to peace in Europe.

Pay : THE DEVIL TO PAY (S.). Tremendous trouble ; a general upheaval.

If you don't post that letter to-night, there'll be the devil to pay.

PAY ATTENTION. Listen and observe intently and carefully.

Pay attention to your teachers, and don't waste your time.

PAY COURT TO. Flatter ; behave like a courtier to a sovereign.

He paid court to the rich widow, and eventually married her.

PAY ONE'S DEBT TO NATURE Old f. Die.

The old man paid his debt to nature forty years ago. See PASS AWAY, etc.

PAY OFF. 1. Pay the whole of what is due.

The old man's paid off his son's debts.

2. Naval. A ship is said to be " paid off " when she returns to port and discharges her crew.

PAY OUT. 1. Punish, in return for some injury. See SERVE ONE OUT.

You may tell lies about me, but I'll pay you out.

2. Nautical. Slacken or loosen a rope.

The sailors paid out the cables, and the ship moved away from the shore.

3. Pay ; disburse money.

We've paid out nearly £500 this month.

7

PAY THE PIPER. Pay whatever the cost, financial or otherwise, may be. Or. Abbrev. of " He who pays the piper should call the tune."

Mary is an extravagant and foolish girl, and her unfortunate husband has to pay the piper.

PAY ONE'S WAY. Pay expenses out of one's income.

I doubt if the business will ever pay its way.

Peace : HOLD ONE'S PEACE. Remain silent.

Hold your peace when a wise man is speaking.

See HOLD ONE'S TONGUE.

KEEP THE PEACE. Refrain from quarrelling, or causing any other disturbance.

His manner was so insulting that I found it difficult to keep the peace.

The magistrate ordered both men to keep the peace for twelve months.

PEACE AT ANY PRICE. A state of peace, whatever has to be sacrificed to obtain it.

He was a weak, lazy man who, where his home was concerned, believed in peace at any price.

PIPE OF PEACE. American Indians celebrated the end of warfare between two tribes or two individuals by smoking a pipe of peace with their recent enemies. See BURY THE HATCHET.

Pearl : CAST PEARLS BEFORE SWINE. Or. Biblical. Present or introduce something of value or beauty to those who are entirely unable to appreciate it.

He took his visitors to the National Gallery, but it was casting pearls before swine.

Peg : PEG AWAY (S.). Continue steadily ; persevere.

If you peg away long enough, you'll be able to learn any language.

PEG OUT (S.). Die.

Old Smith may peg out at any moment.

Penalty : PAY THE PENALTY, or THE DEBT. Suffer what is due and inevitable as the result of an action.

If you drink when you're young, you'll pay the penalty in your old age.

Penny : IN FOR A PENNY, IN FOR A POUND. (Frequently abbrev. to " In for a penny ".) Being slightly involved, one may as well be involved still further.

As we're going to Folkestone, why not cross to Boulogne ? In for a penny——!

PENNY-DREADFUL. An old-f. term for the cheap and sensational magazines of the last century. See BLOOD AND THUNDER.

A PENNY FOR YOUR THOUGHTS. A facetious offer, made to arouse someone who has been silent and distrait.

PENNYWISE. Abbrev. of the proverb, " Penny wise and pound foolish ". Careful in saving small sums, but foolish in the method of doing so.

He refused to spend money in repairing the roof, and now the rain has ruined half his furniture— a plain example of penny wise.

A PRETTY PENNY. A large sum of money.

That house he has bought must have cost a pretty penny.

TURN, or EARN, AN HONEST PENNY. Earn money, usually by extra work, or unusual methods.

I'm trying to turn an honest penny by selling home-made cakes.

Perform : PERFORM THE OFFICE OF. Carry out the duties of.

The captain performed the office of clergyman, and married the young couple on the deck of his ship.

Period : AT NO PERIOD. At no time ; never in the past.

At no period have so many people been interested in politics.

Person : IN PERSON. Personally.

The Queen will open Parliament in person.

Perspective : IN PERSPECTIVE. Viewed or seen from the distance as a past event.

Viewed in perspective, the quarrel seemed to have been very trivial.

Pertaining : PERTAINING or APPERTAINING TO. Connected with. (This phrase is used only formally and in legal documents.)

The house and everything pertaining to it.

Pick : PICK AND CHOOSE. Select.

You haven't time to pick and choose from among so many pictures.

PICK-ME-UP. A quick restorative, after weakness or fatigue.

PICK A QUARREL. Deliberately begin a quarrel.

That dog will pick a quarrel with any other one he meets.
See TRAIL ONE'S COAT.

PICK UP. Acquire by chance ; obtain casually.

I picked up that old oak table in a Welsh village.

PICK ONE'S WAY *or* ONE'S STEPS. Walk deliberately
and carefully among difficulties and obstructions.

We had to pick our way through the mud.

Piece : ALL OF A PIECE. All part of, or connected with.

*His laziness is all of a piece with the rest of his char-
acter.*

A PIECE OF ONE'S MIND. See **Mind,** also WITHOUT
MINCING MATTERS.

GO TO PIECES. Deteriorate completely.

Since his wife's death, Jones has gone all to pieces.

PICK TO PIECES. Lit., Tear into small pieces. Met.,
Analyse ; examine closely with the object of finding fault.

My father picks to pieces every statement I make.

PULL TO PIECES. Lit., As above. Met., similar to
PICK TO PIECES, but more emphatic.

Piecemeal : DESTROY, TEAR, BREAK, CUT UP, *etc.*, PIECE-
MEAL. Divide into small portions ; one portion
at a time.

*The lovely furniture of the palace was smashed piecemeal
by the mob.*

Pig : PIG IN A POKE. Something acquired ignorantly, without
previous examination or knowledge. Usually used
with the verb " buy ". (The word " poke " here
means a pocket or small sack.)

*She bought a pig in a poke when she paid £500 for
those mining shares.*

Pile : MAKE ONE'S PILE (S.). Or. Gold-mining. A man's
" pile " was the amount of gold he accumulated.
Become rich by one's own efforts.

Sir Thomas made his pile selling butter and tea.

Pill : A BITTER PILL. An unpleasant, humiliating or intensely
disappointing fact.

*That she would never love him, in spite of his good looks
and wealth, was a bitter pill to swallow.*

GILD, *or* SUGAR, THE PILL. Do something to make an
unpleasant task or duty less so. Or. The obsolete

custom of gilding pills to make them less offensive to taste or sight.

SWALLOW THE PILL. See BITTER PILL.

Pin : PIN DOWN. 1. Lit., Fix ; fasten firmly.

The house received a direct hit from a bomb, and the unfortunate man was pinned down by a fallen beam.

2. Met., Compelled to deal with some particular fact ; to substantiate a statement.

He admitted that he had been in prison, but I couldn't pin him down to the exact year.

PIN ONE'S FAITH ON. Believe in completely ; trust absolutely.

I pin my faith on the commonsense of the English people.
See SWEAR BY.

PIN ONE'S HOPES ON. Attach one's hopes to ; concentrate one's hopes on.

We are pinning our hopes on having a longer holiday next year.

PIN-MONEY. See **Money.**

PINS AND NEEDLES. The tingling sensation felt in a limb which has become stiff and numb.

I can't walk properly yet, I've pins and needles in my right leg.

Pinch : AT A PINCH. In an emergency ; if absolutely necessary.

We've a good many guests, but at a pinch one or two can sleep in the lounge.

Pink : PINK OF PERFECTION. Absolutely and completely perfect.

Their new cook seems to be the pink of perfection.

Pipe : PUT THAT IN YOUR PIPE AND SMOKE IT (S.). A facetious form of defiance, meaning, "Give *that* your consideration."

I am going to become an artist even if I starve—and you can put that in your pipe and smoke it.

Piping : PIPING HOT. Lit., Hot as water that is " piping " or singing in a kettle just before reaching boiling-point.

He gave us a splendid dinner, piping hot.

Pit : PIT AGAINST. Place in competition against ; compel to fight. In the days of the Roman Emperors, a man with a short sword was frequently pitted against a lion or other wild beast.

Pitch : PITCH INTO (S.).   1. Attack violently, either with one's fists or tongue.

There goes Mrs. Simpson, pitching into her husband as usual.

2. Begin with energy one's work or a meal.

Here's your supper—pitch into it.

PITCH *or* PICK ON.   Decide upon ; choose.

Whenever there's an unpleasant job to be done the chief pitches on me.

PITCH ONE'S TENT.   Lit., To " pitch " a tent is to erect it, usually for a limited period.   Met., To settle anywhere.

We've decided to pitch our tent in London until Christmas.

PITCH A YARN (S.).   Tell a " tall " story, or one difficult to believe.

Bill pitched a yarn about being attacked on his way to the ship.

Pitcher : LITTLE PITCHERS HAVE LONG EARS.   A general warning when children are present.   Small children frequently overhear what they are not intended to know.   (A pitcher is a jug with a handle in the shape of an ear.)

Pity : WHAT A PITY, *or* SHAME !   A general expression of regret.

What a pity that you won't be able to come to the party.

Place : IN THE FIRST PLACE.   Firstly, at the beginning.

In the first place, I must explain that I can't speak English very well.

(Similarly, second, third, etc., place.)

OUT OF PLACE.   Unsuitable ;   in the wrong surroundings.

The little dog looked absurdly out of place in the Royal procession.

TAKE PLACE.   Happen ;   occur.

The wedding will take place next week.

Plain : PLAIN DEALING.   Honest and open business methods.

All his life he believed in plain dealing, and practised it.

PLAIN AS A PIKESTAFF.   Obvious ;   unmistakable.   Or. The pikestaff or long stick carried by pilgrims and on which was fastened a statement of their devotion to Christ.

They're very much in love with each other—that's as plain as a pikestaff.

Play : CHILD'S PLAY. Extremely easy to perform or solve.
This crossword is mere child's play.

PLAY THE DEVIL, *or* DEUCE (S.). Ruin or seriously injure.
This illness will play the Devil with your chance of passing the examination.

PLAY WITH EDGED TOOLS. Incur risk and danger. An "edged" tool is one with a sharp cutting edge.
I warned him that if he threatened the Duke he was playing with edged tools.

PLAY FALSE. Betray ; cheat.
His best friend played him false, and he lost his faith in humanity.

See DOUBLE-CROSS and DOUBLE-DEALING.

PLAY FAST AND LOOSE. Behave recklessly without consideration for others, and regardless of one's promises.
He played fast and loose with his wife's affection for him.

PLAY TO THE GALLERY. Or. Theatrical. Try to achieve popularity among one's inferiors ; degrade one's abilities to obtain popularity.
Finally, playing to the gallery, the candidate finished his speech with a lot of cheap sneers and silly jokes.

PLAY INTO THE HANDS OF. Behave so that one's actions are an advantage to someone else, usually an opponent or enemy.
By neglecting his work, he played into the hands of the man who wanted his job.

PLAY OFF. Use two opponents, one against the other to one's own advantage.
He played off Jones against Smith until both were too angry to attack him.

PLAY SECOND FIDDLE. Be in a subordinate position. The first fiddle is the most important member of an orchestra.
I refuse to play second fiddle to young Simpson.

PLAY TRUANT. Remain away from school.
The two boys decided to play truant and go fishing.

PLAY UP (S.). Support ; follow the example set.
I'm going to assure old Tompkins that we need him on the committee, and you must play up.

PLAY UPON. Take advantage of.
The scoundrel played upon the old woman's love for her daughter.

PLAY UPON WORDS. A pun ; a verbal joke.

PLAYED OUT. Exhausted ; finished ; out of date.
That old plot is completely played out.

Plead : PLEAD THE CAUSE. Speak favourably for ; help by supporting.
I am here to plead the cause of many unfortunate people who cannot plead for themselves.

Please : PLEASE ONESELF. Do as one desires.
I am going home—you can please yourself.

PLEASED AS PUNCH (S.). Extremely pleased.
The baby has its first tooth, and the parents are as pleased as Punch.

Pledge : HOLD IN PLEDGE. To " pledge " is to give a solemn promise. To hold in pledge is to retain something to compel such a promise to be kept.

PLEDGE ONESELF. Make a solemn and formal promise.
I pledge myself to serve the King faithfully.

REDEEM ONE'S PLEDGE. Fulfil such a promise. Also regain something pledged with a pawnbroker by paying the amount due.

TAKE THE PLEDGE. Formally undertake never to drink intoxicants—wine, spirits, beer, etc.

Plentiful : PLENTIFUL AS BLACKBERRIES. Extremely plentiful. Blackberries grow in large numbers in the English hedges in autumn.

Plight : PLIGHT ONE'S TROTH. Old. f. (" Troth " is a variation of " truth ".) Make a formal promise to marry.
They plighted their troth under the old oak-tree.

Plot : THE PLOT THICKENS. The affair becomes more complicated and exciting.

Plough : PLOUGH THE WAVES. Travel, by sail or otherwise, through the sea.
The great liner ploughed the waves on her way to England.

Pluck : PLUCK UP COURAGE. Acquire confidence and conquer fear.
She plucked up courage, and confronted the burglar.

Plume : PLUME ONESELF. Take pride in.
He plumed himself on belonging to the aristocracy.

Pocket : OUT OF POCKET.   Poorer financially.

I am ten shillings out of pocket as a result of the arrangement.

OUT-OF-POCKET EXPENSES.   Expenses incurred and paid in transacting business.

I had to travel to Sheffield, and the out-of-pocket expenses came to over £5.

POCKET, *or* SWALLOW, AN INSULT.   Submit to an insult without protest ; ignore it.

Though furious at the King's words, he decided that it would be wiser to pocket the insult.

POCKET ONE'S PRIDE.   Become humble under compulsion or necessity.

I pocketed my pride and asked my uncle to lend me the fare home.

Point : CARRY ONE'S POINT.   See **Carry.**

A CASE IN POINT.   An example.

Many politicians owe much to their wives ; Gladstone was a case in point.

COME TO THE POINT.   Arrive at the crux, or what is really important.

We talked for an hour before I had enough courage to come to the point and ask her to marry me before I left England.

CULMINATING POINT.   Climax.

The culminating point of the opera was the magnificent singing of the duet in the second act.

A KNOTTY POINT.   A difficult or complicated matter to decide.

Whether the Channel tunnel should be built or not is a knotty point.

MAKE A POINT OF.   Take special care and trouble about.

She always made a point of warming her husband's slippers.

A MOOT POINT.   A point or detail which is unsettled and open to discussion or argument.

The precise centre of England is a moot point.

THE POINT.   The object.

The point of these discussions is that they enable the ministers concerned to get a clear idea of what is happening.

POINT BLANK.   Or. Gunnery.   Direct, without any

qualification. (Fr. *point-blanc*—the white centre of the official target.)

He denied point-blank that he had ever entered the house.

POINT A MORAL. Emphasize some moral truth.

Napoleon's death points a moral to those who would sacrifice everything for power.

POINT OUT. Indicate ; remind a person.

May I point out that you have not yet paid your bill.

A SORE POINT. A subject upon which one is sensitive.

The fact that he is only five feet tall is a sore point with Wilkinson.

STRETCH A POINT. Concede a certain amount.

The landlord is willing to stretch a point, and allow us to stay another week.

POINT OF VIEW. Personal opinion or aspect.

From the smokers' point of view the tobacco tax is too high.

A WEAK POINT. A particular weakness.

The weak point in George's recognition of the burglar is that it was too dark to see the man clearly.

Pole : POLE TO POLE. i.e. From the North to the South Pole. All over the world.

You can hear English spoken from pole to pole.

Polish : POLISH OFF. Finish quickly.

I can polish off the job in five minutes.

Possession : MAN IN POSSESSION. A bailiff, a sheriff's officer ; legally, a man installed by a creditor in the debtor's house until the amount owing is paid.

IN POSSESSION OF. Possessing ; having.

The thief was in possession of a large quantity of stolen property.

See IN THE HANDS OF.

Post : AT ONE'S POST. At one's appointed place, or official position.

The sentry was found sleeping at his post.

LEFT AT THE POST. Or. Racing, the " post " being the starting-post, the point at which a race begins. Hopelessly beaten by other competitors.

At all social functions, poor old Bill is always left at the post.

Pot : GO TO POT (S.). Become totally ruined. Or. The " pot " into which waste metal is put to be melted down.

If you don't attend to your business, it will go to pot.

KEEP THE POT BOILING (S.).   Enable any kind of enterprise, etc., to remain in an active condition.

John has offered to subscribe £20, which will keep the pot boiling for another week or so.

POT-BOILER.   Any literary or artistic work turned out merely to provide money for necessities. See above.

His novels are only pot-boilers ; his best work is as an historian.

THE POT CALLING THE KETTLE BLACK. One person accusing another, of faults of which he is himself guilty.

Smith blamed Jones for careless driving—a bad case of the pot calling the kettle black.

A POT SHOT. A shot fired deliberately at some stationary object.

He took a pot shot at the motionless bird, but missed.

TAKE POT LUCK. See **Luck.**

Pound : POUND AWAY. Work vigorously. Lit., Strike heavily and repeatedly.

If you pound away at the job, you'll have finished before dark.

POUND OF FLESH. Full and complete payment, regardless of circumstances ; the uttermost payment.   Or. Shakespeare's comedy *The Merchant of Venice,* in which Shylock, the Jewish moneylender, claims a pound of flesh rashly promised by a man who cannot pay his debts.

If you borrow from the scoundrel, you may be sure he'll demand his pound of flesh.

Power : MORE POWER TO YOUR ELBOW ! Good luck to your efforts.

So you've decided to be a farmer in Canada ? Well, more power to your elbow !

THE POWERS THAT BE. Or. Biblical. Those in command ; the controllers.

If you want to go to the races, you'll have to ask the powers that be.

Praise : SPARING OF PRAISE. Giving little praise to.
> *The critics are very sparing of praise about Johnson's latest novel.*

Prayer : PAST PRAYING FOR. Impossible to alter, to repair, or to improve.
> *This old suit is past praying for.*

Preparation : IN COURSE OF PREPARATION. Being prepared.
> *The visitors found a magnificent dinner in course of preparation.*

Present : AT PRESENT. At the present time ; now.
> *At present we are living in Richmond.*

Press : PRESS FORWARD. I. Lit., Push in a forward direction.
> *The crowd pressed forward to see the celebrity.*

2. Met., Hasten.
> *I want you to press forward with that work.*

GO TO PRESS, i.e. the printing-press. Usually applied to a periodical, or to a book.
> *"The Weekly Gazette" goes to press on Thursday.*

Pretty : PRETTY GOOD, ACTIVE, *etc.* " Pretty " here is used in the sense of moderately, comparatively. (" FAIRLY " is used with a similar meaning.)
> *Father has pretty good health, considering his age.*

PRETTY WELL, *or* NEARLY, is, however, also used as " almost ".
> *Father will be coming soon—he has pretty well finished his dinner.*

A PRETTY PASS. See **Pass.**

Prevail : PREVAIL UPON. Persuade.
> *The committee hope to prevail upon her Ladyship to attend the concert.*

Prey : A PREY TO MELANCHOLY. Old f. Suffering from melancholy or any similar affliction ; depressed.
> *The old lady has been a prey to melancholy ever since her dog died.*

Prick : PRICK UP ONE'S EARS. Become suddenly alert and attentive, as an animal raises its ears at hearing an unfamiliar sound.
> *He was almost asleep when he heard his own name mentioned, and pricked up his ears.*

Pride : PUT ONE'S PRIDE IN ONE'S POCKET. Same as POCKET ONE'S PRIDE, which see.

Primrose : THE PRIMROSE PATH. The pleasant, easy-going, unthinking way of living. Or. Shakespeare's *Hamlet*, "The primrose path of dalliance ".

He has always followed the primrose path, and his family suffer for it.

Prince : THE PRINCE OF DARKNESS. Satan.

Prison : COMMIT TO PRISON. Formally order to be sent to prison.

The magistrate committed him to prison for a month.

Probability : IN ALL PROBABILITY, *or* LIKELIHOOD. Very probably ; very likely.

In all probability we shall be leaving for Paris next week.

Progress : IN PROGRESS. Being done or undertaken.

Repairs to many of the houses were in progress.

Proof : PROOF AGAINST. Able to resist.

She was extremely pretty, but the young man was proof against the temptation, and did not kiss her.

THE PROOF OF THE PUDDING IS IN THE EATING. Or. Proverbial. The value or wisdom of any action can only be discovered by actual experience.

I think they are foolish to get married, but the proof of the pudding is in the eating.

PUT TO THE PROOF. Test.

The man may be speaking the truth, but we must put his story to the proof.

Properly : PROPERLY. A provincial idiom. Thoroughly ; completely.

It made me properly angry to hear the way he spoke of his mother.

Prospect : IN PROSPECT ; IN VIEW. Being considered.

I have a much better job in prospect.

Pull : PULL OFF (S.). Succeed in completing.

I've managed to pull off a first-class deal with Snooks & Co.

PULL STRINGS. Use private and personal influence.

Alfred had to pull a good many strings to obtain the appointment.

PULL TOGETHER. Work together unitedly. Or. The game of " tug-of-war " in which each " side ", pulling at opposite ends of a rope, tries to drag the other side across the line between them.

If we pull together, success is certain.

PULL ONESELF TOGETHER. Make an effort to regain one's normal mental state.

"Pull yourself together," he told the terrified girl. "We still have a chance of escape."

PULL UP. 1. Noun. A stopping-place where drivers, etc., may stop for rest, food, etc.

There's a good pull-up for lorry-drivers in the next street.

2. Verb. Halt ; stop.

The coach will pull up at Kingston.

PULL UP SHORT. Stop abruptly, and before one intended.

The angry actor was addressing the audience, but had to pull up short when the curtain came down.

Purpose : INFIRM OF PURPOSE. Weak-willed ; unable to decide.

Peter is so infirm of purpose that it is useless to ask him for advice.

ON PURPOSE ; PURPOSELY. Intentionally.

TO THE PURPOSE. Direct to the subject, practically and sensibly.

John never wastes time ; he speaks plainly and to the purpose.

TO NO PURPOSE. Uselessly ; without success.

We begged him not to go out in the storm, but to no purpose.

Put : PUT ABOUT. 1. Worried ; anxious.

He was very put about by the news he received from London.

2. Nautical. Turn in the opposite direction.

The ship put about and returned to port.

3. Circulate ; make publicly known.

It was put about that the Queen was dying.

PUT ACROSS (S.). Successfully narrate, convince or influence.

He told that incredible story to the police, and managed to put it across.

PUT ALL ONE'S EGGS IN ONE BASKET. See **Basket.**

PUT IN AN APPEARANCE. Arrive and be present.

I am glad you were able to put in an appearance at the meeting.

PUT ONE'S BACK UP (S.). See under **Back**.

See RUB THE WRONG WAY; GET ONE'S GOAT; GET ONE'S MONKEY UP.

PUT BY. Save, usually for a special purpose.

I've managed to put by £10 for the holiday.

PUT OUT OF COUNTENANCE. Confuse; disconcert; embarrass.

Cinderella's magnificent ball dress put her jealous sisters completely out of countenance.

PUT DOWN. 1. Cease to hold.

Put down that gun immediately.

2. Suppress.

The General put down the rebellion in six weeks.

3. Store for future use (wine, etc.).

We've put down two dozen bottles of port.

4. Write; record.

Please put down the following facts.

PUT TO DEATH. Execute; kill.

Your orders are to put to death any man caught looting.

PUT TO FLIGHT. Compel to run away.

The victory was complete, and the enemy were put to flight.

PUT ONE'S BEST FOOT, *or* LEG, FOREMOST. See **Foot**.

BE PUT IN, *or* INTO, FORCE. Same as COME INTO FORCE.

PUT FORTH. 1. Announced.

It was put forth that the Queen was only slightly ill.

2. Employ; exert.

We must put forth every effort if the work is to be finished by Monday.

PUT OFF. 1. Delay.

Never put off till to-morrow what you can do to-day.

2. Repelled.

I meant to call on Smith, but was put off by the stories of his rudeness.

PUT OUT. 1. Extinguish.

He put out the lamp.

2. Remove from a house or other building; eject.

He put out the cat.

3. Annoy; perturb.

The old lady seemed put out.

PUT ON AIRS; PUT ON SIDE. See GIVE ONESELF AIRS.

PUT ON THE SCREW (S.). Compel a person by steady pressure (as a screw increases pressure) to do what is desired.

Old Tompkins refuses to pay the money, but I mean to put on the screw and make him.

PUT ONESELF OUT. 1. Take extra trouble.

We always put ourselves out to please grandfather.

2. Be disconcerted or annoyed.

Don't put yourself out because the postman hasn't called.

PUT A STOP TO, *or* **AN END TO.** Terminate ; end.

The Government ought to put a stop to all this official waste.

PUT TO IT ; HARD PUT TO IT. Tested ; confronted with difficulties.

He was hard put to it to decide whether to stay in England or go abroad.

PUT TWO AND TWO TOGETHER (AND MAKE FOUR). Deduce from obvious facts.

Putting two and two together, he realized that his firm would soon be bankrupt.

PUT UP. 1. Receive as a temporary guest ; provide with a bed.

We can easily put you up for the night.

2. Provide for a definite purpose, usually an investment.

I'd like to acquire the business, if my uncle will put up the money.

PUT UP AT. Reside ; live at temporarily.

We put up at the Savoy Hotel when we come to Town.

PUT UP WITH. Endure.

I can't put up with this toothache any longer.

See BEAR WITH.

A PUT-UP AFFAIR. A previously arranged affair ; a plot.

The two men appeared to be quarrelling, but I soon realized that it was a put-up affair, and not genuine.

PUT UPON. Impose upon.

Mary is so good-natured that her friends constantly put upon her.

PUT IN A WORD. Speak in favour of ; recommend.

I shall be grateful if you'll put in a word for my son when he applies for the job.

Q

Qualms : HAVE QUALMS. Have doubts ; feel uneasy.

I had qualms about letting the child go out so late.

Quarter : BEG FOR QUARTER. Implore or beg for mercy.

The beaten enemy begged for quarter, and were well treated.

IN EVERY QUARTER ; IN ALL QUARTERS. Everywhere ; in every direction.

We have received the same welcome in every quarter.

See ON EVERY HAND.

QUARTER ONESELF UPON. Reside with, uninvited, and usually for a considerable time.

My wife's mother has decided to quarter herself upon us.

Quarter-deck : COMING THE QUARTER-DECK (S.). Or. Naval. Behaving arrogantly as a superior. The quarter-deck of a ship is reserved for officers.

If Jones thinks he can come the quarter-deck over me, he's making a mistake.

Queen : QUEEN ANNE'S DEAD ! A sarcastic retort to a piece of information which has been known for a long time. (Queen Anne died in 1714.)

Queer : IN QUEER STREET. In an uncertain position financially ; in financial difficulties. Derived from the custom of writing *Quere* (enquire) against a person's account when it was considered advisable to make enquiries before trusting him.

They say the company is in Queer Street.

QUEER CARD. Or. card-playing. An eccentric and unusual type of person.

The old man was civil, but obviously a queer card.

QUEER CUSTOMER. Similar to above.

Quest : IN QUEST OF. In search of ; to search for.

He came to the City in quest of work.

Question : BEGGING THE QUESTION. Avoiding an argument or decision by bringing forward some immaterial point.

The man is an unscrupulous swindler, and it is begging the question to say that there are plenty of people worse than he is.

See BESIDE THE MARK and NO BEARING ON.

BEYOND ALL QUESTION. Without doubt ; certain.
Russia, beyond all question, is one of the greatest nations.

BURNING QUESTION. A matter requiring an immediate examination and prompt action.
The treatment of young criminals is a burning question.

CALL IN QUESTION. Express doubt about ; challenge.
I call in question the magistrate's right to send that man to prison.

IN QUESTION. Mentioned ; referred to.
The person in question has a very bad character.

OPEN QUESTION. Not certain ; debatable.
The advantage of being a rich man's son is an open question.
See VEXED QUESTION.

OUT OF THE QUESTION. Utterly impossible.
To build a tunnel from England to America is out of the question.

POP THE QUESTION (S.). Old f. and practically obsolete. Propose marriage to, the " question " being " Will you marry me ? "
Mary has been waiting months for George to pop the question, but up to now he hasn't.

VEXED QUESTION. A problem or question very difficult to decide.
The best age for marriage is a vexed question.
Similar to OPEN QUESTION.

Quick : TO THE QUICK. See CUT TO THE QUICK.

Quietus : GIVE A QUIETUS TO. Or. Legal. (A " quietus " is a discharge from some service.) To give freedom from consciousness, or even from life itself.
I gave the villain his quietus.

Quits : See CRY QUITS.

Quod : Prison (S.). (" Quod " is a contraction of " quadrangle ", the enclosure in which prisoners take exercise.)

R

R : THE THREE R'S. Reading, (w)riting and (a)rithmetic— the first elements of education.
His lessons at school were limited to the three R's.

Rack : ON THE RACK. Or. The mediæval instrument of torture. In a condition of acute mental tension ; intensely anxious.

I was on the rack until I received the doctor's report.

RACK ONE'S BRAINS. Similar to CUDGEL ONE'S BRAINS.

RACK AND RUIN ("rack" here = wreck). Complete decay and destruction (usually applied to buildings).

The house has gone to rack and ruin.

Racket : STAND THE RACKET (S.). Face the consequences (usually financial).

We're all going to Paris, and Father has promised to stand the racket.

Rage : ALL THE RAGE. Immensely popular or fashionable.

That shade of blue is all the rage this season.

Rag-tag : RAG-TAG AND BOBTAIL. The lowest level of society. Similar to RIFF-RAFF, which see.

Rain : IT NEVER RAINS BUT IT POURS. Events, fortunate or unfortunate, rarely occur singly.

Mary broke a cup yesterday, Mother dropped a plate this morning, and—it never rains but it pours !— I've just smashed the lid of the teapot.

A RAINY DAY. See **Day.**

Raise : RAISE CAIN (S.). Create a tremendous noise or disturbance.

His wife will raise Cain when she discovers how much he has spent.

RAISE THE WIND (S.). Obtain ready money. Or. Nautical. It is necessary that a wind should "raise" itself for a sailing-ship to move.

I can't raise the wind for a holiday this year.

Rake : RAKE-OFF (S.). Commission ; an agent's share after a purchase has been completed.

He gets a rake-off of ten per cent on every transaction.

RAKE UP. Recall unnecessarily from the past.

Why rake up a scandal that happened so long ago ?

Random : AT RANDOM. By chance ; without deliberate selection.

The explorer chose ten men at random to accompany him.

Range : WITHIN RANGE. Or. Military. Within an effective

distance or area. Near enough to be heard, seen, controlled, etc.

The subject should be within range of his knowledge.

Rank : RANK AND FILE. Or. Military. The ordinary working members of an organization. (Technically, soldiers under the rank of lance-sergeant comprise the rank and file.)

The payment offered to the rank and file is extremely poor.

RISE FROM THE RANKS. See **Rise.**

Rap : NOT WORTH A RAP. Worthless. A " rap " was a halfpenny issued in Ireland in 1721 and actually worth about half a farthing.

RAP ON THE KNUCKLES. A sharp reproof.

The servant received a rap on the knuckles for his carelessness.

RAP OUT. Speak sharply ; snap.

The captain rapped out an order, and the men marched away.

Rate : AT ANY RATE. In any circumstances, whatever has happened or may happen. The phrase is used as a final comment on some event or situation.

The Government, at any rate, is not to blame.

See AT ALL EVENTS ; IN ANY EVENT.

Reach : OUT OF REACH. Beyond the furthest distance to which one can stretch, or (met.) communicate.

We'd telephone to Mary, but she's out of reach.

REACH-ME-DOWNS (S.). Cheap, ready-made clothing.

Read : READ BETWEEN THE LINES. Grasp the hidden significance of something spoken or written.

Reading between the lines, it's plain from Mary's letter that she wishes she had not married him.

Reality : IN REALITY. Actually ; in fact.

He thought her perfect ; in reality she was selfish and vain.

Rear BRING UP THE REAR ; BE IN THE REAR. Travel behind ; be at the back, as the last member of the party.

The Colonel rode in front ; the major brought up the rear.

Reason : BEREFT OF REASON. 1. Insane.

He shouted like a man bereft of reason.

2. Unconscious.

She fell to the ground, bereft of reason.

STAND TO REASON. Be obviously reasonable or logical.

If you go out in the rain, it stands to reason that you'll get wet.

Receive : RECEIVE. Accept as one's social equal, and, as such, invite to dinners, balls, etc.

The Countess refuses to receive her new daughter-in-law.

Reckon : RECKON AMONG. Include among.

I reckon a sense of humour among my greatest blessings.

RECKONING. That which is due, or owing, financially or otherwise.

He paid the reckoning, and they left the restaurant.

RECKON ON. Rely upon. Similar to COUNT UPON.

RECKON WITH. Include in one's plans (usually as an enemy or a difficulty).

If you go swimming this morning, you'll have to reckon with a strong tide.

RECKON WITHOUT ONE'S HOST. Lit., To estimate what one's hotel expenses will be without consulting the landlord. To start any sort of enterprise without knowing what is involved.

He tried to cheat the farmer, but he reckoned without his host—the farmer was much too clever.

Reconcile : RECONCILE ONESELF. Subdue one's dislike or objections.

You must reconcile yourself to getting up early.

Red : LIKE A RED RAG TO A BULL. An exasperation ; an intense annoyance. Or. The belief (widespread but erroneous) that the sight of any red article infuriates a bull.

To the Communist, any reference to the Royal Family was like a red rag to a bull.

RED-HANDED. In the act of doing something wrong. The reference is to a murderer with his hands still stained with the blood of his victim.

We caught the cat red-handed drinking the milk.

RED HERRING. An attempt to divert attention from the chief facts by introducing some detail of no importance. Or. The old trick of drawing a red (dried) herring across the path by criminals when they are being followed by bloodhounds, to destroy the scent.

That account of his visit to the theatre was a mere red herring.

RED-LETTER DAY. Day of rejoicing. From the custom of indicating holidays and important saints' days in red lettering.

Tuesday will be a red-letter day—my daughter is getting married.

RED TAPE. Official and frequently trivial formalities. (From the old custom of Government officials and lawyers tying up their papers with red tape.)

We have given up trying to build a house—there is too much red tape involved.

Reference : IN, *or* WITH, REFERENCE TO. Referring to ; in connection with.

In reference to your letter of yesterday, we cannot accept the offer.

Note.—The phrase is chiefly used in commercial correspondence.

Reflection : DUE REFLECTION. Appropriate time for considering the matter.

After due reflection, we have decided to refuse your offer.

Refresher (*legal*) **:** A sum paid every day to a barrister in addition to his first (retaining) fee.

REFRESHER COURSE. An additional course of studies, following an earlier one, taken to refresh one's memory.

Refusal : THE FIRST REFUSAL. The first chance of buying an object before it is offered elsewhere.

I like the house, and the owner has given me the first refusal.

Regular : REGULAR AS CLOCKWORK. Regular as the movements of a clock.

He comes home every night, regular as clockwork.

Rein : GIVE REIN TO. Allow to escape without restraint.

He gave rein to his joy at meeting his friend.

Relish : NO RELISH FOR. No liking for.

I've no relish for long walks in wet weather.

Render : RENDER (in the sense of " give ").

We hope to render certain services to your company.

RENDER CERTAIN. Make certain; sure.

This medicine will render certain a night's sleep.

Repentance : STOOL OF REPENTANCE. Any conspicuous position in which one is compelled to remain while being censured. Or. The low stool which was once placed in front of the pulpit in Scottish churches, on which anyone who had offended against church law had to sit and listen to the clergyman's rebuke.

Resolution : FORM A RESOLUTION. Determine; definitely decide.

I've formed a resolution never to go to bed later than eleven.

Resolve : BE IT RESOLVED. A legal phrase used in connection with resolutions formally brought before a meeting. Be it resolved = It is resolved. The words of the resolution itself follow.

Respects : IN ALL RESPECTS ; IN EVERY RESPECT. In every way.

The new house is in all respects better than the old one.

PAY ONE'S RESPECTS. Carry out one's social duties by formally calling upon a person.

I hope to pay my respects to his lordship to-morrow.

Rest : REST ON ONE'S LAURELS. Having earned distinction or honours, to remain satisfied and do nothing further.

After a brilliant career at Cambridge, he decided to rest on his laurels and spend a year travelling.

REST ON ONE'S OARS. Or. Rowing. Remain passive, after making progress.

We've sold so many things that we can rest on our oars.

Very similar to REST ON ONE'S LAURELS.

Retreat : BEAT A RETREAT. Depart defeated ; go away ignominiously. Or. Military, from the signal to retreat being given by drum-beats.

I told the boys I would fetch a policeman, and they beat a retreat.

Rhyme : NEITHER RHYME NOR REASON. Nonsense ; rubbish. Or. The author of a worthless volume took it to Sir Thomas More, who told him to turn it into rhyme. When this had been done, More said,

"That will do. 'Tis rhyme now; before it was neither rhyme nor reason."

John's letter doesn't make sense; it is neither rhyme nor reason.

NO RHYME OR REASON. No reason whatever.

There's no rhyme or reason why I shouldn't go to the dance.

Ribbon : BLUE RIBBON. See under **Blue.**

Rid : GET RID OF ; RID ONESELF OF. Dispose of ; remove permanently.

I shall have to get rid of this worn-out carpet.

Ride : RIDE ROUGHSHOD. Proceed without consideration or regard for other people's views or feelings. (A horse is "roughshod" when it is wearing specially roughened shoes.)

The Chairman rode roughshod over all objections to his plans.

Riff-raff : Worthless members of society. (Riff = sweepings, raff = rags. Both words are obsolete Anglo-Saxon.)

We don't want all the riff-raff of London at the meeting.

See RAG-TAG AND BOBTAIL.

Right : BY RIGHTS. Rightly ; justly.

By rights, this house belongs to me.

SERVES YOU RIGHT. See under **Serve.**

RIGHT AS A TRIVET. In satisfactory condition. (A trivet is a metal plate on three legs on which toast, etc., is stood to keep hot.)

Joan was feverish last night, but she's as right as a trivet this morning.

COME RIGHT. See under **Come.**

RIGHT-HAND MAN. Chief assistant or supporter.

Arthur was my right-hand man during the election.

SEND TO THE RIGHTABOUT. Lit., Compel to turn sharply to the right and then depart. Send curtly away.

The beggar asked for money, but I soon sent him to the rightabout.

Ring : RING THE CHANGES. I. Change the order of a limited number of items, so as to produce variety, e.g. mutton, beef, lamb, etc., for dinner. From the variations produced by ringing Church bells in varying order. 2. A swindle, at one time very prevalent, by which a shopkeeper is tricked into giving change for counterfeit coins.

Rise : RISE FROM THE RANKS. Be promoted from a private soldier to a commissioned officer. The phrase is also used in connection with anyone who has risen from a very inferior position to an important one in the same organization.

The Managing Director has risen from the ranks.

RISE IN THE WORLD. Become socially or financially more important.

Brown must have risen in the world ; he's just bought a new car.

RISE WITH THE LARK. Get up early—strictly speaking at sunrise, when the lark begins to sing.

TAKE A RISE OUT OF ANYONE. Make a person look ridiculous, generally by deceiving him.

You'll find it difficult to take a rise out of a Scotsman.

Rob : ROB PETER TO PAY PAUL. Take from one person (or thing) to pay another. (The or. of this phrase goes back to the twelfth century.)

Don't take the drawing-room curtains to make the dining-room look smart—it's merely robbing Peter to pay Paul.

Rock : ROCK-BOTTOM. Lowest possible.

He quoted a rock-bottom price.

ON THE ROCKS (S.). Or. Naval. Lit., Shipwrecked. Applied to financial or other disasters.

They were happy for a year or two, and then their marriage went on the rocks.

Rod : ROD IN PICKLE. A future scolding, or more serious punishment. (The rods with which children were beaten used to be kept in salt water to make them supple and ready for use.)

There's a rod in pickle for young Henry when he comes in from school.

RULE WITH A ROD OF IRON. Govern or control with great severity.

Their father ruled the children with a rod of iron.

Rogue : ROGUE'S MARCH. Lit., The name given to the drum-music played when a bad character is " drummed " out of the army. Commonly used to describe the

stumbling progress of a rebellious prisoner being
dragged along to the police-station.

Roll : ROLL-CALL. The list of names of those who should be
present at some assembly. (See CALL THE ROLL.)

ROLL UP. I. Lit.

Roll up the plans of the City.

2. Met. (S.). Assemble ; appear.

I want all our friends to roll up on this occasion.

Rolling : ROLLING STONE. Or. The proverb, " A rolling
stone gathers no moss," i.e. a wanderer gathers
no riches. One who never settles long in one
place.

Rome : DO IN ROME. Or. The proverb, " Do in Rome
as the Romans do." Adapt yourself to the
habits and customs of those among whom you are
living.

Room : PREFER A PERSON'S ROOM TO HIS COMPANY. Prefer
that he were absent, somewhere else.

*Charles is so bad-tempered that I prefer his room to
his company.*

ROOM AND TO SPARE. Plenty of space.

There's room and to spare in that box for my hat.

Root : ROOT AND BRANCH. Every part ; the whole organization.

*The police are going to put an end to the smuggling,
root and branch.*

THE ROOT OF THE MATTER, TROUBLE, *etc.* The base ;
the foundation of.

*The root of the whole trouble is that the men are
underpaid.*

ROOT OUT. Remove completely ; extract from its
surroundings.

I am going to root out every wasps'-nest in the garden.

Rope : GIVE ONE ENOUGH ROPE. Or. The proverb, " Give
a man rope enough, and he'll hang himself."
Allow a man to continue his mistakes or crimes
until punishment overtakes him.

Ropes : KNOW THE ROPES. Be familiar with the method
and procedure.

Bill had better act as chairman, as he knows the ropes.

Rotten : ROTTEN TO THE CORE. Utterly bad.

The man's morals are rotten to the core.

Rough : ROUGH DIAMOND. An uneducated but worthy person.

Mrs. Juggins is a rough diamond, but she knows how to cook.

ROUGH IT. Live primitively.

If you live in the country, you must be prepared to rough it.

ROUGH ON (S.). Severe on ; a hardship for.

Jack's wife has run away with the man next door— which is rough on Jack.

ROUGHLY. 1. In a rough manner.

The police handled the prisoners roughly.

2. Approximately.

There are roughly half a million people in the city.

SLEEP ROUGH. Sleep out of doors, under haystacks, etc.

Round : GOING THE ROUNDS. A "round" is a regular tour, or "beat", which a watchman or policeman makes to ensure that all is well, or, in the case of a trades- man, to deliver his goods. Used, met., for "cir- culating ; travelling around".

There's a curious story going the rounds about Jenkins.

ROUNDABOUT WAY, ROUTE, *etc.* A straggling, indirect way.

We came into the City by a roundabout way.

ROUND NUMBERS. Strictly speaking, this idiom should refer to complete hundreds, thousands, etc. It is, however, constantly used in the sense of "approxi- mately".

There are in round numbers 1,750 people in the village.

ROUND OFF. Complete ; add a final finish to.

He rounded off the performance with a song.

ROUND ROBIN. A letter or other document, usually of complaint, upon which all those concerned sign their names in a circle, so that everyone has the same responsibility and the leader remains anony- mous.

ROUND-TABLE CONFERENCE. A meeting at which representatives of all parties to a dispute meet on equal terms to discuss matters.

There will be a round-table conference of employers and men to-morrow.

ROUND ON. Blame violently, and frequently un-
deservedly.

*Because you've lost your temper, you needn't round
on me.*

Rout : ROUT OUT.   Compel to come out ; fetch from seclusion
or a hiding-place.

*I'm going to rout out enough young men to make the
dance a success.*

Rub : RUB UP.   1. Polish.

I want you to rub up the silver.

2. Revive one's knowledge of a subject.

I must rub up my Latin for the examination.

RUB UP THE WRONG WAY.   Irritate; annoy.   (From
annoying a cat by rubbing its fur in the wrong
direction.)

Her tactlessness always rubs me up the wrong way.

See PUT ONE'S BACK UP (under **Back**).

Rule : RULE OF THE ROAD.   The general rule governing
traffic.   In England all vehicles go along the road
on the left ; in most other countries on the right.

RULE THE ROOST, *or* ROAST.   Be in the position of one
who issues orders, and is in command.

George's mother rules the roost in the household.

(*Note.*—Rule the roost.—Derived from the cock who
is master of the farmyard " roost ", or hen house.
Rule the roast.—Derived from the cook whose
duty it was to regulate the cooking of the meat
on the kitchen fire.

RULE OF THUMB.   Lit., Measuring lengths by one's
thumb.   Applied to any work in which the
measurements are guesswork based on experience.

RULING PASSION.   The chief incentive in one's life.

*Her ruling passion was to attract the admiration of
young men.*

Run : 1. Verb.   Manage.

He ran a grocery business.

2. Noun.   An extended number of performances or
issues.

The play had a run of 500 nights.

HE WHO RUNS MAY READ.   Or. Biblical.   Applied to
something written so plainly that even a man
running past it could read the words.

IN THE LONG RUN. Eventually.
In the long run, crime does not pay.

ON THE RUN. Being pursued from place to place by the police or military.
The country is crowded with deserters on the run.

RUN ACROSS. Meet casually and unexpectedly.
I don't often run across Smith.

RUN AFTER. Seek ; pursue.
He runs after every pretty girl he meets.
She's a girl who is very much run after.

RUN AGAINST. Similar to RUN ACROSS.

RUN AMUCK, *or* " AMOK ". Dash about wildly and senselessly. Or. Malay. Natives of Malaya " run amuck " when maddened by opium.
The kitten has run amuck with my knitting-wool.

RUN OFF, *or* AWAY, WITH. Steal and depart with.
The assistant has run off with his master's wife and £500.

RUN AWAY WITH THE IDEA. Assume hastily and incorrectly.
I don't want you to run away with the idea that I'm rich.

MAKE A RUNAWAY MATCH. Elope.
The young couple made a runaway match.

RUN COUNTER TO. Be in opposition to.
Your suggestions run counter to what we arranged yesterday.

RUN DOWN. I. Collide with and injure or kill. Similar to RUN OVER.
If you drive so fast, you'll run down some unfortunate pedestrian.

2. Overtake, and frequently capture as well.
They ran down the thief just outside the town.

3. Speak ill of.
She's always running down her neighbours.
See CRY DOWN.

4. Visit.
I'll run down and see you on Monday.

5. In poor health, through overwork, etc.
The poor woman is terribly run down.

RUN TO EARTH. Or. Fox-hunting, from following a fox to its den, or " earth ". Trace to its hiding-place ; of a quotation, its origin.

They ran the murderer to earth in his mother's cottage.
I ran the quotation to earth in Shakespeare's Othello.

RUN ONE'S EARTHLY RACE. Live one's life.

RUN FOR IT. Run for some especially urgent reason.

If you want to meet your father, you'll have to run for it.

A RUN FOR ONE'S MONEY. Time and opportunity in which to be free, or enjoy oneself.

The prisoner was recaptured, but he had had a month's run for his money.

RUN HIGH. Become heated; excited.

Feelings always run high during an election.

RUN IN. Take to a police-station under arrest.

The thief was caught and run in on the same day.

RUN INTO. See RUN ACROSS, also RUN DOWN (1) and RUN OVER (2).

RUN INTO DEBT. Incur debt.

A man who constantly runs into debt is not to be trusted.

RUN LIKE MAD. See under **Mad.**

RUN MAD. Become fantastically exaggerated and unreal.

The plans for rebuilding the City show socialism run mad.

RUN ON. Hasten ahead.

Run on, and see if dinner's ready.

RUN OUT. 1. Come to an end.

My patience has completely run out.

We ran out of coal, and had to burn wood.

2. Cricket. A batsman is "run out" when the ball is thrown against the wicket before he has had time to complete a run.

RUN OVER. 1. Flow over.

The water ran over the edge of the jug.

2. Drive over; collide with.

The train ran over the poor fellow as he was crossing the line.

Similar to RUN INTO.

3. Glance over; read through and check.

You'd better run (your eye) over these instructions before you go.

RUN RIOT. Behave in a completely undisciplined way.
The children in that family run riot.

RUN A RISK. Incur a risk or danger.
You'll run a risk of cutting your feet if you don't wear shoes.

RUN TO SEED. 1. Lit., Grow rank and straggling. As a plant does after it has blossomed. 2. Met., Deteriorate, with an effect of neglect and decay.
A house will soon run to seed if left untenanted.

RUN SHORT OF. Be left without a sufficient supply.
I hate to run short of milk, but the cat knocked over the jug.

RUN THROUGH. 1. Exhaust; squander.
The young spendthrift has run through several fortunes.
2. Read quickly.
I'll just run through these letters, and then we'll go out.
3. Pierce completely.
The needle ran through her finger.

RUN UP. Stitch rapidly.
I'll soon run up this seam.

RUN UP A BILL. Incur debts, usually recklessly.
He ran up a bill for over £100.

RUNNER-UP. The competitor immediately after the winner.
Jim won the swimming race, and Bill was the runner-up.

RUNNING. Consecutive.
We met several days running.
(*Note.*—This adjective invariably follows the noun.)

RUNNING FIGHT. A fight throughout which the defenders are running away and the attackers pursuing them.

RUNNING REMARKS. Comments made while something is being read or spoken.
He read the new regulations amid running remarks from the audience.

Rush : RUSH ONE'S FENCES (S.). Or. Hunting. Be in too great a hurry for results.
Be patient ; don't rush your fences, and she'll marry you yet.

RUSH HEADLONG. Rush recklessly, with all one's energy.
Peter is always rushing headlong from one excitement to another.

S

Sack : GET, *or* BE GIVEN, THE SACK ; BE SACKED (S.). Be dismissed from one's work. Or. Travelling workmen used to keep their tools in sacks or bags. When a man's work was finished he was given back the sack, in which he replaced his tools before going on to seek another job.

If Bill doesn't work harder he'll get the sack.

Sackcloth : IN SACKCLOTH AND ASHES. Or. Biblical. To dress oneself in sackcloth and put ashes on one's head was an indication of mourning and sorrow. Deeply penitent.

I'm in sackcloth and ashes for having forgotten to post the letters last night.

Saddled : SADDLED WITH. Burdened with.

He was saddled with the responsibility of educating three small children.

Said : NO SOONER SAID THAN DONE. Indicative of immediate action, an immediate response.

I asked him for a letter of introduction, and it was no sooner said than done.

Sail : SAIL NEAR, *or* CLOSE TO, THE WIND. Or. Nautical. Go very near to something which is improper or illegal.

The magistrate warned the defendant that he was sailing very near the wind.

SAIL UNDER FALSE COLOURS. Or. Nautical. Pirate ships used to hoist the flags of friendly nations to deceive other vessels. Pretend to be something that one is not.

That young man is sailing under false colours. He pretends to be a gardener, and interested in roses, but the only thing he's interested in is Mary.

SET SAIL. Start on a sea voyage.

The captain set sail for America early in May.

STRIKE SAIL. Or. Nautical. Surrender to someone more powerful. Lit., lower the sails of a ship. In war, to strike the flag is a signal of surrender.

Never strike sail to a threat.

Sally : SALLY FORTH. Come forth, come out, suddenly and dramatically.

The men sallied forth from their hiding-places and attacked the troops.

Salt : SALT OF THE EARTH. Or. Biblical. (" Ye are the salt of the earth ", St. Matthew, ch. 5, v. 13.) The best, most valuable members of society.

An honest, hard-working man is the salt of the earth.

NOT WORTH ONE'S SALT *or* KEEP. Worthless ; not worth the cost of the salary one is paid. (*Note.*— The word " salary " is derived from the Lat. *salarium,* salt. Originally " salt money " was money paid to Roman soldiers in lieu of salt.

TAKE WITH A GRAIN OF SALT. Accept a statement, but with some doubt as to its complete truth.

We take most of what the sailor says with a grain of salt.

Salvation : WORK OUT ONE'S OWN SALVATION. Discover, by experience, the solution to one's problems.

As for Bill, he'll have to work out his own salvation.

Sanctity : ODOUR OF SANCTITY. Lit., The odour of incense surrounding the figures of saints in cathedrals and churches. Met., A general atmosphere of virtue ; virtuous surroundings.

She lived a wicked life, but died in the odour of sanctity

Sand : THE SANDS ARE RUNNING OUT. There is not much time left. Or. The grains of sand running through the hour-glass, once a common substitute for the clock.

You had better confess—the sands are running out.

Satan : SATAN REBUKING SIN. Blaming a person for a fault or sin of which one is also guilty.

George, who spends a pound a week on cigarettes, blames Jane for smoking too much—a case of Satan rebuking sin.

Satisfaction : GIVE SATISFACTION. Satisfy ; be what is required.

I think these stockings will give satisfaction.

Sauce : SAUCE FOR THE GOOSE. Or. The proverb, " What's sauce for the goose is sauce for the gander." What is suitable for one person is equally suitable

8

for another ; the same rule applies to all people in similar circumstances.

If I'm too old to dance, so are you ; what's sauce for the goose——

Save : SAVE APPEARANCES. Prevent or minimize embarrassment ; deal tactfully with any embarrassing situation.

The carpet was very old and shabby ; my aunt, to save appearances, said that it was a family heirloom.

SAVE THE MARK. Or. Archery. When anyone shot especially well, the cry was " God save the mark ! ", i.e., " May God prevent the arrow being displaced by a later shot." Now used to emphasize some ironical statement.

In our free country—save the mark !—you mustn't paint your own front door in your own time with your own paint.

Say : HAVE ONE'S SAY. Say all that one wishes to say in one's own words.

We were all tired of speeches, but the old woman was determined to have her say.

I SAY. An introductory phrase to a remark conveying surprise or special interest.

I say, look at Mary's new hat !

Saying : AS THE SAYING IS ; AS THEY SAY. A half-facetious, half-apologetic excuse for using a hackneyed phrase or cliché.

Well, hard work never hurt anyone, as the saying is.

Scales : SCALES FALL FROM ONE'S EYES. The " scales " are the metaphorical coverings which prevent one from realizing the truth.

Then the scales fell from her eyes, and she saw the man she had loved was a villain.

SCALES OF JUSTICE. The scales traditionally held with each side exactly level by the blindfolded figure of Justice. (The figure is erected over the Central Criminal Court in London, as an emblem of the Law's absolute fairness towards all who are tried there.)

Scarce : MAKE ONESELF SCARCE. Depart quickly, and efface oneself.

Here comes my uncle—you'd better make yourself scarce.

Scene : CREATE, *or* MAKE, A SCENE. Cause any violent emotional disturbance.

Don't lose your temper and create a scene.

Scent : SCENT (A MYSTERY, SCANDAL, *etc.*). Suspect.

Uncle has been making enquiries about George's past ; I'm sure he scents a mystery.

Sceptre : WIELD THE SCEPTRE. Old f. for "reign"; rule as a sovereign.

Queen Victoria wielded the sceptre for over sixty years.

Score : PAY OFF, WIPE OFF, *or* SETTLE OLD SCORES. Cancel an old injury or injustice by inflicting another adequate punishment. "Score" is an Anglo-Saxon word, meaning, lit., a cut or scratch, and debts used to be recorded by making such marks in long sticks. When such debts were paid, the "score" was removed.

He paid off an old score by giving the bully a thorough thrashing.

SCORE OFF. Triumph over ; make one's opponent look foolish or embarrassed.

Jobson scored off Hobson when he told that story of their visit to Paris.

Scorn : POINT THE FINGER OF SCORN. Old f. Sneer at ; speak about with contempt.

Let no one point the finger of scorn at a woman who gives up a fortune to marry a poor man.

Scot : SCOT FREE. See under **Free.**

Scrape : GET INTO A SCRAPE. Get into trouble ; commit some foolish action leading to trouble.

Peter is always getting into some scrape or other.

SCRAPE ACQUAINTANCE WITH. Take special trouble to become acquainted with ; deliberately set out to become friends with.

She was so lonely during her holiday that she would have scraped acquaintance with almost anyone.

SCRAPE TOGETHER. Succeed, with difficulty, in saving a little.

Jones scraped together just enough from his salary to take a week's holiday.

Scratch : BRING, *or* COME UP, TO THE SCRATCH. Or. Prize-fighting. Reach a definite decision ; decide to take definite action. The "scratch" is the line marked in the prize-ring to which the boxers are led at the beginning of a fight.

Peter has not actually asked Jane to marry him, but she hopes to bring him up to the scratch this evening.

SCRATCH TEAM, CREW, *etc.* A number of people collected casually, not regular members.

Although we'd only a scratch team, we won all three matches.

UP TO SCRATCH (S.). Fit to deal with one's work; equal to what is required.

I've had influenza, and am still not up to scratch.

Screw : PUT ON THE SCREW. See under **Put**.

A SCREW LOOSE (S.). Something wrong or irregular.

I can't understand these accounts; there's a screw loose somewhere.

HAVE A SCREW LOOSE (S.). Be mentally deficient, not quite " ALL THERE " (which see).

Scruple : MAKE NO SCRUPLE ; HAVE NO SCRUPLES. Have no hesitation. Frequently applied to some action which might involve some " scruple " or sense of wrong.

The soldiers made no scruple about robbing their prisoners.

Sea : AT SEA. Unaware; confused.

She stayed over an hour, but I am still completely at sea concerning her object in coming to see me.

GET ONE'S SEA-LEGS. Learn to walk successfully on the moving deck of a ship ; accommodate oneself to the rise and fall of the waves.

PUT TO SEA. Leave the shore to start on a voyage.

We put to sea in a leaky old boat called the " Terror ".

SEA OF TROUBLE. Or. Quotation from Shakespeare's *Hamlet* : " To take arms against a sea of troubles." Many heavy troubles.

He looked wretched, as if he were overwhelmed by a sea of troubles.

Seal : ONE'S LIPS ARE SEALED. One is completely silent.

I can tell you nothing ; my lips must be sealed.

SEALED BOOK. A subject completely unknown.

Fifteenth-century art was a sealed book to him.

Season : FOR A SEASON. For a short time.

For a season we shall be apart, to meet again in Heaven.

See FOR A SPACE.

IN SEASON AND OUT OF SEASON. At all times, whether suitable or unsuitable.

He talked of his travels in season and out of season.

OUT OF SEASON. Unseasonable; at a wrong or inappropriate time.

Oysters are out of season in August.

Second : COME OFF SECOND-BEST. Be overcome by a superior force.

The robber attacked the innkeeper, but found that he came off second-best.

SECOND CHILDHOOD. Extreme age, when the mind becomes childish again.

My grandfather is nearly ninety, and in his second childhood.

SECOND NATURE. Instinctive; an action which has already taken place so many times that it has become automatic.

It had become second nature to light the fire and prepare breakfast for her husband.

SECOND THOUGHTS. Or. The proverb, "Second thoughts are best"; later, more mature consideration.

On second thoughts, I won't go to the theatre to-night.

Secret : MAKE NO SECRET OF. State openly, without concealment.

Napoleon made no secret of his hatred for England.

Security : HOLD AS SECURITY. Retain, in case of loss or failure to repay.

The bank are holding the documents as security against the loan.

See : I'LL SEE. I'll consider the matter before deciding.

May John come to tea ?

I'll see.

SEE WITH HALF AN EYE. See immediately, with no effort at all.

One could see with half an eye that she was very ill.

Similar to SEE AT A GLANCE.

SEE FAIR PLAY. Make sure that the rules are obeyed, that there is no cheating.

The two boys began to box, with their father to see fair play.

SEE FIT. Choose ; decide.

I don't see fit to tell you all my plans.

SEE AT A GLANCE. See SEE WITH HALF AN EYE.

SEE HOW THE LAND LIES. Discover the state or condition of affairs.

We'll call on old Brown and see how the land lies.

SEE OFF. Accompany to the starting-place.

We saw him off at the station.

SEE RED. Become infuriated. (It is said that when one person becomes intensely angry with another a red mist floats before his eyes.)

Whenever I hear of a man ill-treating a small child, I see red.

SEE THROUGH.   I. Lit., Perceive through a transparent construction.

I saw him through the window.

2. Met., Perceive the truth, in spite of attempts to deceive.

I saw through the swindle, and refused to have any dealings with him.

3. Ensure that a job is completed.

We are going to see the work through.

(Note alteration in order of words.)

SEE TO. Give one's attention to.

He's seeing to my affairs.

Seed : RUN TO SEED. See under **Run**.

Send : SEND TO THE RIGHT-ABOUT (S.). Or. Military. Dismiss unceremoniously.

If he calls here, I'll soon send him to the right-about.

Sensation : CREATE A SENSATION. Produce a startling effect.

The murder of the king created a tremendous sensation.

Sense : SENSE OF HUMOUR, *etc.* Ability to appreciate what is humorous, etc.

George is a good chap, but he has no sense of humour whatever.

COME TO ONE'S SENSES.   I. Recover consciousness.

She came to her senses in hospital.

2. Recover one's sense of proportion and of what is intelligent and just.

You're talking nonsense; I hope you'll come to your senses later on.

Sensible : SENSIBLE OF. Aware; conscious of.

I am sensible of your great kindness.

Separate : SEPARATE THE SHEEP FROM THE GOATS. Separate decent and respectable people, or (more loosely) those suited to a particular purpose, from those who are the reverse.

We'll go through the list of members, and separate the sheep from the goats.

SEPARATE THE WHEAT FROM THE CHAFF. Separate what is worth keeping from what is rubbish.

Sepulchre : WHITED *or* PAINTED SEPULCHRE. Or. Biblical. One whose virtuous appearance and manner conceals inward vice ; a hypocrite.

The pious-looking old villain is a whited sepulchre.

Serene : ALL SERENE (S.). Quite satisfactory.

How are affairs at home ?
Oh, all serene.

Serve : SERVE SOMEONE RIGHT. Punish justly and appropriately.

He fell through the ice ; it served him right, for we had told him it was dangerous.

SERVE ITS TURN. Prove useful for a limited time.

I used a stick to support me ; it served its turn until I could procure a crutch.

SERVE SOMEONE OUT. Be revenged ; retaliate.

That's a mean trick to have played; I'll serve you out later on.

See PAY OUT (1).

Service : RENDER A SERVICE. Be useful to ; assist.

If you'll deliver this note, you will render me a great service.

Set : SET ABOUT. 1. Begin ; commence.

I'll set about preparing supper.

2. Attack violently. Also SET ON.

The three robbers set about the traveller.

SET ONE'S AFFECTIONS, *or* HEART, ON. Concentrate one's liking upon ; desire intensely.

Mary has set her heart on the big doll in the toyshop.

SET AGAINST. 1. Opposed to.

His parents are very much set against the marriage.
See SET ONE'S FACE AGAINST.

2. Balanced against.

The £5 you've given me now will be set against the £20 you borrowed last year.

SET ASIDE. Disregard; place on one side.
Setting aside the gossip you've heard, admit that she is charming.

SET ONE'S CAP AT. Old f. See under **Cap.**

SET AT DEFIANCE. Defy; completely disregard.
She is one of those artistic women who set convention at defiance.

SET DOWN. Write; place on record.
I will set down the story as it was told to me.

SET BY THE EARS. Exasperate; cause to quarrel.
Don't invite Dorothy—she'll set everyone by the ears within ten minutes.

SET AN EXAMPLE. Exhibit oneself as an example or model to be followed.
Big boys should set an example to small boys in being clean and honest and obliging.

SET ONE'S FACE AGAINST. Oppose firmly.
I've always set my face against cousins marrying, and always shall.

SET FOOT IN. Enter.
I will never set foot in this house again.

SET ON FOOT. Start; initiate.
An enquiry will be set on foot to find out the cause of the accident.

SET FORTH, OFF, OUT. Start; depart.
We shall set forth from London next week.

SET FREE, AT LIBERTY. Release.
The prisoner will be set at liberty as soon as the fine is paid.
See under **Liberty.**

SET ONE'S HAND TO. Old f. Undertake.
Whatever you set your hand to, do as well as you can.

SET ONE'S HOUSE IN ORDER. Arrange one's own affairs properly; correct one's own faults.
She is always grumbling about my untidiness, but she ought to set her house in order first.

SET IN. Begin (applied to something which will continue for some time).
Winter has set in early this year.

SET AT NAUGHT. Disregard completely; defy.
He set at naught every convention of society.

See SET AGAINST and SET ASIDE.

SET OFF. I. Start on a journey.

He set off to London early next day.

2. Make more effective ; embellish.

The roses set off the dark beauty of her hair.

SET ON. See SET ABOUT (2).

SET PHRASE. Formal phrase.

He thanked me in a number of set phrases for my help.

SET PURPOSE. Determined purpose ; one already decided upon.

It was his set purpose to discover his father's old home.

SET AT REST. Cause to subside ; eliminate.

What he told me set at rest all my fears for the girl's happiness.

SET SAIL. See under **Sail.**

SET THE SEAL ON. Complete ; make final. (A legal document is not completed until the principals have signed their names against a seal.)

That pleasant evening set the seal on our friendship.

SET STORE BY. See under **Store.**

SET THE TABLE IN A ROAR. Or. Quotation from *Hamlet* : " Where be . . . your flashes of merriment that were wont to set the table on (mod. usage ' in ') a roar ". Cause shouts of laughter.

The comedian's jokes set the table in a roar.

SET ONE'S TEETH ON EDGE. See under **Teeth.**

SET THE THAMES ON FIRE. Achieve sensational success. (*Note.*—This idiom is always used negatively.)

He'll never set the Thames on fire.

SET TO. I. Noun. Contest ; fight.

There was a set-to between the men, which ended in Bert's winning.

2. Verb. Become active ; busy.

If we set to, we shall soon have the room tidy.

SET UP. I. Formally establish ; cause to exist.

The Prime Minister will set up a committee to investigate the matter.

2. Assume the right.

I don't set up to be regarded as an authority on scarce books.

SET ONE'S WITS TO WORK. Use one's intelligence.

He set his wits to work to discover some way of escape.

Settle : SETTLE DOWN. Become established ; adopt regular habits, live a settled and normal life.

They have settled down very happily in their new home.

SETTLE SOMEONE'S HASH (S.). Destroy ; kill.

The huntsman fired a single shot at the lioness and settled her hash.

See COOK HIS GOOSE ; DO HIM IN ; PUT PAID TO.

Seven : SEVENTH HEAVEN. A state of intense delight or ecstasy. Or. The outmost of the Seven Heavens or " layers " with which it used to be believed that the earth was surrounded.

The old lady was in the Seventh Heaven at meeting her long-lost son.

Shake : SHAKE THE DUST FROM ONE'S FEET. Depart from, usually in contempt or anger.

I shook the dust of the city from my feet.

SHAKE IN ONE'S SHOES. Tremble with fear and apprehension.

The boy shook in his shoes when he saw the cane in the master's hand.

Shakes : NO GREAT SHAKES (S.). Unimportant ; generally inferior.

I've seen her paintings, but they're no great shakes.

Shame : A BURNING SHAME. A great and terrible shame ; one to make the cheeks burn with anger.

It is a burning shame that little children should have to beg in the street.

PUT TO SHAME. Cause to feel ashamed, or inferior.

The boy's playing would have put many a professional pianist to shame.

Share : SHARE AND SHARE ALIKE. Divide everything equally.

The three partners in the business agreed to share and share alike.

Sharp : SHARP PRACTICE. Behaviour which, while still technically legal, practically amounts to swindling.

He's never been to prison, though he's frequently been guilty of sharp practice.

Sheep : BLACK SHEEP. A person with a bad record or reputation. Or. A theory that, as among every flock of sheep there is always one which is black, so in every respectable family there is always one discreditable member.

Arthur has always been the black sheep of the family.
See A BAD HAT.

CAST SHEEP'S EYES. Gaze in a foolish and amorous way at a person (a sheep looks sideways).

There's that young idiot, casting sheep's eyes at his master's daughter.

Sheer : SHEER OFF (S.). Or. Nautical. Move away ; go elsewhere.

He's been waiting outside the house for two hours ; tell him to sheer off.

Sheet : SHEET ANCHOR. Or. Nautical. Chief support. The sheet anchor is the largest and strongest of a ship's anchors.

I earn my living in several ways, but fruit-growing is my sheet anchor.

STAND IN A WHITE SHEET. Behave like a penitent, publicly admitting one's sin, and the justice of the reproof. Or. The custom of compelling a person convicted of certain crimes to stand in a public place clothed in white.

I don't see why I should stand in a white sheet for something I didn't do.

Shelf : ON THE SHELF. No longer required to do active work ; replaced by someone more effective. (Formerly applied to a woman who did not marry.)

The soldier can now find other employment : he is no longer on the shelf.

Shell : SHELL OUT (S.). Pay.

Hurry up, my boy ; it's your turn to shell out to-day.
See PAY UP.

Shield : THE OTHER SIDE OF THE SHIELD. The other point of view or aspect of a question. Or. The legend of two knights who quarrelled as to whether a shield was made of gold or silver—only to discover that one side was gold and the other silver.

You've heard her account of what happened, but there's another side to the shield.

Shift : MAKE SHIFT. See under **Make**.

SHIFT FOR ONESELF. Take care of oneself.

Thanks for your help ; now I can shift for myself.

Shilly-shally : Waste time trying to reach a decision. **Or.** Probably a corruption of " Will I, shall I ? "

Dick hasn't decided whether he will go or stay ; he was always one to shilly-shally.

Shine : TAKE THE SHINE OUT OF. Make appear inferior and unimportant.

Cinderella's dress took the shine out of her sisters'.

Ship : WHEN ONE'S SHIP COMES IN. When one become rich.

I'll buy you a silk dress when my ship comes in.

Shoe : ANOTHER PAIR OF SHOES (S.). An entirely different matter.

I'll lend you five shillings, but a loan of £10 is another pair of shoes.

IN A PERSON'S SHOES. In a similar position to him.

I shouldn't like to be in Robinson's shoes when the manager returns from his holiday.

WHERE THE SHOE PINCHES. The real trouble or worry ; the chief cause of financial anxiety. Or. The saying, " Only he who wears the shoe knows where it pinches."

It is in educating the children that the shoe pinches most.

Shoot : SHOOT AHEAD (*as a boat shoots ahead in a fast-running stream*). Make extremely rapid progress.

The business was started only six months ago, but it has shot ahead rapidly.

Shop : TALK SHOP. Discuss one's business or profession on private and informal occasions.

Gray will talk shop at mealtimes.

Shorn : SHORN OF (*as a sheep is shorn of its wool*).

Shorn of his robe and chain, the Mayor looks a very unimportant person.

Short : SHORT OF. Without sufficient.

I can't offer you tea, as we're short of milk.

SHORT CIRCUIT. Or. An electrical term for deflecting the current along a short route, frequently ending in the wire becoming fused. Deal informally and quickly with an official document, etc., omitting the usual procedure.

If I short-circuit these papers to the Ministry, we should receive a reply within a week.

SHORT CUT. A short way from one point to another, as distinct from the usual one.

The distance by the road is three miles, but there is a short cut through the park.

SHORT-HANDED *or* SHORT-STAFFED. With an insufficient number of helpers ; short of staff.

I'm sorry to keep you waiting, but we are short-handed this week through illness.

IN SHORT. Summarized ; stated briefly.

The man, in short, is not to be trusted.

See THE LONG AND THE SHORT OF IT.

IN SHORT SUPPLY. Available in insufficient quantities to meet the demand.

It is difficult to buy china cups ; they are in very short supply.

SHORT SHRIFT. Very little time for prayer or explanation before inflicting punishment. (To be given " shrift " was to be absolved by a priest.)

They gave the wretched captive short shrift : he was hanged at dawn.

SHORT WEIGHT. Less than was ordered or paid for.

The butcher has given us short weight again.

Shot : LIKE A SHOT. With extreme speed.

The frightened thief dashed away like a shot.

A LONG SHOT, RANDOM SHOT. A casual suggestion ; a mere guess.

" It was you who stole the money," I said. It was a random shot, but the boy turned pale.

Shoulder : GIVE THE COLD SHOULDER TO. Treat coldly and formally ; snub.

The rich friend he had once known so well now gave him the cold shoulder.

See **Coventry.**

HAVE ON ONE'S SHOULDERS. Support ; bear.

It is a terrible responsibility to have on one's shoulders.

PUT ONE'S SHOULDER TO THE WHEEL. Work hard and steadily. Or. The fable of the lazy man who had his cart stuck in the mud. He appealed to Jove for help ; Jove retorted that the man should himself put his shoulder to the wheel and try to move it before appealing to the gods.

If he puts his shoulder to the wheel his business will be a success.

RUB SHOULDERS WITH. Come into intimate contact with ; become acquainted.

STRAIGHT FROM THE SHOULDER. Or. Boxing. Directly and forcibly.

I told that young man, straight from the shoulder, just what I thought of his conduct.

Show : SHOW DOWN. A frank exposure ; an open challenge.

She has been spreading so many rumours and dropped so many hints that it is time we had a show down, and so I asked her exactly where her information came from.

SHOW OFF. Display one's cleverness with the intention of attracting attention and obtaining praise.

Most small children show off in front of visitors.

See PUT ON AIRS ; PUT ON SIDE.

SHOW OF REASON. Apparent justice and logic.

The chef said, with a show of reason, that it was impossible to make an omelette without eggs.

SHOW UP. 1. Expose.

He showed up the villain.

2. Escort someone upstairs.

The visitors have arrived ; show them up.

3. Become increasingly vivid or obvious.

Her dark hair showed up against the white pillows.

Shuffle : SHUFFLE OFF THIS MORTAL COIL. Die. Or. Quotation from *Hamlet* : " What dreams may come when we have shuffled off this mortal coil ".

We must all shuffle off this mortal coil sooner or later.

Shut : SHUT UP (S.). Shut up one's mouth ; stop talking.

His father became tired of the boy's excuses, and told him to shut up.

SHUT UP SHOP (S.). Give up business ; end one's occupation.

He managed a circus, but when the war came he had to shut up shop.

Side : ON EVERY SIDE ; ON ALL SIDES. From every direction, every source.

On every side we have heard approval of the Government's new housing plans.

SIDE WITH. Ally oneself with; openly sympathize with.

I know you will side with me in my dispute with the manager over wages.

Sight: AT FIRST SIGHT. At the first superficial glance; immediately.

They both fell in love at first sight.

IN SIGHT OF. Near enough to see.

We shall soon be in sight of my old home.

IN THE SIGHT OF. In the view of; as seen by.

In the sight of the world, they were a happily married couple.

LOSE SIGHT OF. Lit., Fail to see.

At this distance you lose sight of the town.

Met., Fail to realize, or to remember.

You've lost sight of the fact that you are no longer young.

LOSE ONE'S SIGHT. Become blind.

OUT OF SIGHT. Beyond one's vision.

The car dashed away, and was soon out of sight.

SIGHT FOR SORE EYES (S.). Old f. A very welcome, cheering thing to see.

Come in, my dear, you're a sight for sore eyes.

Sign: SIGN OF THE TIMES. Indication of present-day thought and feeling.

It is a sign of the times that children are taken to listen to debates in Parliament.

Signal: GIVE THE SIGNAL, *or* SIGN. Indicate by sign or speech when some event should happen.

The captain gave the signal for the men to attack.

Signify: IT DOES NOT SIGNIFY. Old f. It does not matter; is of no importance.

The time when we leave does not signify.

Silence: KEEP SILENT, KEEP *or* MAINTAIN SILENCE. Continue to remain silent.

You will have to keep silent throughout the ceremony.

RENDER SILENT. Make silent or incapable of speaking.

The scenery was so beautiful that it rendered even the children silent.

Silk: MAKE A SILK PURSE OUT OF A SOW'S EAR. Change the real character of a person; make a gentleman of one who is naturally low and mean.

They sent their boy to Oxford, but he was born a bully and a cad, and you can't make a silk purse out of a sow's ear.

TAKE SILK. See under **Take.**

Sinews : SINEWS OF WAR. See under **War.**

Sing : SING SMALL. Appear inferior and unimportant.

Cinderella was so charming and so magnificently dressed that she made every other woman at the ball sing small.

See TAKE THE SHINE OUT OF.

SING-SONG. 1. Noun. An impromptu concert, usually held by a community—soldiers, campers, etc.

We had a sing-song round the camp fire after supper.

2. Adjective. Monotonous ; flat and lifeless.

The sentry repeated his instructions in a sing-song voice.

SING THE PRAISES OF. Praise highly and in general terms.

Jack spent half the morning singing the praises of his fiancée.

Single : IN A STATE OF SINGLE BLESSEDNESS. Unmarried.

My uncle lived in a state of single blessedness for nearly a century.

SINGLENESS OF AIM, PURPOSE, HEART. Concentration ; a single object in view.

With complete singleness of aim, Joan of Arc began the task of freeing France from its enemies.

Sink : SINK OR SWIM. Rely on one's own efforts.

As for George, I am going to let him sink or swim.

Sit : SIT UP (S.). Be startled.

That dress of yours will make the neighbours sit up.

SIT UP FOR. Wait after the usual bedtime for somebody's return.

We shall probably be late coming home, so don't sit up for us.

Six : AT SIXES AND SEVENS. Muddled ; in a state of confusion.

We have only just moved into the house, and everything is at sixes and sevens.

SIX OF ONE AND HALF-A-DOZEN OF THE OTHER. An affair in which both sides deserve equal blame or merit.

The magistrates listened to the story of the quarrel between the two women, and decided that it was six of one and half-a-dozen of the other.

Skeleton : SKELETON IN THE CUPBOARD. A disgrace which the family or community does its best to conceal.

I've always guessed that the Watsons had a skeleton in their cupboard.

Skin : ESCAPE BY THE SKIN OF ONE'S TEETH. Only just escape. See NARROW ESCAPE.

Slap : SLAP IN THE FACE. A rebuff ; an insult.

It was a slap in the face to Cinderella to be told she was not going to the ball.

SLAP-UP (S.). First-class ; splendid.

We went to the hotel and had a slap-up dinner.

Sleep : SLEEP ON A MATTER. Allow a night to pass before finally deciding.

I'll sleep on the matter, and write to you to-morrow.

SLEEP LIKE A TOP. Sleep peacefully and deeply. (When a top is spinning at its greatest speed, it appears motionless and is almost soundless.)

SLEEPING PARTNER. One who invests enough to become a partner in a business, but takes no active share in it.

Sleight : SLEIGHT OF HAND. Extreme manual dexterity and quickness. (The phrase is generally used in connection with conjuring and in performing an illusion.)

By sleight of hand he made an entire pack of cards disappear.

Slide : LET THINGS SLIDE, *or* DRIFT. Do nothing ; take no active steps.

It is useless to ask Father to help ; he'll merely let things slide.

Slink : SLINK AWAY. Retreat silently and ignominiously.

I saw him slink away as I approached.

See SNEAK OFF and TAIL BETWEEN ONE'S LEGS.

Slip : GIVE THE SLIP. Escape, and remain uncaptured.

He tied a string to the dog's collar in case the animal should give him the slip.

See SLIP THROUGH ONE'S FINGERS.

MAKE A SLIP, *or* SLIP UP. Make a slight (but frequently vital) error.

You've made a slip somewhere in these accounts.

MANY A SLIP. Or. The Greek proverb, "There's many
a slip 'twixt the cup and the lip." Many things
may happen to prevent a desired or expected
result.
*He seems sure that he will pass the examinations, but
there's many a slip.*

SLIP THROUGH ONE'S FINGERS. Escape ; be lost.
*I had the chance of becoming rich, but let it slip through
my fingers.*

SLIP OF THE PEN. An error in writing.
*By a slip of the pen he wrote, " Queen Victoria died
in 1801."*

SLIP OF THE TONGUE. A verbal error.
*The Chairman spoke of Mr. Gladstone as a great
Labour leader—a slip of the tongue.*

Sly : ON THE SLY. Secretly and artfully.
*I thought he was my friend, until I found he was
trying to ruin me on the sly.*

Small : SMALL BEER. Or. Shakespeare's *Othello* : " To
suckle fools and chronicle small beer ". Trivial ;
unimportant.
The news is all very small beer.
Frequently used negatively.
He thinks no small beer of himself (i.e. He thinks
himself important.)

SMALL TALK. See **Talk.**

Smoke : END IN SMOKE. Have no result ; end in nothing.
*The committee discussed various improvements, but it
has all ended in smoke.*

Snake : SCOTCH THE SNAKE. Make ineffective and negative.
(To " scotch " is to wound seriously, but without
killing.)
*There were rumours that he was bankrupt, but after
his wife had given a party that snake was
scotched.*

SNAKE IN THE GRASS. A hidden or hypocritical enemy.
*I never trusted her ; she has always been a snake in
the grass.*

Snap : SNAP ONE'S FINGERS AT. Disregard ; treat with
contempt.
*He was one of those who snap their fingers at all
regulations.*

Sneak : SNEAK OFF, *or* AWAY. Depart furtively.
  See SLINK AWAY and TAIL BETWEEN ONE'S LEGS.

Sneeze : NOT TO BE SNEEZED AT. Not to be treated as unimportant or insignificant. (*Note.*—This idiom is always used in the negative.)
> *The firm pays me £10 a week, which isn't to be sneezed at.*

Snuff : UP TO SNUFF. See under **Up.**

So : JUST SO ; QUITE SO. I agree ; it is as you have stated.
> *Jane is a nice girl, and nice girls should marry.*
> *Quite so.*

  AND SO FORTH. Similar objects ; in a similar way, etc.
> *He dealt in chairs, tables, and so forth.*

  Similar to AND SO ON ; ET CETERA.

  SO-LONG (S.). Good-bye ; farewell till we meet again.

  SO-SO. In inferior health ; not very well.
> *Old Mrs. Huggins seems very so-so this morning.*

  SO-AND-SO. Such and such a person. Used as a general substitute for the specific name of a person or thing.
> *Choose a hat that suits you, no matter what Mrs. So-and-so is wearing.*

  Similar to SUCH-AND-SUCH A PERSON. See also WHAT'S-HIS-NAME.

  SO TO SPEAK ; IN A MANNER OF SPEAKING. Speaking generally, without being literally exact ; speaking with a certain amount of metaphorical exaggeration.
> *When the old man comes home in a temper, he turns the whole house upside down, so to speak.*

Sober : SOBER DOWN. Become more serious-minded and reliable.
> *The boy will sober down as he grows older.*

  2. Recover from a temporary attack of hysteria or drunkenness.
> *We put him on the bed to sober down.*

  SOBER-MINDED. Serious ; with a sense of responsibility.

Soft : SOFT SAWDER ; SOFT SOAP (S.). Complimentary, flattering words.
> *Don't think you're going to persuade me by using soft soap.*

SOFT SPOKEN. Gently and politely speaking.
> *She's a pleasant, soft-spoken girl.*

Sold : SOLD (S.) ; SOLD A PUP (S.). Swindled ; cheated.
> *If you paid £5 for that watch, you were sold.*

Soldier : SOLDIER OF FORTUNE. Originally a professional soldier who hired himself as such to any country. A wanderer who lives by his wits.

Solecism : COMMIT A SOLECISM. Misuse a word or phrase ; make a mistake in syntax. Or. An Athenian colony settled in Soli in Cilicia, which forgot the purity of their native tongue. (*Note.*—This phrase is frequently used in connection with a social *faux pas.*)

Some : SOMEBODY, SOMEONE, SOME PERSON, SOMEHOW, FOR SOME REASON, SOMETHING, OR OTHER. " Other " is here used as a vague alternative to an unspecified individual or thing, i.e. somebody or other = " any person ".
> *Somebody or other has left the gate open.*

Song : FOR A SONG ; A MERE SONG. Extremely cheap ; at a merely nominal price. Similar to CHEAP AS DIRT.

Soon : SOONER OR LATER. Eventually ; in the end.
> *If you drive like that, sooner or later you'll have an accident.*

See BEFORE LONG.

Sooth : SOOTH TO SAY. Old f. To speak plainly and truthfully.
> *Sooth to say, I don't really care for modern music.*

Sop : SOP TO CERBERUS. A bribe or concession given to console an opponent. Or. The Greek and Roman custom of putting a cake in the hands of a dead person to give to Cerberus, the three-headed dog of Pluto, guardian of the infernal regions.
> *I told him, as a sop to Cerberus, that he might keep his car in my garage.*

Sort : A GOOD SORT. A good fellow.
> *Jimmy is a good sort ; he'll always help a friend.*

OUT OF SORTS. Not in good health, depressed and irritable.
> *The chief's feeling thoroughly out of sorts this morning.*

See OFF COLOUR.

Soul : CALL ONE'S SOUL ONE'S OWN. Act freely ; indulge in one's spiritual and moral desires.

He is so dominated by his wife that he daren't call his soul his own.

(*Note.*—This phrase is almost invariably used in the negative.)

NOT A SOUL. Absolutely no-one.

When I reached the station, there was not a soul on the platform.

Sour : SOUR GRAPES. Something referred to with contempt only because it is out of reach and unattainable. Or. Æsop's fable of the fox who, after vainly trying to reach some grapes he wanted, consoled himself by saying that they were sour.

Miranda says she doesn't want to go to Paris, but I fancy it is merely sour grapes.

Sow : SOW THE SEEDS OF. Originate ; begin.

Reckless living when one is young often sows the seeds of ill-health later on.

Space : FOR A SPACE. Similar to FOR A SEASON.

Spade : CALL A SPADE A SPADE. Speak quite plainly and without refinement.

To call a spade a spade, young Smith is a coward and a liar.

Spanner : THROW A SPANNER IN THE WORKS. Interfere with, and check another person's plans. (A spanner is a small tool used for turning metal " nuts ".) Similar to PUT A SPOKE IN ONE'S WHEEL, which see.

Speak : PLAIN SPEAKING. Uttering one's real and un-flattering opinion.

There was a good deal of plain speaking, and they parted in anger.

See NOT TO MINCE MATTERS, and HARD WORDS.

SPEAKS FOR ITSELF. Demonstrates without words ; requires no explanation.

The healthy look of a boy who has plenty of fresh air speaks for itself.

SPEAKING LIKENESS. A vivid and realistic likeness

SPEAK VOLUMES. Convey much, while actually saying little or nothing.

The glance she gave him spoke volumes.

STRICTLY SPEAKING. Speaking exactly, or according to a rule or promise.

Strictly speaking, her name is Brown, not Jones.

Strictly speaking, I ought not to tell you this.

Spick : SPICK AND SPAN. Extremely neat and tidy. Or. Nautical. A " spick " is a spike or nail, a " span " a chip of wood ; a spick-and-span ship is one in which all wood and metal is new.

Spike : SPIKE A PERSON'S GUNS. Take some sudden action which ends opposition. Or. Military. Old-fashioned cannon were fired by applying a light to the "touch-hole", one bored into the near end of the barrel. The object of an attacking enemy was always to hammer a spike of iron into this hole, making the cannon useless.

When I told him that I would never consent to his marrying my daughter, he spiked my guns by saying, " We were married last week."

Spin : SPIN OUT. Draw out ; prolong.

I tried to spin out the conversation until Mary came home.

SPIN A YARN. Or. Nautical. Tell a story.

The old man could spin many yarns of his youth.

Spirit : CALL UP SPIRITS. Summon from some other world the spirits of dead people.

Spite : IN SPITE OF. Despite ; notwithstanding.

We're going to get married, in spite of the opposition of her family.

Splash : MAKE A SPLASH (S.). Cause a sensation, excitement.

We're going to make a splash by giving a big party on John's birthday.

Splice : Marry (S.). Or. Nautical. Strictly speaking, to " splice " is another form of " split ", to divide. Its normal meaning, however, is to join, particularly to join the ends of two ropes, which have to be divided or untwisted for that purpose.

Joan and Peter were spliced last month.

(*Note.*—This idiom is always used in the objective case.)

SPLICE THE MAINBRACE (S.). Or. Naval. Take a stimulating drink to keep one's spirits up. The " mainbrace " is the rope which fixes the main (or chief) mast in position.

Spoil : SPOILING FOR A FIGHT.   Anxious and eager to quarrel or fight.

I realized at once that my enemy was spoiling for a fight.

Sponge : SPONGE ON.   Systematically and constantly obtain money from one's friends.

He's done no work for years, and lives by sponging on his relations.

Spoon : BORN WITH A SILVER SPOON IN ONE'S MOUTH.   Born of rich parents.

Peter has never had to work : he was born with a silver spoon in his mouth.

Spot : SPOT (S.).   Discover.

We soon spotted George in the crowd.

SPOT THE WINNER.   Bet successfully.

I was lucky enough to spot the winner in the two o'clock race.

SPOT CASH.   Immediate payment in cash.

I've sold my bicycle for £5, spot cash.

ON THE SPOT.   1. At that particular place ; there.

The police were on the spot within ten minutes.

2. Immediately ; without delay.

He drew a revolver and shot his enemy on the spot.
See THERE AND THEN.

Spout : UP THE SPOUT (S.).   In the pawnshop ; pawned. (The "spout" is the channel up which goods upon which money has been lent are sent to the store-room, to remain until claimed.)

The poor chap can't come to the reception ; his best suit is up the spout.

Sprat : A SPRAT TO CATCH A MACKEREL.   A small gift or concession made in the hope of obtaining a large one.

The manager has sent me tickets for the theatre—obviously a sprat to catch a mackerel.

Spur : ON THE SPUR OF THE MOMENT.   Suddenly, without previous consideration.

On the spur of the moment I asked Susan to marry me, and she said " Yes ".

WIN ONE'S SPURS.   Perform an action leading to special distinction.   Or. The conspicuous act of bravery by which a knight obtained his rank and the golden spurs which indicated it.

He won his spurs for running while at Oxford.

Square : ALL SQUARE. Level ; equal.

> *If I give you a shilling, we shall be all square.*

ON THE SQUARE (S.). Honest ; genuine.

> *I don't think he's on the square.*

See FAIR AND SQUARE.

SQUARE A MAN. Bribe him.

> *Don't try to square a policeman—it always does more harm than good.*

Stable : LOCK THE STABLE DOOR. Take precautions when the accident they are to prevent has already happened. Or. The proverb, " It is useless to lock the stable door when the steed is stolen."

> *After the burglary she put fresh fastenings to the windows, but it was locking the stable door.*

Staff : OVER-STAFFED. With more employees than are needed.

UNDER-STAFFED. The reverse. See SHORT-HANDED.

STAFF OF LIFE. Bread.

Stake : AT STAKE. Dependent upon what is about to happen.

> *It was a tremendously important interview ; my whole future was at stake.*

Stand : IT STANDS TO REASON. It is logically clear and certain.

> *It stands to reason that two people cannot live as cheaply as one.*

STAND AGHAST. Be shocked, appalled.

> *I stand aghast when I see the ruin the bombs did to London.*

STAND ALOOF. Remain detached ; refuse to share or co-operate with.

> *All but one of us helped in the work ; only Peter Wilkins stood aloof.*

See STAND OUT (I).

STAND ASIDE. I. Lit., Stand where the progress of others will not be impeded.

> *If you'll stand aside, these people can pass.*

2. Met., Give someone else an opportunity.

> *He might have married Marjory, but he stood aside because his brother loved her.*

STAND BY. I. Wait in a state of readiness.

> *The troops have been ordered to stand by.*

2. Support by word or deed.

He stood by his friend through all his troubles.

STAND ON CEREMONY. Behave stiffly and ceremoniously. (Usually used in the negative.)

Don't stand on ceremony—this is an entirely informal meeting.

STAND A CHANCE. Have any possibility.

I don't think your horse stands a chance of winning.

STAND CORRECTED. Admit to being wrong.

I am sorry for the mistake—I stand corrected.

STAND ON ONE'S DIGNITY. Show—often absurdly—a sense of one's importance.

The Mayor stood on his dignity, and insisted on leading the procession in his official robes.

STAND FAST, *or* FIRM. Remain immovable.

If the troops stand firm till sunset, the battle is won.

STAND ONE'S GROUND. Refuse to change one's statements or opinions.

The police tried to make her admit that she had made a mistake, but the girl stood her ground and said that she had seen the burglar.

STAND, *or* STICK, TO ONE'S GUNS. Or. Military. Similar to above.

STAND ON ONE'S OWN FEET, *or* LEGS. Accept full responsibility for one's own actions; accept no assistance.

My uncle offered to help me, but I told him I would rather stand on my own legs.

STAND IN A PERSON'S LIGHT. Prevent his advancement; spoil his career. Usually used in the negative.

I don't wish to stand in George's light if this trip to Africa is going to help him in his work.

STAND-OFFISH. Haughty; consciously superior; curt.

The Director's manner was very stand-offish.

STAND OUT. **1.** Remain in opposition; refuse to co-operate.

The conspirators did their best to persuade all the men to join them, but three stood out.

See STAND ALOOF.

2. Be conspicuous.

The statue stands out against the trees.

STAND OUT FOR. Insist upon.

The workmen are standing out for higher wages.

See STICK OUT.

STAND OVER. 1. Stand near, usually to enforce an order.

She stood over the boy while he washed his face.

2. Put aside for a time.

The accounts can stand over till next week.

STAND ON ONE'S RIGHTS. Insist upon one's legal rights.

If he stands on his rights, he can claim all his wife's savings.

STAND SAM (S.). Pay all expenses.

Order some beer—it's my turn to stand Sam.

See STAND TREAT.

STAND IN THE SHOES OF. See under **Shoes.**

STAND IN GOOD STEAD. Prove useful to.

This old coat will stand me in good stead if the weather turns cold.

STAND TO. Similar to STAND BY (1).

STAND TREAT. Almost identical with STAND SAM, but with an added sense of generosity.

We'll go to the theatre, and I'll stand treat.

STAND UP FOR. Support openly, by speech or action.

He stood up for his brother.

See STICK UP FOR.

STAND UP TO. Confront boldly; oppose.

If the lawyer tries to bully you, stand up to him.

STANDING DISH. A dish which is served regularly.

Roast beef was at one time a standing dish in English homes.

Standstill : AT A STANDSTILL. No longer moving or functioning.

During the strike, all work in the factories was at a standstill.

Star : A great or popular performer. Or. The names of famous actors are emphasized by stars in electric lights outside theatres in which they are performing.

STAR TURN. A " turn " or act by a famous performer. Frequently applied to any conspicuous or successful incident.

The star turn of the party was George pretending to be old Aunt Emily.

Stare : STARE ONE IN THE FACE. Confront ; be evident and obvious.

You said you couldn't find the key ; it's staring you in the face.

Start : A FRESH START. A new beginning.

Let's make a fresh start, and be friends.

Stave : STAVE IN. Smash inwards.

These rocks would stave in the side of any ship.

Steal : STEAL A MARCH ON. Or. Military. Gain an advantage for which one's adversary was not prepared.

He stole a march on his enemies, and betrayed them to the king.

STEAL UPON. Creep softly upon.

What are these sounds which steal upon my ear ?

Steer : STEER CLEAR OF. Or. Nautical. Avoid ; evade.

If you want to steer clear of trouble, my boy, don't get married.

STEER A MIDDLE COURSE. Avoid extremes ; act moderately, and compromise.

Step : PICK ONE'S STEPS. See PICK ONE'S WAY.

RETRACE ONE'S STEPS. Return in the direction one had come.

He retraced his steps, looking for the purse.

STEP BY STEP. Slowly and methodically.

Step by step she taught the little dog to obey her.

STEPPING-STONE, *or* STONES. Lit., Stones in a stream used to enable one to cross with dry feet. Met., Anything which may help to lead one to greater wealth, power or goodness.

The post of junior clerk may prove a stepping-stone to partnership in the firm.

Stick : STICK IT (S.). Endure ; persevere under difficulties.

This road is terrible, but if we can stick it we shall save over a mile.

STICK-IN-THE-MUD. An unenterprising, unambitious person.

Farmer Juggins is a regular old stick-in-the-mud.

STICK AT NOTHING. Stop at nothing ; be restrained by no scruple or impediment.

She is one of those women who will stick at nothing to get what she wants.

STICK OUT. Same as STAND OUT (2).

STICK OUT FOR. Same as STAND OUT FOR (1), which see.

STICK IN ONE'S THROAT *or* (S.) GIZZARD. Lit., Choke one. Met., cause disgust or aversion.

> *It sticks in my throat to have to say " Sir " to a man who was my father's valet.*

STICK UP FOR. Same as STAND UP FOR.

Stiff : STIFF AS A POKER, AS A RAMROD, AS BUCKRAM. Rigid ; formal. (Buckram is a particularly stiff kind of cloth used in binding books.)

> *The old lady sat upright, stiff as a poker, and glared at me.*

Still : STILL LIFE. A phrase applied by artists to compositions in which there is no life at all—flowers, fruit, game, etc.

STILL WATERS RUN DEEP. Proverb. Streams which flow silently are usually deep. Quiet, undemonstrative people are frequently those whose real ambitions and plans are most successfully concealed.

Stock : ON THE STOCKS. Or. Shipping. Being made, but not finished.

> *I have two novels on the stocks.*

STOCK STILL. Absolutely motionless.

> *The boy stood stock still, too terrified to breathe.*

See A DEAD STOP.

STOCK-IN-TRADE. Lit., A tradesman's stock, or supply of goods for sale. Met., Any possession, tangible or otherwise, which one employs in one's business or profession.

> *Her stock-in-trade consisted of plenty of confidence, a knowledge of French, and a charming smile.*

TAKE STOCK OF. Consider the value or possibilities of.

> *He took stock of his present position as a prisoner of the king. It was not a very cheerful stock-taking.*

Stone : LEAVE NO STONE UNTURNED. Use every possible effort to find out ; investigate thoroughly.

> *The police will leave no stone unturned to discover the murderer.*

See LEAVE NO AVENUE UNEXPLORED.

STONE BLIND *or* DEAF. Totally blind or deaf. Also, with the same effect, STONE COLD and STONE DEAD. (But not, for some reason, stone dumb.) See LOSE ONE'S HEARING.

STONE'S-THROW. A short distance—theoretically, as far as one can throw a stone.

The house was within a stone's-throw of the sea.

Stoop : STOOP TO CONQUER. Or. Goldsmith's comedy, *She Stoops to Conquer.* Humiliate oneself to achieve success in the end.

Stop : A DEAD STOP. A complete and sudden halt.

The car came to a dead stop in the middle of the road. See STOCK STILL.

Store : SET STORE BY. Value ; attach importance to.

I've kept all your mother's letters, as I know you set store by them.

Storm : BOW TO THE STORM. Yield to public indignation.

The Town Council wanted to close the gardens on Sunday, but they bowed to the storm and said they might be opened after ten o'clock.

STORM IN A TEACUP. Much excitement and trouble over a trivial matter.

The people next door are continually quarrelling, but it is usually a storm in a tea-cup.

Straight : KEEP A STRAIGHT FACE. See under **Face.**

STRAIGHT AWAY ; STRAIGHT OFF. Immediately.

Mr. Smith is at home and will see you straight away.

STRAIGHT FROM THE SHOULDER. See under **Shoulder.**

STRAIGHT TIP (S.). Or. Betting. A definite hint ; also private and accurate information.

Take a straight tip from me, and have no further dealings with the company.

Strain : STRAIN AT A GNAT AND SWALLOW A CAMEL. Or. Biblical. Object to some trivial matter while condoning or permitting a far greater offence.

He is enraged if George is five minutes late for breakfast, but sees nothing wrong in his coming home hopelessly drunk the night before—a perfect example of straining at a gnat and swallowing a camel.

STRAIN ONE'S EYES. 1. Make an extra effort to see.

If you strain your eyes, you can just see the church.
2. Tire one's eyes.

Don't strain your eyes by reading such small print.

Straw : CLUTCH AT A STRAW. Or. The saying that a drowning man will clutch at even a straw to save himself.

Grasp at anything, however trivial, to escape disaster; gain hope from the slightest sign that may appear favourable.

" I was a friend of your father's," said the visitor, and the condemned man, clutching at a straw, looked up with a gleam of hope in his eyes.

THE LAST STRAW. Or. The proverb, " It is the last straw that breaks the camel's back." Any final unendurable event; a culminating injury.

You borrow money, do no work, and—the last straw— persuade my daughter to run away with you.

MAKE BRICKS WITHOUT STRAW. See under **Brick.**

A MAN OF STRAW. See under **Man.**

NOT CARE A STRAW, *or* TWO STRAWS. Care nothing at all.

Susan says she hates me—I don't care two straws.

A STRAW WILL SHOW WHICH WAY THE WIND BLOWS. A trivial thing will indicate what is likely to happen.

All the workmen have touched their caps to Leonard since his uncle died; a straw which shows which way the wind blows.

Stream : GO, *or* DRIFT, WITH THE STREAM. Follow the example of the majority.

All the people I know are voting for Johnson; I shall probably go with the stream and do the same.

Stretch : AT A STRETCH. With an effort; only by straining one's resources.

We can manage to entertain ten people at dinner at a stretch.

Stricken : STRICKEN IN YEARS. Old f. Aged.

She was stricken in years when I first met her.

Strides : MAKE RAPID STRIDES. Progress quickly (a stride is a long step).

His new novel is making rapid strides.

Strike : STRIKE A BARGAIN. Reach an agreement.

I'll strike a bargain with you, and exchange your horse for my car.

STRIKE THE HAPPY MEDIUM. Arrive at the best possible compromise.

John wanted white walls and Mary wanted light yellow, so they struck the happy medium and painted them cream.

She is neither too friendly nor too formal, but strikes the happy medium.

STRIKE HOME. Strike a vital blow; strike directly at the heart or emotions.

He raised his sword and struck home.

Her mother's reproaches struck home, and the girl burst into tears.

STRIKE IN. Interrupt; intervene suddenly.

We were discussing music when Mary struck in with, " I'm tired of talk, I want my dinner."

See BUTT IN.

STRIKE WHILE THE IRON IS HOT. Take advantage of a suitable opportunity.

Meeting old Robinson, I decided to strike while the iron was hot, and I asked him if he would like me for a son-in-law.

STRIKE OFF. 1. Remove from an official list or record.

His name was struck off the register of doctors.

2. Print (illustrations, etc.).

Two hundred copies of the etching were struck off.

STRIKE OUT. 1. Make violent movements with one's arms or legs.

The swimmer struck out for the shore.

2. Similar to STRIKE OFF (1).

STRIKE TERROR, FEAR, *etc.* Create terror; terrify.

His fierce expression would strike terror in any child.

String : STRING TOGETHER. Lit., Link, as by a string or cord. Met., Arrange in sequence.

I've strung together a few verses on the political situation.

Strong : STRONG BOX. A metal box designed to protect valuable papers from fire or thieves.

STRONG WATERS. Old f. Spirits, wines and other intoxicants.

My son, refrain from strong waters.

Struck : STRUCK ALL OF A HEAP (S.). Met., Stunned; utterly astonished.

We were struck all of a heap when Peter walked in.

Stuck : STUCK UP (S.). Vain; arrogant.

Millicent is a silly, stuck-up child.

Study : IN A BROWN STUDY. See under **Brown**.

Stumble : STUMBLE UPON. Discover by chance.

I stumbled upon some interesting old letters in Grand-father's desk.

Stump : STUMP ORATOR. Or. America. A wandering political or other public speaker who addresses his audience from a tree-stump or some similar platform. An open-air speaker.

Stung : STUNG, WOUNDED *or* CUT TO, THE QUICK. See under **Cut.**

Subject : A SORE SUBJECT. A subject about which one is particularly sensitive.

We didn't discuss his son's absence, as we knew it was a sore subject.

Submerged : BELONGING TO THE SUBMERGED TENTH. Or. It was formerly estimated that one-tenth of the population of England lived in hopeless poverty. A person without sufficient money, a decent home or social position ; a tramp, a pauper. See DOWN AND OUT.

Such : SUCH-AND-SUCH A PERSON. See SO-AND-SO.

SUCH BEING THE CASE. Considering the present state of affairs.

Such being the case, we were very lucky to have a house of our own.

Suggestion : THROW OUT A SUGGESTION. See DROP A HINT.

Sum : SUM UP. Or. Legal. Give a final résumé and analysis of what has occurred. A judge " sums up " when each side has stated its case.

One may sum up the situation by saying we are living in a condition of uneasy peace.

Summer : SUMMER TIME. The official alteration of " Greenwich " time, in order to allow more hours of daylight in summer to be used.

Sun : UNDER THE SUN. In the whole world.

There's nothing new under the sun.

Sure : MAKE SURE ; MAKE CERTAIN. Render absolutely certain.

I will make sure that the letter leaves to-night.

SURE ENOUGH. In accordance with something anticipated.

I said you'd come, and sure enough here you are.

sure as fate. Beyond a doubt, with absolute certainty.

As sure as Fate, I shall get a letter to-morrow telling me to go home.

Surprise : TAKEN BY SURPRISE. Suddenly surprised ; astonished.

She was so taken by surprise at his rudeness that she burst into tears.

Suspense : IN SUSPENSE. In a condition of uncertainty.

We shall be in suspense until we receive further news.

Swallow : SWALLOW UP. Engulf ; cause to disappear.

An earthquake can swallow up an entire town.

His wife's debts swallowed up all his savings.

Swear : SWEAR BY. See PIN ONE'S FAITH ON and PUT ONE'S FAITH IN.

SWEAR LIKE A TROOPER. Use particularly bad language. (A trooper is a soldier, a member of a troop of horse.)

When I told the old woman I had come to arrest her son, she swore like a trooper.

Sweep : MAKE A CLEAN SWEEP OF. Get rid or dispose of everyone or everything concerned.

The new manager is going to make a clean sweep of the old staff.

Swell : SWELL THE RANKS OF. Add to an already large number of people or things.

George has lost his job, and now swells the ranks of the unemployed.

Swim : GO SWIMMINGLY ; GO WITH A SWING. Proceed smoothly and well ; become a complete success.

I am sure your party to-morrow will go swimmingly.

Swing : IN FULL SWING. Making full progress.

The fête was in full swing when the storm came.

Swoop : AT ONE FELL SWOOP. In one complete and sudden disaster.

She lost her husband, her son and her home at one fell swoop.

Sword : SWORD OF DAMOCLES. A disaster liable to occur at any moment ; a threat to one's peace and happiness. Or. The Story of Damocles who, being invited by Dionysius to a splendid feast, looked

9

up from his seat to see a sword suspended above his head by a single hair.

PUT TO THE SWORD. Executed.

The savage king put all the prisoners to the sword.

T

T : TO A " T ". Exactly. The allusion is to the T-shaped piece of wood used by carpenters to make sure that joists are exactly at right angles.

This measurement is correct to a T.

Similar to TO A HAIR.

Tackle : Undertake (usually with difficulty).

I'll tackle the job as soon as I have time.

Tag : TAG RAG AND BOBTAIL. See RAG TAG AND BOBTAIL.

Tail : TAIL BETWEEN HIS LEGS. Completely cowed and humiliated, like a frightened dog.

My father sent the bully away with his tail between his legs.

Take : TAKEN ABACK. Disconcerted ; surprised.

The man was utterly taken aback when the police recognized him.

TAKE AFTER. Resemble, physically or otherwise.

Mary takes after her father, and is very musical.

TAKE BACK. Withdraw.

I take back everything I said.

TAKE A BACK SEAT (S.). Become less important and prominent ; be supplanted.

Now that the President has arrived, the Vice-President will have to take a back seat.

TAKE THE CAKE, *or* THE BISCUIT (S.). See " THE LIMIT ", to which it is very similar, though the meaning is not identical.

TAKE CARE. Be careful.

Take care that you don't slip on the frosty road.

TAKE A CUE. Or. Drama. Understand a hint. The " cue " is the word which indicates when the actor is to appear.

TAKE DOWN. 1. Lit.

Take down that book (or *take that book down*) *from the shelf.*

2. Met., Record ; write.

Take down this letter, please.

TAKE DOWN A PEG (S.). See **Peg**.

TAKE ONE'S FANCY. Charm ; attract ; interest.

I saw nothing in the shop to take my fancy.

TAKE FLIGHT ; TAKE TO FLIGHT. Depart quickly.

The bandits, hearing footsteps, took to flight.

TAKE IN GOOD (BAD) PART. Accept good-naturedly (or angrily).

I hope you'll take my advice in good part.

TAKE IN HAND. Undertake.

The workmen will take the repairs in hand next week.

TAKE TO HEART. Be seriously affected.

He has taken your words to heart, and will try to be more careful in future.

TAKE HEED OF *or* TO. Attend ; be warned by.

Take heed of what I've told you, and do not go out after dark.

TAKE HOLD OF. Seize ; grasp.

The boy took hold of the ladder, and began to climb.

TAKE IN. 1. Mislead ; deceive.

We were completely taken in by his story.

2. Buy regularly.

I take in the " Gardeners' Magazine ".

3. Receive, as a means of livelihood.

Old Miss Brown takes in lodgers when she can get them.

4. Escort to a dining-room, etc.

Our host took in the Duchess as the principal guest.

TAKE A LIKING, DISLIKE, FANCY, *etc.*, TO. The same as " like ", etc., except that the effect is rather more emphatic and spontaneous.

TAKE OFF. 1. Mimic.

He took off the headmaster perfectly.

2. Rise from the ground.

The aeroplane will take off at three o'clock.

TAKE ONESELF OFF. Depart, generally abruptly or indignantly.

They took themselves off without saying good-bye.

TAKE OFFENCE, *or* UMBRAGE. Be annoyed ; angry.

He always takes offence at any kind of criticism.

TAKE ON. 1. Accept responsibility for.
I've taken on the organization of our Hospital Fête.
See TAKE UPON ONESELF.

2. Grieve (S.). Old f.
*Don't take on so—you'll find plenty of other girls to
choose from.*

TAKE OUT. 1. Obtain the issue of (in a legal sense).
I am taking out a patent for the invention.

2. Extract.
The dentist took out five of Mary's teeth.

3. Accompany (for a walk, etc.) ; in charge of.
Father isn't at home ; he's taken out the dog.

TAKE IT OUT OF ONE. Exhaust ; weaken.
So much hill-climbing takes it out of me terribly.

TAKE OVER. Take the place of someone else.
*You watch the house until ten o'clock, and then I'll
take over.*

TAKE PAINS, *or* TROUBLE. Make a considerable effort.
I took pains to explain the facts clearly.

TAKE PART IN. Share ; co-operate ; act with others.
Her ladyship takes part in all local entertainments.

TAKE A PERSON'S PART. Support ; identify oneself
with.
The boy's mother will naturally take his part.

TAKE PLACE. Happen ; occur.
The race will take place to-morrow.
See DOING.

TAKE THE ROUGH WITH THE SMOOTH. Accept philo-
sophically both pleasant and unpleasant things.
*If one becomes a soldier, one must be ready to take
the rough with the smooth.*

TAKE THE SHINE OUT OF (S.). Cause to appear inferior ;
supersede.
Mary's new hat takes the shine out of yours.
See TAKE A BACK SEAT.

TAKE SIDES. Support one adversary against another.
*A judge should remain impartial, and not take
sides.*

TAKE SILK. Become a Queen's Counsel, an honour
which entitles a barrister to wear a silk gown in
Court, instead of the cloth one previously worn.
The new judge took silk ten years ago.

TAKE ONE'S STAND. Decide upon a mental attitude ; base one's argument.

I take my stand on the fact that all men are born free and equal.

TAKE STOCK OF. Examine thoroughly and in detail.

He decided to take stock of the present condition of affairs.

TAKE BY STORM. Or. Military. Capture by a violent attack.

The city was taken by storm at the end of the day.

TAKE TO. Form a liking for.

The baby took to the kitten at once.

See TAKE A LIKING TO.

TAKE TO ONE'S BED. Go to bed, usually for some time, as the result of illness, etc.

My husband feels so ill that he has taken to his bed.

TAKE TO TASK. Blame ; reprove.

His wife took him to task for his laziness.

TAKE TOO MUCH. Become intoxicated.

Though Bill often visits the public-house, he never takes too much.

TAKE IN TOW. Or. Nautical. A disabled vessel is " taken in tow " when she is attached to another and towed through the water. Met., Take charge of ; be responsible for.

Poor old Bill seems to have taken his wife and most of her family in tow.

TAKE ON TRUST. Believe without evidence or proof.

We are prepared to take on trust the story you have told us.

TAKE UP. 1. Arrest.

Young Parker has been taken up for betting in the street.

2. Absorb ; occupy.

Attending to a husband and six children takes up most of her time.

3. Lift.

We will take up the carpet and send it to be cleaned to-morrow.

TAKE UP THE THREADS. Resume after an interruption.

She came home from a long holiday to take up the threads of her old life.

TAKE UP WITH. Become friendly or intimate with.

Since Peter left her, the girl has taken up with several other boys.

TAKE UPON ONESELF. Assume or accept responsibility without being asked.

I've taken it upon myself to ask the Bishop to dinner.

TAKE THE WILL FOR THE DEED. Accept the desire to be kind and helpful, even if nothing practical results.

We'd have been delighted to ask you to dinner on Tuesday, but unfortunately we've promised to dine in town, so you'll have to take the will for the deed.

Tale : TALE-BEARER. One who spreads rumours, and who tells malicious stories of other people.

TELL ITS OWN TALE. Need no explanation.

The canary's feathers in the cat's mouth tell their own tale.

TELL TALES OUT OF SCHOOL. Reveal another person's private affairs ; discuss them with inappropriate people, or at inappropriate times.

Jane, telling tales out of school as usual, has been telling people about Mary's coming divorce.

THEREBY HANGS A TALE. Or. Quotation from Shakespeare's *The Taming of the Shrew*. With that event is connected a story.

I met Mary on her way to Peter's house ; and thereby hangs a tale.

UNFOLD A TALE. Old f. Narrate a story.

I could unfold a tale of tragedy and terror.

Talk : IDLE TALK. Foolish, useless talk ; gossip.

SMALL TALK. Talk concerning trivialities ; formal and polite conversation.

The Duke of Wellington once said that he had no small talk when conversing with Queen Victoria.

TABLE-TALK. Conversation of the friendly and entertaining type which takes place among intimates at a meal. Applied especially to the talk of famous people.

TALK OVER. 1. Discuss.

We talked over his plans for the future.

2. Convince ; bring to one's own way of thinking.

He wouldn't come at first, but we talked him over.

TALKING OF—— As we are discussing——

Talking of money, have you paid the tailor's bill yet ?

Tall : A TALL ORDER (S.). An order or request difficult to carry out.

The chief wanted me to leave for America in two days. I pointed out that it was a tall order.

TALL STORY. One difficult to believe ; an exaggerated and improbable story.

He told me that when in India he shot ten tigers in one day—a tall story, even for Smith.

Tape : GETTING A MAN TAPED (S.). Being aware of the character and past record of a person. Or. Using a measuring-tape to record for medical and other purposes the physical dimensions of a man.

Smith thinks nothing is known about him, but I am told that the authorities have him taped.

Tar : TARRED WITH THE SAME BRUSH. Having the same defects.

She is horribly mean, but all her family are tarred with the same brush.

Tartar : CATCH A TARTAR. Catch an unexpectedly violent and difficult enemy.

When the police arrested the woman, they found they had caught a tartar.

Taste : A TASTE FOR. A natural appreciation of, or liking for.

I have no taste whatever for Japanese art.

See AN EAR FOR and AN EYE FOR.

Tear : (Pron. TAIR). TEAR TO TATTERS, RIBBONS, *etc.* Tear roughly into small pieces.

The flag was torn to tatters by the gale.

Tears : (Pron. TEERS). BATHED, DROWNED *or* DISSOLVED IN TEARS. Weeping excessively.

The unhappy woman, drowned in tears, told her story to the magistrate.

CROCODILE TEARS. Hypocritical tears ; tears shed by one who is not, in fact, grieving at all. Or. The legend, based on the sucking and oozing sounds made by the movement of crocodiles in the swampy ground in which they live, that the animals deliberately weep noisily, so that travellers go to rescue what they imagine to be a lost child.

The new king shed crocodile tears on hearing of his father's death.

REDUCE TO TEARS. Compel to weep by pity or distress.

The old man's story reduced Mary to tears.

Teens : IN ONE'S TEENS ; 'TEEN AGE. At any age from thirteen to nineteen inclusive.

Teeth : IN THE TEETH OF. In spite of ; without regard to.
We married in the teeth of her parents' opposition.

MAKE SOMEONE'S TEETH CHATTER. Cause one to tremble or shiver so much that the upper and lower teeth click together.
The bitter north wind made their teeth chatter.

SET ONE'S TEETH ON EDGE. Lit., Cause a grating or tingling sensation around one's teeth, through their contact with acid, etc. Met., Cause a general discomfort at some particularly harsh sound, or by embarrassing action or speech.
For Heaven's sake oil that squeaky wheel—it sets my teeth on edge.

SHOW ONE'S TEETH. Indicate anger or annoyance (as an animal shows its teeth when enraged).
The old man was civil enough when we first met, but showed his teeth when I asked him for a job.

SKIN OF ONE'S TEETH. See under **Skin.**

Tell : TELL ONE'S BEADS. Say a series of prayers as one passes one's fingers over the beads of a rosary ; say the Rosary. (" Tell " in this sense means " count ".)

TELL OFF. 1. Select a number of persons by name for a special purpose.
The captain told off six men to act as escort to the prisoners.
2. (S.). Reprove. Express one's views frankly and unfavourably.
I told off young George for keeping me waiting.

TELL THAT TO THE MARINES (or, more correctly, THE HORSE MARINES, such a corps being non-existent, as Marines are a sea-going force). Tell that story to someone who doesn't exist, since no one who does exist is likely to believe it.

Temper : LOSE ONE'S TEMPER ; BE OUT OF TEMPER. Exchange one's good temper for a bad temper ; be angry, irritable, in an unpleasant mood.
The old woman was completely out of temper.

Ten : TEN TO ONE. It is ten chances to one that it will happen ; very probably. (Similarly other numbers.)
Tell him you've broken the vase ; ten to one he won't be angry.

Tenterhooks : ON TENTERHOOKS. In a state of acute anxiety or suspense. Tenterhooks are hooks on which cloth is stretched after being woven.

The students were on tenterhooks to hear the result of the examination.

See ON THORNS.

Terms : COME TO TERMS. Reach a formal and businesslike arrangement.

If you're willing to sell your house, we can soon come to terms.

See CRY QUITS.

COUCHED IN TERMS. Expressed in words.

What he said of his wife was couched in terms of deep affection.

ON GOOD, *or* BAD, TERMS. "Terms" means the condition or state of affairs existing between two people or groups of people.

The Robinsons have always been on bad terms with their neighbours.

Thank : THANK GOODNESS, HEAVEN, *etc.* A general ejaculation of gratitude.

Thank goodness it hasn't rained to-day!

THANK ONE'S (LUCKY) STARS. The stars are supposed to protect a person and bring good fortune—and the reverse.

You may thank your lucky stars that you weren't in the house when the bomb fell.

THANKS TO. Owing to ; because of.

Thanks to Father's generosity, we are flying to Paris.

NO THANKS TO. No credit or gratitude is due to.

It's no thanks to you that the house wasn't burnt down.

(*Note.*—The phrase is always used to indicate blame.)

That : AT THAT. Thereupon ; following that statement.

I told Peter I hated him, and at that he immediately turned and left the room.

THAT'S THA (S.). A concluding emphasis to a statement.

I won't marry Peter, and that's that.

THAT IS TO SAY. To express differently, or more fully (= the Latin *id est*).

He's a cutler—that is to say, a man who sells knives and sharp tools.

Thick : IN THE THICK OF. In the densest, most congested part. Lit. and Met.

We were in the thick of the crowd at the Coronation.
Don't disturb me—I'm in the thick of a job.

THROUGH THICK AND THIN. Through every trouble or difficulty, good fortune or bad fortune.

His wife said she loved him, and would follow him through thick and thin.

Thing : JUST THE THING ; THE VERY THING. Exactly what is needed or appropriate.

This feather is just the thing for your hat.

OF ALL THINGS. From among all the things which might have happened, *this* has occurred.

And now we're told—of all things !—that we shall have to leave the house.

TAKING ONE THING WITH ANOTHER. Weighing the advantages against the disadvantages ; considering all the circumstances.

Taking one thing with another, we are better off in England than in France.

TAKING THINGS AS THEY ARE. As things are. See SUCH BEING THE CASE.

THE THING (TO DO). The fashion ; socially correct.

I hear it's the thing to carry a muff this season.

See IT ISN'T DONE (under DO).

Think : I DON'T THINK ! (S.). Used as a term of ironic dissent.

Her father was a nobleman—I don't think !

THINK BETTER OF IT. Abandon an unwise decision.

He was going to fight the policeman, but thought better of it, and walked quietly away.

THINK FIT, *or* THINK PROPER. Decide ; consider suitable or appropriate. (The phrase is frequently used ironically.)

The young man, having no job and no money, thought fit to get married.

THINK HIGHLY, *or* MUCH OF. Admire.

The directors think highly of Smith.

THINK LITTLE, *or* NOTHING, OF. 1. Treat casually ; regard as normal.

In Australia, one thinks nothing of riding fifty miles to a dance.

2. Regard as worthless.

George thinks nothing of his wife's work in the home.

THINK NO END OF. Have a very high opinion of.

We think no end of our new chauffeur.

THINK NO MORE OF. Forget.

He had deceived her, and she would think no more of him.

THINK NO SMALL BEER (S.). Have a high opinion ; be proud of.

That young fellow thinks no small beer of himself.

THINK OUT. Meditate upon ; consider.

We must think out some other way of paying our debts.

THINK SCORN OF. Old f. Scorn ; regard contemptuously.

I think scorn of any man who will not defend his home.

WAY OF THINKING. Point of view ; personal aspect.

According to my way of thinking, all wars do more harm than good.

Thorns : ON THORNS. In a state of acute mental discomfort or anxiety.

He was on thorns, fearing that his mother would ask where he had been.

See ON TENTERHOOKS.

A THORN IN THE FLESH, *or* IN ONE'S SIDE. An infliction ; an annoyance which one has to endure. Or. The custom of the ancient Pharisees of putting thorns in their garments to prick their legs when walking.

That old aunt who lives with the Wilkinsons is a permanent thorn in the flesh.

Thorough : THOROUGH-PACED. Complete ; without qualification. (Usually applied unflatteringly.)

King John was a thorough-paced villain.

Thought : QUICK AS THOUGHT. Instantly.

Quick as thought, he struck at his enemy.

TAKE NO THOUGHT FOR. Or. Scriptural. Do not worry or concern yourself about.

Take no thought for your future needs ; I will attend to them.

TAKE THOUGHT. Consider thoroughly.

Take thought before offending a rich man.

Thread : THREAD OR EDGE ONE'S WAY. Move to one's destination through narrow or crowded streets.

We threaded our way through the cheering crowds to the station.

Threshold : ON THE THRESHOLD. Lit., The "sill" (horizontal piece of wood or stone) that forms the bottom of the door-frame at the entrance of a building. Met., The beginning of anything.

He felt he was on the threshold of solving a tremendous mystery.

Through : BY MEANS OF.

He obtained work through his own efforts.

THROUGH WITH (S.). Finished with.

I'm through with Emily Jones—she's deceived me too often.

Throw : THROW DUST IN THE EYES OF. Obscure the facts ; mislead.

She said she was going to post a letter, but that was only to throw dust in the eyes of her parents.

THROW A FIT (S.). Lit., Have a fit. Met., Become highly agitated or excited.

Father will throw a fit when he hears that the house has been burgled.

THROW ONESELF AT THE HEAD OF (*applied to women only*). Show a man that she is anxious to marry him.

The silly girl is throwing herself at young Pawson's head.

See SET ONE'S CAP AT.

THROW IN. Give in addition.

The herrings were ten a shilling, and the fishmonger threw in an extra one.

THROW LIGHT UPON. Make plainer.

This information may throw light upon the mystery of the Duke's death.

THROW OFF THE SCENT. Or. Hunting. Distract from what is of true importance, from the true facts.

The police were completely thrown off the scent, and arrested the wrong man.

See RED HERRING.

THROW IN THE SHADE. Supersede; render inconspicuous.

Olivier's acting threw that of every other actor in the shade.

THROW OUT A FEELER. Find out by a preliminary question or hint.

He threw out a feeler to discover what chances there were of his becoming a partner in the business.

THROW OVER. Abandon; discard; have no further association with.

He was engaged to the rich Miss Watson, but she threw him over.

THROW UP THE SPONGE. Or. Prize-fighting. Surrender; abandon abruptly; admit complete defeat. (The sponge used to bathe the boxers' faces is thrown into the air when the loser admits his defeat.)

You've still a chance of winning a scholarship; don't throw up the sponge.

Thumb : UNDER ONE'S THUMB. Under one's control or influence.

She has her husband completely under her thumb.

Thunder : THUNDERS OF APPLAUSE. Applause so noisy and continuous that it suggests thunder.

There were thunders of applause when the curtain fell.

THUNDERSTRUCK. Overcome with astonishment. See MOON-STRUCK.

Tick : HALF A TICK (S.). See **Jiffy.**

ON TICK (S.). On credit; without immediate payment.

We bought our deal chairs on tick.

Ticket : THAT'S THE TICKET (S.). That's good; well done!

And you'll go home to-morrow to your father and mother? That's the ticket!

Tickle : TICKLE TO DEATH (S.). Extremely amused.

The family will be tickled to death to hear that old Miss Juggins is marrying Sir John.

Tide : TIDE OVER. Continue until changed and usually improved conditions take place.

We'll try to tide over with the old carpet until the spring.

Tie : BLACK TIE. A black tie worn with a black waistcoat and dinner-jacket. (The idiom is used as indicating the whole outfit.)

WHITE TIE. Similarly, a white tie worn with white

waistcoat, coat with " tails ", and black trousers—
the more formal evening dress.

Are you wearing a black or white tie at the dinner ?
Oh, white.

Time : AT THIS TIME OF DAY.   At the present state of affairs ;
at this point.

At this time of day it is absurd to treat girls of sixteen
as if they were small children.

AT TIMES ;   FROM TIME TO TIME.   At intervals ;
occasionally.

He seems at times to recognize us.

See NOW AND THEN ;   NOW AND AGAIN.

BEAT TIME.   The action of a conductor indicating the
" beats " in the music with his baton.

BEFORE ONE'S TIME.   1. Before one was born.

Dickens died in 1870—before your time.

Compare BORN BEFORE ONE'S TIME.

2. Too early.

He was here before his time.

BIDE ONE'S TIME.   Wait patiently.   (" Bide " is an
abbrev. of " abide " = stay, remain.)

If we bide our time it will all come right.

FOR THE TIME BEING.   Temporarily ;   during the time
that is immediately coming.

We are going to Rome as soon as we can, but are staying
in London for the time being.

See IN THE MEAN TIME ;   FOR THE NONCE.

A GOOD TIME.   1. A highly pleasurable time.

Jane and Joan are at Brighton, having a thoroughly
good time.

2. A considerable period.

I am going into the town, and shall not be back for a
good time.

HARD TIMES.   Times of poverty, suffering, or discomfort.

He went through hard times when he was young.

HIGH TIME.   Fully time.

It is high time that you earnt your own living.

HIGH OLD TIME (S.).   A gay and unconventional time.

We had a high old time at George's party.

IN COURSE OF TIME.   Eventually, after some time had
passed.

In course of time they married and lived happily together.

IN TIME.   I. Before it is too late.
The doctor came in time to save her life.
2. After some considerable time had passed.
In time he forgot all about her.

IN GOOD TIME.   Early; with time to spare.
Be at the station in good time.

IN THE NICK OF TIME.   Just in time; almost, but not quite, too late.
The door of the tiger's cage was shut in the nick of time.

IN NO TIME, *or* LESS THAN NO TIME.   Very soon; almost immediately.
We shall be ready in less than no time.

See HALF A TICK; TWO-TWOS; HALF A JIFFY.

MANY A TIME.   Repeatedly; frequently.
Many a time we walked by the river.

ONCE UPON A TIME.   Some time ago; in the past. (The traditional beginning to children's stories.)
Once upon a time there lived a king with three sons.

OVERTIME.   Extra time; additional hours of work for which payment is usually made.

PART-TIME.   Time which does not occupy all the usual working day.
Marjory has a part-time job taking care of young children.

PRESSED FOR TIME.   Short of time; very busy.
I can't stay more than ten minutes, as I am pressed for time.

STATED TIME.   A time already fixed.
At the stated time the ship will leave the harbour.

TAKE TIME BY THE FORELOCK.   Act promptly and without delay. (Time is always represented as an old man, bald except for a " forelock " or tuft of hair over his forehead.)   See STRIKE WHILE THE IRON IS HOT.

TIME IS DRAWING ON.   It is growing late.
Time is drawing on; we ought to leave in ten minutes.

TIME'S UP (S.).   The stated time has come to an end, is finished.
Time's up—you must say good-bye.

TIME OF DAY.   Old f.   The time, the hour.
What's the time of day?   Ten past two.

TIME GROWING SHORT.   Very similar to TIME DRAWING ON.

TIME OF LIFE. Age.

At my time of life I can't be expected to dance.

TIME OF ONE'S LIFE. The best and most enjoyable moment of one's life.

I had the time of my life at the party.

TIME ON ONE'S HANDS. Time to waste, to spare; superfluous time.

As I had a good deal of time on my hands, I decided to explore the City.

THE TIMES ARE OUT OF JOINT. Or. Shakespeare's *Hamlet*. Affairs in general are out of harmony; unhappy and uncomfortable.

He felt that the times were out of joint, and the world was a miserable place.

TIME OUT OF MIND; TIME IMMEMORIAL. Longer than can be remembered.

Farmers have fed their sheep here time out of mind.

(*Note.*—Legally, " time immemorial " is equivalent to any period not later than the reign of Richard I.)

TIMES OUT OF NUMBER, *or* WITHOUT NUMBER. Many times; times beyond counting.

You've been told times without number to wash your hands when you come to dinner.

TIMES, DAYS, YEARS, *etc.*, TO COME. In the future.

In times to come we shall all travel to work in planes.

WORK AGAINST TIME. Use special efforts to finish a piece of work within a stated time.

We are working against time to complete the house by Christmas.

Tip : A STRAIGHT TIP (S.). Definite and accurate information; also (frequently) a plain warning.

He got the straight tip from Wilson—work harder, or you'll lose your job.

TIP THE WINK (S.). Warn; give a signal.

I'm going to sleep ; tip the wink when the chief is coming.

Tiptoe : ON TIPTOE. Standing on the tips of one's toes; used, met., to indicate a state of excitement and tension.

The village was on tiptoe to meet the new Vicar and his wife.

Tip-top; topping (S.). Excellent; the best of its kind.
We had a tip-top breakfast at the hotel.

Tit for tat : Or. Said to be derived from the Dutch *dit vor dat* = " This for that ". An equivalent; something, frequently unpleasant, given in return for something else.
The little girl tore her brother's book, and tit-for-tat he hid her doll.

Tittle-tattle : Idle, chattering gossip.
According to village tittle-tattle, the squire was going to marry his cousin.

To : TO AND FRO. (= To and from.) From one spot to another and back again.
The sentry paced to and fro.
See BACKWARDS AND FORWARDS.

Together : TOGETHER WITH. With; also.
I am selling the house, together with the furniture.

Token : BY THE SAME TOKEN. Further; moreover.
The thieves were caught, and by the same token sent to prison.

Tom Tiddler's Ground. Or. Said to be derived from " Tom the Idler's Ground ". An imaginary place in which unlimited wealth can be obtained with very little effort. (*Note.*—Children play a game beginning, " I'm on Tom Tiddler's ground, picking up gold and silver.")
The unscrupulous dealer found London a regular Tom Tiddler's ground.

Tongue : GIVE TONGUE. Or. Hunting. Hounds are said to " give tongue ", or utter their peculiar cry, when the fox is seen. Met., Repeat; report.
I wouldn't give tongue to such gossip.

HOLD ONE'S TONGUE. Become silent; cease to speak.
" Hold your tongue ! " cried my mother, and I said no more.

ON THE TIP OF ONE'S TONGUE. On the verge of being spoken; almost but not quite uttered.
It was on the tip of my tongue to tell him my secret, but I was too frightened.

TONGUE-TIED. Silent through embarrassment or fear.
The boy stood tongue-tied in front of the master.

WITH ONE'S TONGUE IN ONE'S CHEEK. Without meaning what one says; insincerely.

He said he was terribly sorry, but I knew he spoke with his tongue in his cheek.

Tooth : A SWEET TOOTH. A liking for sweet things—jam, sugar, etc.

Arthur, who has a sweet tooth, spent two shillings on chocolates.

TOOTH AND NAIL. With extreme fierceness.

She attacked the old man tooth and nail, for coming down late for breakfast.

Top : TOP OF ONE'S BENT. See under **Bent.**

TOP SPEED ; FULL SPEED. As fast as possible.

The car dashed through the town at top speed.

TOP OF THE TREE, *or* LADDER. The highest point in one's business or profession.

Jevons has reached the top of the tree as a surgeon.

TOP UP (S.). Finish ; conclude.

I'm going to have chicken for lunch, and top up with an ice.

Topsy-turvy : From the Anglo-Saxon " top side " and " turn away ". Inverted, the normal position reversed.

The driver's seat was a wooden box put topsy-turvy on the front of the cart.

See UPSIDE DOWN.

Toss : TOSS UP. Decide by spinning a coin. See HEADS OR TAILS.

A TOSS-UP. A complete uncertainty ; as likely as unlikely.

It's a toss-up whether we meet again.

Touch : IN TOUCH WITH. In communication, or contact, with.

I am in touch with the police, and they'll be here in ten minutes.

LOSE TOUCH. Cease to have any communication with.

I used to see Williamson fairly often, but I've lost touch with him lately.

TOUCH AND GO. Extremely doubtful or precarious.

It was touch and go whether we should escape.

A TOUCH OF THE TAR-BRUSH (S.). A trace of negro blood.

She is so dark that I'm sure there's a touch of the tar-brush in the family.

TOUCH UP. Restore or improve by a number of small touches with a brush or pen.

Pete is busy touching up that old picture he bought.

TOUCH UPON. Refer to briefly.

The preacher touched upon the restlessness of the present time.

Tower : TOWER OF STRENGTH. A great support and help.

Miss Brown was a tower of strength at the concert.

IN A TOWERING PASSION, *or* RAGE. Dominated by tremendous danger.

The King was in such a towering rage that his courtiers were terrified.

Track : BEATEN TRACK. Lit., A pathway which has been beaten or flattened by many feet. Met., A regular routine ; customary procedure.

The candidate, leaving the beaten track of politics for a time, entertained the audience with stories of his early life.

MAKE TRACKS (S.). Hurry away.

I'm going to make tracks for the post office at once.

Trade : OF A TRADE. Following the same occupation.

Are both of you stamp-collectors, too ? Then we're three of a trade.

Trail : TRAIL ONE'S COAT. Attempt to start a quarrel or argument. To trail or drag one's coat behind one was an accepted method of issuing a general challenge ; any person stepping on the coat was considered to have insulted its owner.

That quarrelsome Irishman has been trailing his coat for the last half-hour.

TRAIL OFF. Become weaker and feebler.

He began by shouting, but his voice trailed off into a mere whisper.

Train : IN THE TRAIN OF. Among those in an inferior position accompanying a great personage.

In the train of the cardinal were many bishops and priests, as well as his personal servants.

Tread : TREAD ON ONE'S CORNS (S.). Accidentally say or do something to cause embarrassment.

I'm afraid I trod on old Jaggers' corns when I asked him what his son was doing.

TREAD A MEASURE. Old f. Take part in a formal dance.

The quadrille is beginning; let us tread a measure.

Treasure : TREASURE UP. Retain, as something precious and valuable.

We should treasure every moment of such a day as this.

Trial : GIVE A TRIAL, TRY OUT. Test.

We've decided to give the new soap a trial.

Tribute : PAY TRIBUTE. Lit., To pay a fixed amount to a ruler or other governor. Met., Admit one's indebtedness to some helper or benefactor.

I am delighted to pay tribute to all that Mrs. Smith has done for the parish.

Trice : IN A TRICE. Old f. A " trice " is, lit., a period of time equal to one-third of a second, or a 180th of a minute. Very quickly.

Don't go—I'm coming in a trice.

Trivial : THE TRIVIAL ROUND. The routine of everyday life ; the succession of small regular duties. Abbrev. of lines from Keble's well-known hymn, " The trivial round, the common task, will furnish all we need to ask ".

Trot : TROT OUT (S.). Quote ; exhibit ; produce in support.

He trotted out the old proverb that there's no time like the present.

Trouble : TROUBLE BREWING. Trouble is likely to occur.

I'm afraid there's trouble brewing over that speech you made at the meeting yesterday.

TROUBLE IN STORE. Trouble likely to occur at some later time.

I am afraid you have trouble in store with that child.

Truce : HOLLOW TRUCE. A truce which is merely an interval during which both sides prepare for further fighting.

A TRUCE TO. An invitation to abandon the subject.

You speak of the equality of man. A truce to this nonsense !

Trump : TRUMP-CARD. Or. Card-playing. " Trump " is an abbrev. for " triumph ", and a trump-card is a " triumph " or winning card.

Then he played his trump-card. If she wouldn't go to America with him, he would go alone.

TRUMP UP. Falsely state; tell maliciously and untruthfully.

He came to me with a trumped-up story about my brother.

TURN UP TRUMPS. See under **Turn**.

Trumpet : BLOW ONE'S OWN TRUMPET. Boast of one's own work or actions.

He spends most of the time blowing his own trumpet.

FLOURISH OF TRUMPETS. Preliminary ceremonies and announcements, as a herald proclaiming some matter of importance.

The new hotel was opened with a flourish of trumpets.

Truth : THE NAKED, PLAIN, SIMPLE, SOBER, *or* STARK TRUTH. The truth, and nothing but the truth. (The figure of Truth is represented as a naked woman, living in the depths of a well.)

ARRIVE AT THE TRUTH. Discover what really occurred.

Six months passed before I was able to arrive at the truth about the accident.

Try : TRY CONCLUSIONS. Start a struggle that must have a definite ending.

The Government is certain to try conclusions with the House of Lords.

TRY ONE'S HAND AT. Attempt.

I'm going to try my hand at cooking while Jane is away.

TRY ON. 1. Put on a garment to see if it fits.

You'd better try on the coat before you buy it.

2. (S.) (with hyphen). An impudent attempt.

He asked me to lend him some money, but it was merely a try-on.

Tuck : TUCK IN (S.). (*Verb.*) Have a good meal. (*Noun.*) A good meal.

I took him to the restaurant, ordered lunch, and told him to tuck in.

TUCK UP. Wrap closely in bedclothes, etc.

The boy's mother came into the bedroom every evening to tuck him up.

Tug : Tug-of-war. See PULL TOGETHER.

Tune : SING A DIFFERENT TUNE. Behave in a different way.

When he hears that his partner has been arrested, he'll sing a different tune.

TO THE TUNE OF. At a cost of.

The town is building a new hall to the tune of twenty thousand pounds.

Tuppenny-ha'penny : A TUPPENNY-HA'PENNY *or* TWO-PENNY HALFPENNY AFFAIR. A trivial affair ; one of no importance.

The trouble between the women is a tuppenny-ha'penny affair.

Turn : AS IT TURNED OUT. As it resulted ; happened ; as the sequel.

Everyone thought farmers would be ruined by the war, but as it turned out they were more prosperous than before.

DO A GOOD, *or* BAD, TURN. Help (or the reverse).

I thought I would do Mary a good turn by minding the baby.

You did me a bad turn when you introduced me to Watson.

GIVE SOMEONE A TURN. Old f. Startle ; shock.

It gave Mother a turn when Alfred arrived from Edinburgh yesterday.

TAKE A TURN. Pass from one state of health to another.

The injured man took a turn for the worse on Monday, and died yesterday.

TAKE TURNS ; TAKE IT IN TURNS. Act in rotation or regular order.

We took turns in guarding the treasure.

TURN TO ACCOUNT *or* GOOD ACCOUNT. Use ; make use of successfully.

I can turn to good account all this timber.

TURN ADRIFT. Or. Nautical. Cast out to wander. A vessel is adrift if it is floating without control wherever the winds and current may take it.

The brutal landlord turned the widow and her child adrift in a snowstorm.

TURN AGAINST. Change from like to dislike ; regard with aversion.

He became so irritable and impatient that many of his old friends turned against him.

TURN ASIDE. Alter the direction in which one is going. Temporarily leave one occupation for another.

The Professor would turn aside from his studies to play with his little grandson.

TURN ONE'S BACK ON. Deliberately ignore.

The penitent boy turned his back on the unhappy past and began a new existence.

TURN THE CORNER. Pass a crisis successfully.

The patient has turned the corner, and will recover.

TURN DOWN. 1. Lit., Fold over and flatten down.

He turned down the collar of his coat.

2. Met., Refuse or decline definitely.

He was poor but proud, and turned down every offer of help.

TURN OF EVENTS. Change in the course of events, or happenings.

A year later, owing to a strange turn of events, I found myself in Paris again.

TURN OF EXPRESSION. Phrase or sentence.

The stranger from Scotland used many turns of expression which were new to his listeners.

TURN ONE'S HAND TO. Undertake a variety of work, or work that is not one's normal occupation.

I'm a carpenter by trade, but I can turn my hand to brick-laying or painting.

TURN AN HONEST PENNY. See under **Penny.**

TURN IN. Go to bed.

The travellers were so fatigued that they all turned in early.

TURN INSIDE OUT. Lit., Turn so that the inner is outside, and vice versa. Met., Examine or explore with extreme thoroughness.

I've turned my desk inside out, but cannot find the missing paper.

TURN OFF, *or* ON. Stop or start the supply by turning a tap.

Please turn off the wireless.

TURN OUT. 1. Display.

The Lord Mayor's show was a magnificent turn-out.

2. Manufacture.

We can turn out twenty gross of cups a week.

3. Compel to leave ; evict.

The family were turned out of their cottage because they could not pay their rent.

4. Empty ; usually to tidy.

He turned out his desk.

5. The final fact; the outcome (used at the end of a narration).

It turned out that he was George's father.

6. Extinguish (a light) by turning a tap (similar to TURN OFF).

TURN OUT WELL. Succeed in life.

He's a sensible and clever boy, and ought to turn out well.

TURN, TILT THE SCALES. Lit., Make the scale fall, and so register something slightly heavier than the weight on the opposite side.

He turned the scale at eleven stone.

Met., Finally decide some matter which is in doubt.

The evidence given by his friend turned the scale, and the boy was set free.

See TURN THE TABLES.

TURN THE TABLES. Reverse the position.

The sudden arrival of the police turned the tables; the villains who had kept us prisoners were themselves captured and led away.

TURN TAIL. Turn and run away.

When the thief heard the police he turned tail and fled.

TURN OF THE TIDE. Lit., The point at which the sea ceases to flow out and begins to flow back, or vice versa. Met., The point at which success is followed by failure, or vice versa.

For Napoleon the turn of the tide came soon after he divorced Josephine.

TURN AND TURN ABOUT. First one, then the other, for equal periods.

George and I kept watch, turn and turn about, for an hour at a time.

TURN TURTLE. Turn upside down in the sea.

The great ship turned turtle and sank.

TURN UP. Arrive; appear.

Our guests did not turn up until nearly midnight.

TURN UP ONE'S NOSE. Sneer.

Now she has become rich she turns up her nose at plain food.

TURN UP TRUMPS. Prove of great and vital service.

We couldn't have afforded to get married if Jack's rich uncle hadn't turned up trumps.

TURN UPON. Blame or attack.
The old woman turned upon me suddenly and accused me of cheating her.

Twiddle : TWIDDLE ONE'S THUMBS. Waste one's time. See KICK ONE'S HEELS

Twinkle : TWINKLING OF AN EYE. Very quickly. ("Twinkling" means a rapid twist or turn, and is of the same origin as "wriggle".)

Twister : (S.). One who "twists", or systematically cheats.
Don't trust Ernest—he's a regular twister.

Two : IN TWO-TWOS (S.). In a moment ; almost instantly.

Two-way : Or. Electrical. Operating, according to choice, in two directions—e.g. the same light being switched on and off from the top or bottom of a staircase. See CUT BOTH WAYS.

U

Unappropriate : UNAPPROPRIATED BLESSING. Old f. Unmarried woman, usually elderly. Old maid.

Unbosom : UNBOSOM ONESELF. Confess one's private thoughts ; reveal one's hopes and fears.
That evening, when we were alone, the boy unbosomed himself.

Under : COME UNDER. Be classified with.
Cups and saucers come under crockery.

FALL UNDER. Met., Similar to COME UNDER.

UNDER THE ROSE. Tr. of the Latin *sub rosa*—privately ; secretly. Or. The rose is the emblem of silence.
It was whispered, under the rose, that the King was insane.

UNDER WAY. See **Way.**

Understanding : COME TO AN UNDERSTANDING. Agree and co-operate, after discussions and explanations.
The two men held opposing views, but eventually came to an understanding.

Also, (old f.) AGREE TO MARRY.

ON THE UNDERSTANDING, *or* WITH THE UNDERSTANDING. According to an agreement, instruction, etc.

You may go to the dance, on the understanding that you are back before midnight.

Up: ALL UP. See under ALL.

UP AND ABOUT. Well enough to leave one's bed after an illness.

UP IN ARMS. Indignant ; resentful.

She was up in arms at the mere idea of obeying her husband.

UP AND DOING. Active ; busy.

We must be up and doing if we are going to catch the train.

UPS AND DOWNS. Good times and bad times.

We all have our ups and downs.

UP-END. Place so that the small or narrow end is uppermost.

We shall have to up-end the box to get it out of the room.

UP TO THE EYES. Submerged.

I am up to the eyes in work.

See UP TO THE HILT.

UP TO THE HILT. To the limit, the greatest possible extent. The hilt is the handle of a sword, at which the blade ends.

The property is mortgaged up to the hilt.

UP TO THE MARK (S.). In one's normal state of health ; capable of doing one's ordinary work.

John does not seem up to the mark this morning.

(*Note.*—This idiom is more frequently used in the negative.)

COME UP TO THE SCRATCH. See **Scratch.**

UP TO SNUFF ; UP TO A THING OR TWO (S.). Old f. Alert ; shrewd.

Jenkins may be old, but he's up to snuff.

UP TO SOMETHING. Privately planning ; plotting some scheme.

I guess by the look on her face as she went out that Belinda is up to something.

UP STAGE (S.). Theatrical term, meaning the front of the stage, the position of most prominence. Applied, met., to anyone behaving haughtily and aggressively.

Sally Brown has become terribly up stage since she had tea with a countess.

UP TO YOU (S.). The responsibility is yours.
It's up to you to win this fight.

UP A TREE (S.). In a state of desperation.
I've had my wallet stolen, and am completely up a tree.

Upon : UPON WHICH. When this occurred.
The boy admitted that he stole the fruit, upon which his father thrashed him.

Upper : UPPER HAND. See under **Hand.**

THE UPPER TEN. Abbrev. of Upper ten thousand, the ten thousand people who in the Victorian era represented the wealthy aristocracy of England. A phrase now almost obsolete.

Uppers : ON ONE'S UPPERS. Very poor ; completely destitute. (The reference is to shoes or boots. When the sole is completely worn out the wearer is walking on the "uppers" or upper layers of leather.)
Sam lost his job six months ago, and he's now on his uppers.

Upside : UPSIDE DOWN. Inverted. See TOPSY-TURVY.

Upsides : UPSIDES WITH. Aware of ; familiar with.
You can't expect me to be upsides with all these new regulations.

Use : MAKE USE OF. Utilize, employ.
We can make use of these bricks to build a statue.

USED UP. Lit., Finished.
The food is used up.

Met., Exhausted ; with no energy or strength remaining.
He is completely used up through lack of food.

Uttermost : THE UTTERMOST FARTHING. The last amount, however small, that is owing.
The debt shall be paid to the uttermost farthing (paid until there is nothing left to pay, and the debt has ceased to exist).

UTTERMOST PART(S). The furthest, most distant parts.
I will follow him to the uttermost parts of the earth.

V

Vain : IN VAIN. Ineffectively ; without any result.
He shouted in vain for help.

Vale : VALE OF TEARS. Old f. Or. Quotation from a seventeenth-century poem. The world; the earth.

He lived for many years in this vale of tears.

Valour : THE BETTER PART OF VALOUR. Discretion. Or. The proverb, "Discretion is the better part of valour."

The general decided on the better part of valour, and surrendered.

Value : SET A VALUE ON. Estimate the value of.

I asked him to set a value on the pictures.

Van : IN THE VAN. Or. Nautical, from the French *avant*. Abbrev. for "vanguard"; the foremost or leading position. In the front.

Our firm is always in the van with improvements.

Variance : AT VARIANCE. In a state of quarrelling or disagreement.

The two families are always at variance with one another.

Vasty : VASTY DEEP. Old f. Large areas of deep water; the sea or the ocean.

Veer : VEER ROUND. Or. The wind, which "veers" or varies. Change one's opinions completely.

At first Father agreed with me; then he veered round and agreed with Mother.

Veil : BEYOND THE VEIL. Beyond human sight and knowledge; in the next world.

He has passed beyond the veil, and we shall hear his voice no more.

DRAW A VEIL OVER. Remain silent about; conceal.

The boy was sent into the study, where the headmaster was waiting with a cane, and I will draw a veil over what followed.

TAKE THE VEIL. Become a fully initiated nun.

Vengeance : WITH A VENGEANCE. To an excessive degree.

There will be trouble with a vengeance when his father hears what happened.

Vent : GIVE VENT TO. Give expression to; allow one's emotions to escape.

The old man gave vent to his anger when he heard the news.

Ventilate : VENTILATE A GRIEVANCE. See AIR A GRIEVANCE.

Venture : AT A VENTURE. By chance ; without consideration or knowledge.

He chose the book at a venture from the shelves.

Verdict : BRING IN, *or* RETURN, A VERDICT. The legal phrase for a jury recording a decision.

The jury brought in a verdict of guilty.

Very : THE VERY THING. See JUST THE THING.

VERY WELL. See under **Well.**

Vested : VESTED INTEREST. Permanent rights.

The old man has a vested interest in the farm.

Vet. : Abbrev. for " Veterinary surgeon ", one who examines and cures sick animals. Now frequently used as a verb in the sense of examining and, where necessary, correcting any form of work.

I shall be glad if you'll vet this essay I've written.

View : BIRD'S-EYE VIEW. A comprehensive view from above, such as a bird would obtain.

You get a bird's-eye view of Paris from the Eiffel Tower.

BRING INTO VIEW. Reveal to one's sight.

The telescope can bring into view objects a mile distant.

TO HAVE IN VIEW. To be contemplating, planning.

We have in view a new hospital for seamen.

IN VIEW OF. After consideration of.

In view of what you tell me about London, I shall not go there.

IN MY VIEW. In my opinion.

In my view, war is a game in which both sides lose.

MEET A PERSON'S VIEWS. Do as he desires.

We will do everything we can to meet your views.

ONE-SIDED VIEW. A prejudiced and limited outlook.

King Charles unfortunately took an entirely one-sided view of the situation. See also ONE-SIDED.

TAKING A LONG VIEW. Planning over a long period.

Taking a long view, we are buying land to build a new factory ten years hence.

Virtue : BY, *or* IN, VIRTUE OF. As a result or consequence of.

By virtue of his position, the Lord Mayor is the chief magistrate in the city.

Visit : VISIT THE SINS ON (Or. Biblical). Punish a person for the sins someone else has committed. " I will visit the sins of the fathers upon the children."

It isn't right to visit the sins of my brother on me.

A VISITATION OF PROVIDENCE. An event beyond the power of human beings to influence.

A visitation of Providence in the form of an earthquake destroyed the town.

Vital : THE VITAL SPARK. Old f. Life ; vitality.

She lay motionless ; the vital spark had fled.

Voice : GIVE VOICE TO. Express ; state publicly.

I am sure I am giving voice to what we all feel in wishing our Chairman a quick recovery.

RAISE THE VOICE. Speak more loudly.

Please raise your voice when addressing an audience.

Similarly LOWER THE VOICE. Speak more softly.

STILL, SMALL VOICE. Or. Biblical (I Kings xix. 12). Conscience ; one's inward knowledge of what is right.

AT THE TOP OF ONE'S VOICE. As loudly as possible.

The sergeant shouted at the top of his voice.

A VOICE IN THE MATTER. A share in the control ; a right to express one's views.

Before you and Frank decide to get married, remember that I have a voice in the matter.

Vulgar : THE VULGAR HERD. Ordinary people. (The phrase is generally used either ironically or snobbishly.)

The vulgar herd cannot be expected to appreciate my poems.

W

Waif : WAIFS AND STRAYS. Originally referring to lost or abandoned children ; now applied also to sayings or quotations whose origins or authors cannot be traced.

Wait : WAIT UPON. 1. Pay a formal visit (a social inferior to a superior).

Be good enough to inform her Majesty that I will wait upon her on Monday.

2. Attend to the wants of.

The dinner was good, but there weren't enough people to wait upon the guests.

Wake : IN THE WAKE. Or. Nautical. In the footsteps or path of. The "wake" is the track left by a vessel as it passes through the water.

Famine follows in the wake of war.

Walk : A WALK-OVER. An extremely easy victory.

The next race ought to be a walk-over for the Frenchman.

Wall : FIGHT WITH ONE'S BACK TO THE WALL. Fight desperately ; make a final defence.

We're fighting with our backs to the wall to win the election.

BE DRIVEN TO THE WALL. See GO TO THE WALL.

Wane : ON THE WANE. Or. Astronomy : a star " wanes " when its light decreases. Diminishing ; decreasing in power.

Her influence over him was on the wane.

War : SINEWS OF WAR. Money, which is necessary in every war, as, similarly, the sinews in one's body enable one to exercise force.

We'd like to spend the holiday in Rome, but we haven't the sinews of war.

See THE NEEDFUL, THE WHEREWITHAL.

WAGE WAR. Conduct war.

The English waged war with Napoleon.

WAR TO THE KNIFE, *or* THE DEATH. A bitter and ruthless struggle.

It was war to the knife between the two women who loved him.

Wash : WASH ONE'S DIRTY LINEN IN PUBLIC. Discuss one's family scandals and disgraces in public.

All the village knows that Mr. Snooks has been to prison; Mrs. Snooks has no hesitation in washing her dirty linen in public.

WASH ONE'S HANDS OF. Refuse any responsibility for.

Do as you like ; I wash my hands of the whole business.

WASH-OUT *(with hyphen)* (S.). Complete failure.

I tried to make my living as an artist, but it was a wash-out.

WASH OUT *(without hyphen)*. Lit., Remove by washing.

I've washed out the stain on your coat.

Met., Obliterate.

He tried, by good conduct, to wash out memories of the past.

Watch : ON THE WATCH. In a state of watchfulness. See ON THE ALERT.

SET A WATCH. Arrange for systematic watching.

If we set a watch, we shall probably catch the thief.

WATCH AND WARD. Watch, and at the same time guard from interference.

The policeman kept watch and ward over his prisoners.

Water : HOLD WATER. 1. Lit., Contain without leaking.

That pail will hold water.

2. Be true and capable of being tested.

His account of the robbery won't hold water.

(*Note.*—No. 2 is almost always used in the negative.)

IN HOT WATER. In trouble.

Jack, as usual, is in hot water.

OF THE FIRST WATER. Originally applied only to the finest precious stones. Of the finest possible quality ; to the greatest degree.

The defendant is a liar of the first water.

MAKE ONE'S MOUTH WATER. Be intensely attractive, delightful to eat or see.

The diamonds in that jeweller's shop make my mouth water.

THROW COLD WATER ON. Depreciate ; discourage.

We want to start a fish shop, but Father is inclined to throw cold water on the idea.

Way : ACROSS THE WAY, STREET, ROAD, *etc.*

On the opposite side, a short distance away.

ALL MANNER, ALL SORTS, ALL KINDS OF WAYS. A large variety of ways.

The new lodger will be useful in all manner of ways.

BY THE WAY. Incidentally. The phrase—one of the most useful in the English language—is used when a speaker wishes to pass abruptly from one subject to another which has little or no connection with it.

By the way, I am leaving early to-night.

GET IN THE WAY, *or* GET OUT OF THE WAY. Obstruct, or the reverse.

Please get out of my way.

GET INTO THE WAY OF. Acquire the habit of doing.

You'll soon get into the way of walking barefoot.

GIVE WAY. 1. Lit., Break.

The railings gave way, and three people fell in the river.

2. Met., Yield.

He begged his mother to come, and at last she gave way.

GO ONE'S OWN WAY. Follow one's personal desires, without accepting guidance or advice.

It is waste of time warning him—the fool is determined to go his own way.

See HAVE ONE'S OWN WAY; FOLLOW ONE'S OWN DEVICES.

GO THE WAY OF ALL FLESH. Die.

HAVE ONE'S OWN WAY. Do as one wishes.

I want to go to London, and I mean to have my own way.

IN A WAY. In certain respects; to a certain extent.

He considers his wife clever, and in a way he's justified.

IN THE WAY. Obstructing; forming an obstruction.

I can't empty the bottle—there's a piece of cork in the way.

A LONG WAY OFF. Very distant.

Those hills are a long way off.

MAKE ONE'S WAY. 1. Progress; travel on one's journey. 2. Succeed in one's profession.

That young man will make his way in the world.

MAKE WAY. Lit., Step aside.

Make way for his Highness.

Met., Retire from office.

I shall make way for a younger man.

ON THE WAY. Coming, *en route.*

OUT OF THE WAY. See under OUT.

OVER THE WAY. Same as ACROSS THE WAY.

UNDER WAY (*frequently, but incorrectly, written "Weigh"*). Or. Nautical. Beginning; moving; starting.

We have several plans under way.

WAYS AND MEANS. Methods of overcoming difficulties.

I hope we can find ways and means of getting to the seaside.

WING ONE'S WAY. Travel swiftly, as a bird flies.

The telegram winged its way with the news.

Weak : THE WEAKER SEX. The female sex; woman. Same as FAIR SEX.

Wear : FAIR WEAR AND TEAR. A legal phrase. The normal lessening in value due to constant use.

Apart from fair wear and tear, the bicycle is in excellent condition.

WEAR AWAY. Cause to disappear by friction. Lit. or Met.

The leather on the writing-case was completely worn away.

WEAR ONE'S HEART ON ONE'S SLEEVE. See under **Heart.**

WEAR OFF. Diminish and finally disappear.
The effects of the shock will soon wear off.

WEAR ON. Pass or diminish slowly.
The hours wore on ; night came.

WEAR OUT. 1. Lit., Render useless by wear.
My boots are worn out.
2. Met., Exhaust.
The poor woman had not slept all night and was completely worn out.

Weather : MAKE HEAVY WEATHER OF (S.). Treat as though it were a very serious matter.
Peter is making very heavy weather over Jane's engagement.

UNDER THE WEATHER. Unwell or depressed, or both.
Poor Uncle John seems rather under the weather to-night.

WEATHER THE STORM. Survive. (" Storm " is frequently used for financial and other troubles.)
Trade is very bad, but we shall weather the storm.

Wedge : THE THIN END OF THE WEDGE. A small or trivial beginning which is likely to develop into something of much greater importance.
The workmen are demanding extra payment for difficult work—it is the thin end of the wedge.

Weigh : WEIGHED IN THE BALANCE (i.e. ON THE SCALES) AND FOUND WANTING. Or. Biblical (Daniel v. 27). Applied to one whose fault or weakness has been discovered.
We thought him trustworthy, but when serious trouble came, he was weighed in the balance and found wanting.

See THE WRITING ON THE WALL.

Well : AS WELL. Also.
Come early, and bring your sister as well.

VERY WELL. A general expression of agreement and assent.

WELL AND GOOD. Similar to above.

WELL-AFFECTED. Old f. Friendly.
The King showed himself well-affected towards the enemy.

WELL-BUILT, *or* **WELL SET UP**. Physically well-constructed ; fit.

He was a well-set-up man of forty.

WELL-FAVOURED. A rather old-fashioned phrase for " handsome ".

A well-favoured young man opened the door.

WELL-FOUNDED. Justifiable.

He had a well-founded belief that his cousin was cheating him.

WELL, I NEVER ! Abbrev. of " Well, I never heard anything so extraordinary ! " A common expression of astonishment.

And Ben is marrying the widow ? Well, I never !

WELL-LINED PURSE. Plenty of money.

One needs a well-lined purse to stay at the Ritz Hotel.

WELL OFF. See under OFF.

WELL-ROUNDED, *or* **TURNED, PHRASES, SENTENCES,** *etc.* Elegant and graceful speech.

The Mayor welcomed his Highness in well-rounded phrases.

WELL-TO-DO. Fairly rich.

West : GO WEST (S.). Die ; or become destroyed, or useless.

My old raincoat has gone west.

(The phrase originated in the 1914–18 War.)

What : I TELL YOU WHAT. I make this suggestion.

I tell you what—let's go to London.

KNOW WHAT'S WHAT. Be able to discriminate between what is of value and use, and what is not.

You won't deceive George, he knows what's what.

WHAT'S-HIS-NAME ; WHAT DO YOU CALL HIM ? A substitution for a name one has forgotten.

This morning I met that tall man with red hair—old what's-his-name.

See also SO-AND-SO.

Wheel : PUT A SPOKE IN ONE'S WHEEL. Interfere with one's plans.

If that girl is intending to marry John, his mother will soon put a spoke in her wheel.

See THROW A SPANNER IN THE WORKS.

WHEELS WITHIN WHEELS. Small, often unknown motives and influences, which contribute to the general result.

I tried to obtain the appointment for John, but found there were so many wheels within wheels that it was hopeless.

Wherewithal : THE WHEREWITHAL ; THE NEEDFUL. Money.

We can't get married—we haven't the wherewithal.

See RAISE THE WIND, and SINEWS OF WAR.

Whether : WHETHER OR NO. Whether or not.

He could not decide whether or no to return home.

While : A LITTLE WHILE. A short time.

I'll telephone you in a little while.

Whistle : WET ONE'S WHISTLE (S.). Indulge in a drink—*not* usually of water.

George decided to wet his whistle before he went on the stage.

WHISTLE FOR. Give up any hope of obtaining.

If you want a house in this village, you'll have to whistle for it.

Whit : NOT A WHIT. Not at all. (The phrase is practically always preceded by " not ".) A " whit " is actually a speck, the smallest visible particle of matter.

White : WHITE, *or* PURE, AS DRIVEN SNOW. Absolutely white. Driven snow is snow that has been " driven ", or blown, by the wind.

WHITE AS A SHEET. Extremely pale ; colourless.

When she heard the news, she turned as white as a sheet.

White-livered : (S.). Cowardly. (See also—illogically—YELLOW.)

Whole : GO THE WHOLE HOG (S.). Insist on having all or the best obtainable.

He went the whole hog, and occupied the most expensive suite at the Grand Hotel.

ON THE WHOLE. Used when summarizing the entire subject.

I think, on the whole, we had better stay at home.

Why : THE WHY AND WHEREFORE. The reasons for any action or the existence of any condition.

I never understood the why and wherefore of their marriage, but they seem extremely happy.

Wide : WIDE AWAKE. 1. Lit., Entirely awake. 2. Met., Alert, aware.

He is a very wide-awake young man where business is concerned.

Note use of hyphen in (2).

GIVE A WIDE BERTH TO. Avoid.

It is advisable to give a wide berth to small and shabby lodging-houses.

WIDE OF THE MARK. Or. Shooting. Inaccurate.

You're very wide of the mark if you think I want to marry Phyllis.

Widow : WIDOW'S WEEDS. The black dresses, etc., formerly made of crepe, worn by a widow.

Wigging : GET A WIGGING (S.). Be severely blamed.

You'll get a wigging for leaving the door open.

Wild : WILD GOOSE CHASE. A practically hopeless search or other enterprise.

George has gone to the fair to find his brother, but it's a wild goose chase.

Wildfire : SPREAD LIKE WILDFIRE. (Or. Naval.) Become known with extreme rapidity. " Wildfire ", also known as " Greek fire ", was an inflammable mixture very difficult to extinguish. It was used in fighting at sea.

The news of the victory spread like wildfire.

Wile : WILE, *frequently incorrectly written " while "*, AWAY THE TIME. Pass or occupy the time amusingly.

We wiled away the time singing comic songs.

Will : AT ONE'S OWN SWEET WILL. Exactly as one pleases.

One is allowed to wander about the grounds at one's own sweet will.

HAVE ONE'S WILL. Do as one wishes.

Though I may refuse at first, my wife will have her will in the end.

A WILL OF ONE'S OWN. Spirit, determination, of one's own.

Our baby is only a month old, but he's already shown that he has a will of his own.

WILLY-NILLY. (Abbrev. of the old " will-he, nill-he ".) Whether one wishes or not.

Willy-nilly, every youth must serve as a soldier for three years.

Win : WIN OVER. Convert to one's own point of view ;
persuade to become one's ally.

Napoleon won over the generals in the army.

Wind : GET WIND OF. Obtain early information about something that is likely to happen.

*Wellington got wind of Napoleon's plans, and altered
his own.*

GET THE WIND UP. Become scared ; frightened.
Or. Air Force 1914–18.

*I get the wind up every time I walk along that road in
the Park.*

ILL WIND. Or. The proverb, " It is an ill wind that
blows nobody any good."   It is a very unfortunate
event which is of no benefit : someone is almost
sure to profit from a loss. (The phrase is
usually uttered consolingly, or with a sigh of
resignation.)

*The rain has spoilt our picnic, but the ducks are
enjoying themselves ; it's an ill wind.*

IN THE WIND. An indicated possibility.

It's in the wind that he will be the next Prime Minister.
*Our train is stopping just before the frontier ; I wonder
what's in the wind.*

RAISE THE WIND (S.). See **Raise.**

TAKE THE WIND OUT OF ONE'S SAILS. **1.** Disconcert.
*Uncle Silas suddenly took the wind out of Jim's sails
by asking when he was getting married.*

2. Gain an advantage over.

*We were very proud when George became mayor, but
Ernest took the wind out of George's sails by
becoming a Member of Parliament.*

WHICH WAY THE WIND BLOWS. See under **Cat.**

WIND UP (*pron.* WYND, *as to wind up a clock*). Conclude ;
bring to an end.

This dance will wind up our entertainment.

Wing : CLIP THE WINGS. See under **Clip.**

TAKE UNDER ONE'S WING. Protect (as a hen takes her
chickens under her wing). Chaperon.

*Young Thompson is certain to succeed if Sir George
takes him under his wing.*

Wink : WINK AT. Tactfully ignore.

The chief winks at a good many small irregularities in our department.

Wise : IN NO WISE. Or. Biblical, obsolete in ordinary conversation. In no way.

To tell lies will in no wise help you.

Wish : WISH TO GOODNESS. A polite and ladylike version of " Wish to God ! " Wish intensely, emphatically. (Goodness is similarly used in " Hope to goodness " and " Trust to goodness ".)

I wish to goodness you'd come down to breakfast punctually.

WISH A PERSON JOY. Wish him, or her, luck ; congratulate.

WISH A PERSON JOY OF. Hope he may find some pleasure or satisfaction in. (*Note.*—The idiom is always used ironically.)

Old Miss Snooks is a detestable person to have as a visitor, and I wish you joy of her.

Wishy-washy : Similar to MILK-AND-WATER.

Wit : ADDLE ONE'S WITS. Make one's mind hopelessly confused. (" Addled " is applied to an egg upon which the bird has been sitting for some time, and then has deserted it.)

The problems involved are enough to addle any man's wits.

AT ONE'S WITS' END. See under **End.**

HAVE, *or* KEEP, ONE'S WITS ABOUT ONE. Be alert and observant.

One needs to have one's wits about one in crossing a street in London.

Withers : WRING ONE'S WITHERS. Cause acute distress. (The " withers " of a horse are the muscles joining the back and shoulders, and these are often made painful (" wrung " in Shakespeare's *Henry IV*) by a badly-fitting saddle.)

The girl's pitiful history would wring one's withers.

Within : WITHIN CALL OR HAIL. Near enough to hear the sound of a voice.

He is a man with a violent temper, and I should be glad if you would remain within call.

WITHIN REACH ; WITHIN EASY REACH. Accessible ;

capable of being reached, physically or by communication.

There are shops within easy reach of the house.

Wolf : CRY WOLF. See under **Cry.**

KEEP THE WOLF FROM THE DOOR. Live without suffering acute poverty.

He earns scarcely enough to keep the wolf from the door.

WOLF IN SHEEP'S CLOTHING. A plausible deceiver ; one whose apparent harmlessness conceals his true character. Or. Biblical : also Æsop's fable, in which a wolf covered himself with the sheep's skin and succeeded in deceiving a herd of sheep— but not the shepherd.

George behaves like a friend but he's merely a wolf in sheep's clothing.

Wonder : FOR A WONDER. Surprisingly ; astonishingly.

George, for a wonder, arrived early.

NINE DAYS WONDER. An event which causes great excitement for a short time and is then forgotten.

The Duke's marriage to the milkmaid was a nine days wonder in the county.

Wool : BE WOOL-GATHERING Allow one's thoughts to wander.

Finish your work—you've been wool-gathering.

See DAY-DREAMING.

Word : AS GOOD AS ONE'S WORD. Faithful in keeping a promise.

She said she would marry him when he came out of prison, and was as good as her word.

COIN A WORD. Invent a word.

That unpleasant Mrs. Snooker was—to coin a word— behaving very snookily.

HARD WORDS. Harsh and unpleasant statements, not necessarily true.

The brothers quarrelled, and hard words passed between them.

See NOT TO MINCE MATTERS ; PLAIN SPEAKING.

HAVE WORDS. Quarrel.

Must you always have words with Miriam when you meet ?

HIGH WORDS. Angry words.

She heard high words in the library, and dared not go in

IN SO MANY WORDS. Verbally and explicitly.

He told me, in so many words, that he was leaving for London to-morrow.

LEAVE WORD. Leave a message.

Leave word at the office about your holiday plans.

A MAN OF HIS WORD. One who can be trusted to keep a promise.

SAY A GOOD WORD FOR; PUT IN A GOOD WORD FOR. Speak in favour of.

He offered to say a good word for me with the prison Governor.

SPARING OF WORDS. Terse and curt in speaking or writing.

I must be sparing of words, for there is little time for talk.

TAKE AT ONE'S WORD. Accept a statement literally, and as the truth.

When the hotel manager promised us a first-class dinner, we foolishly took him at his word.

UPON MY WORD! Exclamation, expressing astonishment.

Upon my word, this is an extraordinary story!

WORD FOR WORD. Exactly as spoken or written; verbatim.

This is, word for word, the message he gave me.

A WORD IN THE EAR. A private statement, or hint.

A word from me in the ear of His Majesty, and the Duke will be ruined.

WORD OF MOUTH. Verbally; spoken, as contrasted with written speech.

The General informed me by word of mouth that peace would shortly be arranged.

WORD-PERFECT. Exact, absolutely accurate.

The actor is word-perfect in his part.

A WORD TO THE WISE. Latin: *verbum sapienti.* A hint or suggestion which an intelligent hearer is expected to act upon.

" A word to the wise," said our host. " Don't go into the haunted room at midnight."

Work : AT WORK ON. Engaged or employed on.

I'm at work on a new life of Nelson.

DONKEY-WORK. Rough or hard work, necessary at the beginning of a task. (A " donkey-engine " is a small engine which supplies power for minor work on board ship.)

You have only to arrange the furniture in your room—the cleaners have done all the donkey-work.

FANCY WORK. Ornamental and trivial articles, chiefly sewn or knitted.

MAKE SHORT WORK OF. Finish quickly.

The new girl makes short work of the washing.

WORK ONE'S PASSAGE. Or. Nautical. Earn a privilege or advantage by doing work in return. A passenger who has no money to pay his fare and works as a seaman instead, is said to work his passage.

WORK UP. 1. Create by degrees.

From one small shop, he worked up to a very fine business.

2. Rouse or excite.

It was a thrilling play, and the audience became very worked up.

WORK UPON. Exert influence upon.

That politician can work upon his hearers' emotions until they are prepared to vote for anything he suggests.

See WROUGHT UPON.

World : ALL THE WORLD AND HIS WIFE. Everyone ; all the people there are.

All the world and his wife seem to be present.

ALL THE WORLD OVER. Universally ; everywhere.

A girl who is both pretty and charming is popular all the world over.

MAKE THE BEST OF BOTH WORLDS. Satisfy two opposing demands ; compromise.

George loves his family, but he also likes spending his time with his men friends, and tries to make the best of both worlds.

A MAN, *or* WOMAN, OF THE WORLD. An experienced person ; one familiar with the customs and habits of Society.

THE WAY OF THE WORLD. The customary behaviour of mankind, especially civilized, sophisticated mankind. (The phrase is generally used ironically.)

Most of his rich acquaintances ignored him when he was poor, as is the way of the world.

Worm : EVEN A WORM WILL TURN. Or. Proverbial. Even
the weakest person may be goaded into defiance
or rebellion.

*But at last the worm turned, and the old servant refused
to obey his brutal master.*

WORM IN. Insinuate.

*Now he has made a fortune, he will, I expect, try to
worm his way into Society.*

WORM OUT. Discover by persistent questioning.

*By the end of the week he had wormed out her
secret.*

Worst : AT THE WORST. In the worst possible circumstances ;
even if the worst happens.

*Let's start in spite of the rain ; at the worst we can only
get wet.*

Worth : WORTH ONE'S SALT ; WORTH ONE'S KEEP. See under
Salt. (*Note.*—This idiom is generally used in
the negative.)

WORTH WHILE ; WORTH ONE'S WHILE. Worth spending
time or trouble over.

*I would try to sell the business, but it isn't worth
while.*

Wrap : WRAPPED UP IN. Entirely devoted to ; absorbed in.

He is wrapped up in his business.

Write : WRITE OFF. Or. Commercial. Treat as no longer
of any value.

*The shares are unsaleable ; we had better write them
off.*

Writing : THE WRITING ON THE WALL. Or. Biblical. The
writing on the wall was the warning given to
Belshazzar. A plain indication that unless the
man who receives it alters his conduct, the end
will be disaster.

*All his friends recognized the writing on the wall—
John's extravagance was leading straight to ruin.*

Wrong : GET HOLD OF THE WRONG END OF THE STICK (S.).
Be completely mistaken.

*You've got hold of the wrong end of the stick—Jane,
not Marjory, is marrying George.*

Wrought : WROUGHT UPON. Similar to WORK UPON, but
used only in the past tense.

Y

Year : ALL THE YEAR ROUND. Throughout the year.

    We have breakfast on the verandah all the year round.

    (*Note.*—Charles Dickens founded a magazine with this title.)

    YEARS OF DISCRETION. An age at which one is supposed to have acquired a certain amount of wisdom and discretion.

    You'll know better when you've reached years of discretion.

Yellow : YELLOW AS A GUINEA. A guinea—twenty-one shillings—was a gold coin slightly larger than a sovereign. The yellow, of course, refers to its colour, and has no connection with its value.

    The old woman looks terribly ill—her skin is as yellow as a guinea.

    YELLOW-LIVERED. Cowardly. There is a tradition that the liver of a coward has a streak of yellow in it. See WHITE-LIVERED.

Yeoman : YEOMAN SERVICE. Sound and excellent work.

    The general did yeoman service in re-organizing the artillery.

AMERICAN IDIOMS

THE selection of these has provided several problems.

Firstly, American idioms, carried by the winds of travel across the Atlantic, flourish so readily on English soil that within a year or so it is difficult to remember their origin.

Secondly, very many of them consist of single words with highly specialized meanings. And such words do not, strictly speaking, come within the scope of this book.

Finally, there remains the difficulty of selecting from an immense collection those phrases which are most likely to prove of value to the average student, either English or foreign.

Account : NO-ACCOUNT. Of no value ; worthless.
>   *Tell that no-account fellow that he is dismissed.*

Ace : ACE IN. Attract attention.
>   *She's a girl would ace in anywhere.*

All : ALL-FIRED (S.). Extreme, or extremely. Or. Said to be a corruption of " Hell-fired ".
>   *That's an all-fired pretty hat Jane's wearing.*

>   ALL IN. 1. Exhausted.
>   *The girl's eyes closed. I saw that she was all in.*

>   2. Inclusive (Eng. and American).
>   *The rent will be $200 a month, all in.*

>   ALL SET. Ready, fully prepared.
>   *We're all set for the journey.*

Ambulance : AMBULANCE CHASER (S.). An unscrupulous type of lawyer who hurries to the bedside of anyone injured in an accident, and induces him to authorize the lawyer to recover what damages he can, in return for an agreed percentage of the amount obtained.

Ante : ANTE UP ; PONY UP (S.). Settle the account, pay what is due. (" Pony " is an old-fashioned slang term for money.)
>   *You'll have to ante up for the drinks.*

Apple : APPLE SAUCE (S.). Humbug ; insincere talk. See **Boloney**.

Back : BACK AND FORTH. Eng. equiv. "To and fro". Going and returning regularly from one place to another.

Every day he travelled back and forth from New York to Washington.

Boiled : BOILED SHIRT. Starched white shirt worn on formal occasions with a black or white bow tie.

Boloney : BOLONEY. Similar to APPLE SAUCE.

Cake : FLANNEL CAKE. A soft, thin cake, generally eaten with sandwiches.

Can : CAN-OPENER (S.). A cheap car.

Carpet : CARPET-BAGGER. Derogatory term applied to a newcomer to a district, arriving with political ambitions and consequently regarded with suspicion and contempt. Or. The migration of many northern adventurers to the South after the Civil War in U.S.A.

Check : CHECK OUT (*or* UP). Settle one's account at a hotel and depart.

CHECK UP. Audit. Examine for purposes of comparison.

A check-up of the passengers showed that only ten were British.

Community : COMMUNITY CHEST : A fund raised by a group of people for some special object, frequently religious.

COMMUNITY CHURCH. Members of different denominations who have decided to unite as one congregation.

Dandy : DANDY TRAP. A loose stone that tilts up when trodden upon.

Dime : DIME NOVEL. Eng. equiv. "Penny Dreadful". Crude, paper-bound thrillers, read chiefly by boys and uneducated persons.

Door : DOOR TENDER. Hall porter ; official stationed at the door of flats, etc.

DOOR YARD. Eng. equiv. "Back yard". The patch of ground near the back door of a house.

Down : DOWN COUNTRY. The area near the mouth of a river or sea.

DOWN EAST. The New England States.

DOWN TOWN. The business quarter of a town. See UP TOWN.

Drag : DRAG-PULL. Personal influence.

The family has considerable drag-pull in Kentucky.

Drop : GET THE DROP ON (S.). Lit., Shoot before one's enemy has a chance of shooting. Met., Be in a superior position to deal with one's enemy.

I've got the drop on George. I'll be seeing the Chief on Monday.

Drug : DRUG STORE. Nominally, " chemist's shop ", but in America one that also deals in non-intoxicating drinks, ice-creams, sandwiches and other miscellaneous goods.

Figure : FIGURE OUT. Estimate ; reckon.

We figure out we shall reach Chicago on Wednesday morning.

Four : FOUR-FLUSHER (S.). A boaster.

FOUR HUNDRED, THE. An expression, dating from 1890, and based on a casual reference to the élite of New York as being limited to 400 families. (English equiv. The Upper Ten Thousand.)

Frame : FRAME HOUSE ; COTTAGE, *etc.* One built with a framework of timber, to which wood boards (" shingles ") are nailed for the walls.

Garbage : GARBAGE CAN (*or* BARREL). Eng. equiv. Dust-bin, the receptacle into which household refuse is placed, later to be removed by the official paid to collect it.

Get : GET BY. Eng. equiv. " Get away with ", or " Pull off ". Succeed in ; accomplish.

I didn't think he'd get by with his scheme of re-organizing the business.

GET THE GATE (S.). Eng. equiv. " Get the sack ". Be dismissed from one's post or job.

GET ONE'S DANDER (S.). Exasperate ; make angry.

It gets my dander to hear people sneering at the President.

GET (*or* BE HANDED) THE FROZEN MITT. Be received coldly and contemptuously ; be snubbed.

GET THE MITTEN (S.). More correctly, " Give the mitten ". Or. Fr., based on an old ironical custom of giving an unwelcome lover a pair of *mitaines* (mittens) instead of the lady's hand for which he asked. Be rejected as a suitor.

Poor Jake has been terribly depressed since Susan gave him the mitten.

GO-GETTER. One who concentrates upon his own progress ; who " has an eye to the main chance ".

Young George is a go-getter ; he will be managing a business of his own before he's thirty.

Grab-Bag. Eng. equiv. " Lucky Dip ", or Bran Tub. A tub or similar vessel filled with bran, sawdust, etc. in which a number of small objects are buried, and into which, on payment of a small sum, customers plunge their hands and draw out whatever they grasp.

Graduate : GRADUATE NURSE. A trained, officially qualified nurse.

Hall : HALL BEDROOM. Bedroom above the entrance hall.

Hand : HAND-ME-DOWNS (S.). Eng. equiv. Reach-me-downs or Off the Peg. Ready-made clothing.

Hard : HARD-BOILED (S.). Eng. equiv. Hard-headed. Practical ; sophisticated.

George is a hard-boiled man of business.

HARD LIQUOR (whisky, brandy, rum, etc.) containing a high proportion of alcohol, as distinct from beer, light wines and non-intoxicating (" soft ") drinks.

HARD MONEY. Money in the form of coins, as distinct from paper.

HARD SAUCE. Any sauce not in liquid form.

Hold : HOLD DOWN. Keep ; retain.

He is a good workman, and will hold down his job.

HOLD UP. Lit., A robbery in which the victim is ordered to hold up his hands above his head so that he has no opportunity of resisting. Met. Any abrupt and violent method of obtaining money or power.

The bandits held up the express (i.e. stopped it by threatening the driver), *while they robbed the passengers.*

The landowner, taking advantage of a recent law, held up the Government for twenty thousand dollars before consenting to part with his property.

Home : HOME-FOR-RENT (S.). Widow.

Hot : HOT DOG. A bread roll split and buttered, with a hot sausage inserted between the halves.

Jump : JUMPING ROPE. Eng. equiv. Skipping-rope. That used in the game of skipping.

Kentucky : KENTUCKY CARDINAL. A small North American bird with brilliant red plumage. Name derived from the scarlet robe worn by cardinals of the Church of Rome.

Lawn : LAWN PARTY. Eng. equiv. Garden party. A party, frequently informal, held in the open air.

Let : LET DOWN ONE'S HAIR. Relax ; behave informally.

    LET UP. 1. Stop ; cease.

    He's a man who, having begun a job, will never let up until it's finished.

    2. Relax one's efforts.

    There will be no let-up in our determination to provide more houses.

Limited : LIMITED EXPRESS. Fast and luxurious train which carries only passengers prepared to pay extra fares for speed and comfort. See PARLOUR CAR.

Maid : MAID OF HONOUR. Eng. equiv. Chief bridesmaid. Not, as in the past, personal attendant upon a queen when she appeared in public.

Mail : MAIL MATTER. In the U.S.A. this consists of 4 classes —1st class, letters ; 2nd class, officially recognized newspapers and periodicals ; 3rd class, printed matter and parcels not over 8 oz. in weight ; 4th class, anything else that may be sent by post.

Mason : MASON AND DIXON'S LINE. A line based on a survey made in 1763–6 by two Englishmen, Mason and Dixon. It was accepted as defining the boundary between Maryland and West Virginia, following a dispute between those states, and was originally marked by milestones, on one side of which was carved the arms of William Penn, and on the other side those of Lord Baltimore. Until the abolition of slavery it was generally accepted as the dividing line between free and slave-owning States.

Measure : MEASURE UP TO. Reach the level or standard of.

    No girl is ever likely to measure up to Henry's standards of beauty.

Muscle : MUSCLE INTO. Thrust one's way, frequently by illegal methods, into a business or profession.

Tom Smith is a newcomer, but he has already muscled into the political circles that control the town.

Night : NIGHT STICK. A short, heavy truncheon used by policemen on night duty.

Oil : OIL-CAN (S.). An unattractive or unpopular girl.

Old : OLD COLONY. Massachusetts.

OLD DOMINION. Virginia.

OLD GLORY. The national flag, the Stars and Stripes.

Once : ONCE OVER. A brief, superficial examination.

I gave the car the once-over before we started.

One : ONE-HORSE. Inferior ; of little importance.

Mother lives in a one-horse town near Boston.

Out : AT OUTS. Disagreeing with.

Mary is at outs with John over their holiday.

Owl : OWL TRAIN. One leaving the terminus between midnight and dawn. Similarly, Owl Taxi, one available for hire during those hours.

Packet : PACKET. A packet (S.). A considerable sum.

The old man made a packet out of his gold-mining shares.

Pail : PAIL. The full dinner-pail. Symbol of general working-class prosperity.

Every labourer dreams of plenty of leisure and a full dinner-pail.

Parlour : PARLOUR CAR. A luxuriously-fitted railway car for the use of which an extra charge is made. See LIMITED EXPRESS.

Patrol : PATROL WAGON. Eng. equiv. Police-van, or " Black Maria ". The vehicle in which prisoners are taken to the police-station or jail.

Pay : PAY-ROLL. Eng. equiv. Salary list. List of a firm's employees and their salaries.

Penalty : PENALTY ENVELOPE. One used for Government business, and upon which no postage-stamp is necessary. (Eng. equiv., one marked " O.H.M.S.") A " penalty " is charged when it is unofficially and improperly used.

Pipe : PIPE-LAYING (S.). Eng. equiv. Wire-pulling. Exerting private influence for political and similar purposes.

After a good deal of pipe-laying, Thomson got himself appointed Chairman of the Committee.

Plate : PLATE LUNCH (*or* DINNER). A meal in which, to save time, the entire course—meat, vegetables, etc.—is heaped on one plate.

Play : PLAY THE RACES. Bet on horse races.

Pony : RIDING ON A PONY. Using a translation (or crib) to help one, illegally, to pass an examination.

He would have failed if he had not been smart enough to ride on a pony through his Greek prose.

Poor : POOR WHITES. Originally applied to the white families living in the Southern States of America, but possessing no slaves. Later used indiscriminately of the shiftless, lazy and generally discreditable white inhabitants of the South.

Prairie : PRAIRIE SCHOONER. The large, old-fashioned two-horse wagon in which early settlers in America packed themselves, their families and their possessions, and, followed by their cattle, travelled westward.

Prudential : PRUDENTIAL COMMITTEE. One elected to deal especially with the financial affairs of a company.

Public : PUBLIC ENEMY. A modern term, roughly equivalent to the old English word " outlaw ", applied to a criminal for whose arrest the Government offered a reward. The first person officially designated as Public Enemy No. 1 was Al Capone, the reward being $25,000. The next was Dillinger, shot down in Chicago by Federal Police in 1934.

Quaker : QUAKER CITY. Philadelphia, founded by William Penn, the Quaker.

Real : REAL ESTATE. Land and houses. REALTOR. Eng. equiv. House-agent, one who deals in such property.

Right : RIGHT OF WAY. Eng. equiv. of Permanent way, the track along which a train or trains run.

Room : ROOMING HOUSE. Eng. equiv. Lodging-house, as distinct from a hotel or boarding-house in which the inmates have their meals.

Row : ROW OF BEANS. Eng. equiv. Row of pins or Two pins. Of little, or no value. Almost always used in the negative sense.

I don't care a row of beans for your objections.

Saloon : SALOON-KEEPER. Eng. equiv. Public-house keeper ; Landlord.

Say : SAY-SO. Expression of opinion ; also decision.

> *I don't expect to be allowed any say-so in the matter.*
> *You have the final say-so.*

Scratch : SCRATCH-PAD (*or* BLOCK). Eng. equiv. Scribbling-block. Pad of paper used for making rough notes.

Shingle : PUT UP ONE'S SHINGLE. Eng. equiv. Put up one's brass plate—the engraved plate used by doctors, dentists, etc., that indicates one's profession and qualifications.

Shoe : ON A SHOE-STRING. With very small or inadequate capital.

> *He started the business on a shoe-string and is now a millionaire.*

Shoot : SHOOT TO DEATH. Shoot dead.

> *The robber was shot to death as he tried to escape.*

Short Order. Eng. equiv. In no time. Very quickly ; almost at once.

> *They extinguished the blaze in short order.*

Shot : BIG SHOT, *or* NOISE (S.). Important and/or influential person.

Side : ON THE SIDE. As well as ; in addition to.

> *We were invited to dinner, and on the side, to a concert afterwards.*

Also used with a sinister implication.

> *The boys made a good deal on the side by gambling.*

SIDE-BURNS. Short whiskers worn with a moustache and ending at the angle of the jaw.

SIDE-WALK. Eng. equiv. Pavement, which word in America for the Eng. " Road ".

> *The stands erected to see the procession filled the side-walk, and pedestrians were compelled to tramp along on the pavement.*

Silent : SILENT PARTNER. Eng. equiv. Sleeping partner (which see).

Sit : SIT DOWN HARD UPON. Eng. equiv. Set one's face against (which see).

Station : STATION HOUSE. Eng. equiv. Police-station.

Step : STEP LIVELY. Move quickly.

> *If you don't step lively we shall miss the train.*

STEP ON THE GAS (S.). Lit. Step on the accelerator of a car, increasing its speed. Met., Quicken one's action ; hasten ; hurry.

Stop : STOP BY *or* IN. Eng. equiv. Look in ; Drop in. Visit casually when passing.

As he approached his old home, he thought he would stop by for a few moments.

Straight : STRAIGHT TICKET. Election idiom. To vote for all the Candidates of one's party—a thing impossible in England—by making a cross in the top of a list of candidates.

Straw : STRAW VOTE. An unofficial vote, usually taken shortly before an election with the object of revealing the general trend of public opinion. More commonly known in England as a Gallup Poll.

String : A STRING TO IT. A statement or agreement to which some condition is attached.

He said he would support the candidate but I'm certain that there's a string to it somewhere.

STRING TIE. A narrow necktie fastened in front with a small bow.

Tell : TELL GOODBYE. Eng. equiv. Bid farewell (which see).

Thus : THUS AND SO. A curiously redundant idiom, the English equivalent being " thus " or " so " only.

Many people would behave thus and so if this happened.

Tie : TIE UP WITH. Eng. equiv. Join forces with (which see).

Town : ON THE TOWN (Obs.). Eng. equiv. On the parish. Supported by the parish authorities ; living in an institution for paupers.

Up : UP AND COMING. Youthfully alert and self-confident.

Anne was a smart up-and-coming girl of sixteen.

UP TOWN. The superior or residential area of a town.

Wash : WASH-RAG. Eng. equiv. Face-cloth. A small square cloth used for washing one's face and hands.

Way : WAY-STATION ; WAY TRAIN. A railway station of minor importance frequently equiv. to the English halt. WAY TRAIN. Eng. equiv. Slow train, is one which stops at such stations.

White : WHITE WINGS. Colloquial name for New York street cleaners, who are equipped with white uniforms.

Wide : WIDE OPEN. Applied to a town or city when the laws against immorality, drinking, etc., are openly disregarded.

The Mayor is largely responsible for this town being the most wide open in the county.

Woods : TAKE TO THE WOODS. Run away from one's responsibilities, especially in connection with voting.

> *On election day half those who have said that they are going to vote for Thompson will probably take to the woods.*

Yellow : YELLOW DOG. An utterly contemptible person.

> *The defendant is a yellow dog and unfit for any decent post.*

A YELLOW DOG FUND. One used for purposes of bribery.